WESTERN ESOTERICISM IN CONTEXT IV

The Celestial Art

Essays on Astrological Magic

Edited by
AUSTIN COPPOCK AND DANIEL A. SCHULKE

THREE HANDS PRESS
2018

Jacket cover images (*The Celestial Spheres*, 2017, and *Dragon's Eye*, 2017), and title frontispiece (*Stargazer*, 2017) by Joseph Uccello.
Jacket and interior book design and typesetting by Joseph Uccello.
Fine edition designs by Daniel A. Schulke.

Printed in the United States of America.

ISBN 978–1945147173 (softcover)

Three Hands Press
www.threehandspress.com

CONTENTS

Acknowledgements

The editors thank those good souls who assisted the manifestation of this book. Our copy editors, Kaitlin Coppock and Robert Fitzgerald were both instrumental in preparing the final typescript, and to them all gratitude is due. To our writers, we extend our appreciation for their patience, as well as their willingness to explore the further bounds of esoteric astrology. We also thank Joseph Uccello for his original artwork, which elegantly embodies the *numen* resulting from the union of heaven and earth. Finally, for inspiration and encouragement, thanks to Michael Howard, who understood the essential communion of angelical and astrological sorcery.

Introduction

SOME SAY THAT the sky has a language, that the stars and planets are its letters, and its mandalic, cyclical patterns the grammatical structure. Astrologers read the sequence of human events and experiences from its text. Its stories, when told here on earth, reproduce the events described in the skies. The pattern of light above rearranges the world below.

Though the firmament can be said to be a text, it is not a stone tablet, but a living tome. It is a constantly changing grimoire, an ever-changing book of spells written in the language of angels, demons, gods and monsters. Like all such books of magic, its text embodies specific powers available to the magician, diviner, and sorcerer. The apprehension of these powers, and their effective translation from potential to active, comprises the Celestial Art.

Yet this Art has become rare indeed. Recent centuries have not been kind to astrology, nor to magic. In addition to their individual abuse at the hands of history, the two have also become estranged, impoverishing and limiting them both. Fortunately, the recent Renaissance in each field has served not only to restore them individually, but also to reveal their historical, practical, and conceptual entanglement. Though conceived by Hermeticists as sister-sciences, their relationship is not that of siblings, but of lovers, for each completes the other, and when united, they give birth to the Celestial Art itself.

For this Art to become clear, to speak and figurate in the manner of the heavens, we must begin in two places. The first of these is historical: to ignore the understanding of past practitioners is to condemn ourselves to the dubious proposition of reinventing the wheel. Although we might succeed in discovering such a simple machine, the Art requires wheels upon wheels, for the sophistication of its clockwork dwarfs that of the common timepiece. This volume thus contains essays that work up and down the textual timeline of astrological magic, dusting away at carefully excavated material and in the process revealing new translations of ancient wisdom-teachings, timelines clarified and repaired, and clear expositions of classic texts.

While it would be foolish to disregard the knowledge of those who came before, what has been passed on is not the Art entire, but that which has managed to survive the years. The Art itself must be performed in the present, by practitioners of the current age. This volume lends ample space to these contemporary perspectives, which shed light on matters both practical and paradigmatic. The theory of the Art may be unchanging, but their application to a world in constant flux demands adaptations and strategies only implied by historical texts. It is not merely the conditions of practice that change, but also the cosmology which contains it. New discoveries about the nature of the physical reality may deepen our understanding of the universe's star-flecked body, but they demand to be reconciled with more ancient visions, as the highest potential of the Art requires a coherent cosmology.

Astrological magic is the act of reconciling heaven and earth, and so sets tasks of that nature before us. Past and present must find union, and so must theory and practice be married. Each of the following essays attempts this perilous union of above and below in its own way. They are thus not merely about the Art, they are examples of it. It is the sincere hope of the editors that the constellation of pieces offered here serves to reconcile the doctrines of astrology and magic, thus facilitating the restoration of the Celestial Art to its rightful place, and ultimately, awakening the reader to their own potential power to participate in and shape the continually unfolding congress between heaven and earth.

—AUSTIN COPPOCK AND DANIEL A. SCHULKE

A Feast of Starlight

Reflections on Stellar Magic

Austin Coppock

With holy voice I call the stars on high, pure sacred lights and genii of the sky.
    Celestial stars, the progeny of Night, in whirling circles beaming far your light,
Refulgent rays around the heav'ns ye throw, eternal fires, the source of all below.
    With flames significant of Fate ye shine, and aptly rule for men a path divine.
In seven bright zones ye run with wand'ring flames, and heaven and earth compose your lucid frames:
    With course unwearied, pure and fiery bright forever shining thro' the veil of Night.
Hail twinkling, joyful, ever wakeful fires! Propitious shine on all my just desires;
    These sacred rites regard with conscious rays, and end our works devoted to your praise.

—ORPHIC HYMN VI
TO THE STARS[1]

THE TRADITIONAL TEXTS of astrological magic, such as the *Picatrix*, *Gayat Al Hakim* and the *Three Books of Occult Philosophy* are, in the majority, books of *planetary* magic. They spend their reams primarily on the powers of the seven visible planets, enumerating the many images and poems by which they might be called, and the metals and stones that would receive them. This focus on the planets and their powers is not a special prejudice of books on astrological magic, though, it is also the bias of the entire tradition of horoscopic astrology, whose earliest texts date back to the 1st century BCE.

---

1 Thomas Taylor, trans.

Though often referred to colloquially as the 'science of the stars,' the stars play only a supporting role in the tradition of 'Western' astrology. This emphasis on the planetary extends even to the sidereal traditions of astrology, such as those of India. In such systems, the stars are used to determine the placement of the signs of the zodiac, and then asked to step back politely and let the planets do the talking.

There are reasons for this. The first of which is that the stars move little, if at all, during the lifespan of a human being. They therefore cannot be used to give auguries about the shifting tides of fortune which characterize human life. If anything, their constancy stands as a counterpoint to the maelstrom of human experience. The planets, on the other hand, mirror this dynamic tumult. Spinning through their courses, they speed up, slow down and even reverse course in our sky. They brighten and dim, advance and retreat, and are thus the perfect celestial proxy for the circles along which we run.

The stars, on the other hand, are unceasing in their stability. They earn the title by which they are called, 'The Fixed Stars,' with their lack of apparent motion and the constancy of their light. Those that twinkle or shift are in the minority, and especially recognized for even these minute motions.

Yet the stars have power. The earliest human ritual edifices are aligned with the stars. It is not the planets' cycles to which the pyramids, ziggurats and standing stones are consistently oriented. It is the stars. The stone megaliths of humanity's yesterday provide a mute testimony to the importance of the stars, pointing upward like enormous, silent fingers. Yet while they indicate, they do not explain.

For more we must engage the stories of times and people past. The oldest stories provide some clues as to why these great stones were erected in sight of particular stars. Many tales speak of the great teachers of mankind descending from the stars. The Vedas look at the 7 stars of the Big Dipper and see 7 immortal sages, each of whom bestowed upon mankind gifts of wisdom and earthly power. The teaching star-sage is not a motif confined merely to India. The skies over China, Mesopotamia and many others also glittered with tutelary spirits, though not all lands saw the knowledge-givers as uniformly benevolent. The *Book of Enoch* tells of the Watchers, the angels who descended to earth not only to teach, but also to mate. That knowledge which fell to earth on beams of jeweled light, like Prometheus, put divine flame in human hands. Such power gives off the nuclear heat of starfire, and smells of burnt fingers.

As the great monuments and myths attest to, there is both power and knowledge in the stars, of a nature and quality that the planets cannot be substituted for. The attainment of congress with these radiant points and the subsequent transmission of intelligence and power via them is well within the purview of astrological magic. Not only that, but the stars provide a bridge to an older stratum of skylore and celestial magic, a time when the planets' orbits were not yet familiar.

Yet the methods for connecting to the stars and directing their power in the extant canon of astrological magic are underdeveloped and incomplete when compared with the wealth of planetary lore which the texts present. There is material, though, and however partial it is, it can be used as a starting point for building a more complete method. Let us then conduct a survey of issues relevant to the praxis of stellar magic, using traditional material, when available, as a jumping-off point for further consideration.

ARISE

Key to all astrological magic, be it planetary or otherwise, is timing. The method for timing the right moment to approach a stars' power given in the *Picatrix* and many subsequent works is relatively simple, when compared to the painstaking calculations necessary for planetary work. Find the moment when the Moon conjoins a given star, and then wait for the two to reach the highest point in the sky together.

Yet if we look to those cultures whose sky lore focuses on the stellar rather than the planetary, such as the ancient Egyptians, we find a tremendous emphasis on the rising, culmination and setting of the stars. From the vantage of any given place on earth, each star has a set of calendar dates for when it rises in the East, just before the morning Sun. This phenomenon, referred to as heliacal rising, reliably occurs on the same calendar day for the span of 72 years, approximately one human life. This moment when a star arises to herald the dawn, after a period of invisibility, is a crucial moment in the cyclical relationship between us and the stars. It should be noted that it is to these key heliacal risings, as well as to culminations and settings, that the stellar megaliths were often built to align with.

Sadly, these most significant moments of emergence for the stars are neglected in the canon of traditional astrological magic. Yet with a little work this understanding of visual phase can easily be reunited with astromagical praxis. Bernadette Brady, in *Brady's Book of Fixed Stars*, writes extensively on how to calculate these times for any given location. With some study, a local yearly calendar of heliacal risings, culminations and settings can be constructed for any star. The dates are subject to precession, yet they will slide by only a few days over the next few centuries. By aligning the Moon's position with these yearly power points, stellar potency is increased.

By considering the cycle of a given star's visibility, we establish a more intimate, rhythmic understanding of its relationship with our place on earth. Furthermore, by doing so we align ourselves with the most ancient of sky-watchers, for whom the stars' appearances and disappearances anchored both myth and ritual.

LANGUAGE

To reach out to any entity, one must first know its name, or at least a name it will answer to. Unfortunately, the current state of our star lore has a special problem with names. Many stars are still referred to by mangled transliterations of the names they had in medieval Arabic. These names are often not even the proper words in their original language, much less terms that offer an entry point to the stars' identity and power. Translating these titles, in some cases, provides some clarity, but the star names are often reliant on the context of an ecosystem of stories that are themselves obscure. It is an undigested portion of a thousand-year old inheritance of knowledge, still sitting somewhere in the culture's intestines.

To truly work with the stars, we must understand their identities. Yet even proper translations of star names often offers us little more than an indication of what constellation they are part of. 'The Goat's Tail' is more informative than 'Deneb Algedi,' but it does not reveal the deep identity of the star.

To this end, certain sects of esoteric Taoism, part of whose praxis depended on stellar work, maintained separate star lists from the population at large. The secret names and identities of the stars were collected so that they could be called upon in practice. Though the lists of the esoteric Taoists may or may not be useful to a contemporary practitioner of astrological magic, the logic behind the assembly of such lists is both clear and attractive.

The issue of identity is inextricably connected to the way that one approaches, and addresses, a star during a working. Traditional texts provide a set of rhetorical strategies for conjuring the power of the planets, but do not provide cognate methods for calling on stellar power. Yet the addresses to the planets might provide us with oratory models applicable to the stars. Take, for example, the call to Venus from the *Picatrix*:

> *Peace be upon you Venus, O Happy Bosomed Lady, the Cold, the moderate in humidity, the clean, the beautiful, the aromatic, the generous in joy, the owner of jewels, gold, happiness, dancing, singing, decoration...I also call you in all your names in Arabic Aye ZAHRA, in Persian ANAHEED, in Roman APHRODITE, in Greek TIYANA, in Indian SURFAH...*

Notice the use of the second-person, 'you' language, which implies a conscious, listening subject on the other side of the dialogue. Furthermore, that celestial 'other' is recognized for having qualities of personality. It is not merely that Venus rules over cleanliness, Venus is herself clean. It is not merely that Venus rules pleasant smells, she is herself aromatic. These calls, which are in practice quite effective, provide a mode of address to each planetary power, as well as an excellent sketch of their likes, dislikes, powers and personalities. In doing so, they provide a method through which intimate communion with each planetary power might be achieved. Sadly, the *Picatrix* does not include similar petitions to the stars.

In the *Three Books of Occult Philosophy*, Agrippa suggests a personal mode of address to planetary powers, though of a different sort. While the *Picatrix* provides speeches, complete with a syncretic ambivalence about divine names, *Three Books of Occult Philosophy* mobilizes the well-trod identifications between the Greco-Roman gods and the planets by suggesting that one use the Orphic Hymn associated with the appropriate deity to attract a planet's attention. As in the *Picatrix*, no cognate method is given for the stars.

One might be tempted to assume that the absence of stellar calls was because the method is not appropriate, but thousands of years of lore directly contradict that assertion. Every tradition has as its foundation the figures and stories of the stars. Many deities dwelt within stars before they descended to the planetary realm.

Those who would seek communion and empowerment with the stars would thus be right in searching out their stories, names and personalities, as the knowledge of true names and identities has long been a key to the magical art. From this research and the greater intimacy of communion which results, one can expand their understanding of each star and its power well beyond the mere sentences which the canon of astrological magic provides.

Though it is beyond the scope of this essay to provide exhaustive commentary on the identity of each of the stars, the oratory strategies which both the *Picatrix* and Agrippa employ for the planets can be implemented with the stars with little difficulty.

THE PICATRIXAN MODE OF ADDRESS

The *Picatrix'* planetary conjurations begin with a description of the planet's light and motion and the earthly qualities which they give rise to. Mars' ruddy light and his warlike qualities are inseparable. Thus a stellar oration might begin with its quality of light. Let us use Sirius for an example, the brightest star in the sky. Sirius flames with a brilliant white light, and it would be a serious omission to leave that fact out of any address to the star. Thus, we might begin:

Sirius, incandescent white, whose brilliant torch sets fire to night...

The planet's motion is also a component of their conjurations. Though the stars do not move as the planets, they do have two types of motion. The first is yearly motion. Each star has a period of visibility and invisibility in a given location. The rising, culmination and setting times of the stars was of great importance to many ancient cultures, the Egyptians and Polynesians among them. Sirius, for example, heliacally rose at a time near the Summer solstice in ancient Egypt and was used as a marker for when the flooding of the Nile would occur. The star's cyclical appearance and its meaning, if any, to cultures past is a way of incorporating motion into the address:

Brilliant one, the deluge was long yours to unleash...

The other type of stellar movement is precessional, which occurs on an approximately 26,000 year cycle. Although precession affects all stars, it does so unevenly. One of Sirius' useful qualities for calendars is that it precesses much more slowly than most other stars:

Though your starry brethren whirl and spin, you walk slow and unperturbed through the aeons...

In addition to the quality of light and motion which a given star possesses, its location is important. Describe both the constellation it is a part of, as well as those it nears:

Light of the Great Hound, you follow the giant Orion through the night sky…

Many of the Behenian stars have gods, goddesses and stories associated with them. Here research will lead you to a number of names and tales. The *Picatrix* gives a useful, ambivalent and syncretic model for utilizing multiple sources. The planets are addressed using multiple names, from multiple cultures. Here we might adapt this, saying of Sirius:

The people of the Pyramids called you Sopdet, hound-rider and guarantor of the land's fertility. The Polynesians called you the body of the Great Bird, Manu. The Scandinavians called you Lokabrenna—Loki's Torch. To the Chinese, you are the Celestial Wolf.

Then finalize with the fact that though it is known by many names in many times, there is a unity which lies behind the names and faces, and it is to this unity you speak. The rhetorical strategy presented in the *Picatrix* is useful precisely because it does not rely on any one name or culturally specific mythopoesis. It is a method native to a multicultural period, and thus may be of especial value to those seeking a way in amidst a panopoly of conflicting stories.

AGRIPPA'S MODE OF ADDRESS

In contrast to the mode of address presented in the *Picatrix*, one might also utilize a stars' identification with a single figure from a particular mythos. This strategy, presented by Agrippa for use with the planets, will work for stars that have strong mythologies and whose associated deities have extant liturgies. It is also the most sensible approach for those whose magic operates primarily within the context of a particular pantheon.

For one example of this method we might use the chief star of the constellation Ophiucus, Rasalhague. This constellation was explicitly identified with the divine healer Asklepius during the classical era. The single snake twining around Asklepius' staff and the snake with which Ophiucus grapples are one and the same. The astrologer Bernadette Brady, in *Brady's*

Book of Fixed Stars, when discussing the subject, finds repeatedly that the pattern associated with an entire constellation often concentrated in its brightest star. Rasalhague often prominently placed in the charts of those called to the healing arts. Once a sufficient case can be made for identification, existing odes and liturgies can then be mobilized in a ritual address to the star. In the case of Rasalhague and Asklepius, one can simply look to the surviving Orphic Hymns:

> *Great Esculapius, skill'd to heal mankind, all-ruling Pæan, and physician kind;*
> *Whose arts medic'nal, can alone assuage diseases dire, and stop their dreadful rage:*
> *Strong lenient God, regard my suppliant pray'r, bring gentle Health, adorn'd with lovely hair;*
> *Convey the means of mitigating pain, and raging, deadly pestilence restrain.*
> *O pow'r all-flourishing, abundant, bright, Apollo's honor'd offspring, God of light;*
> *Husband of blameless Health, the constant foe of dread Disease the minister of woe:*
> *Come, blessed saviour, and my health defend, and to my life afford a prosp'rous end.*

THE THIEF AND THE POET

To these established modes of address we might add the tremendous amount of poetry written about the stars, for the glittering hoard above is one of poetry's most enduring themes. Do not fear to raid the treasure house of literary history, for in that act there is great reward but no punishment. The history of Hermeticism is nothing if not a magpie mania of clever acquisition and combination.

Though there are many poems not specifically written as conjurations that may serve, there are some poets and practitioners which have done us the favor of composing odes to the stars. Andrew Watt's *Behenian Poems,* for example, provides a trove of material.

There is also the matter of composing one's own ode. Although much attention is given to the construction of ritual implements such as wands or altarpieces, the composition of conjurations is often held to be outside the practitioner's authority. Yet there is little as satisfying or potent as building a bridge to the stars with one's own words. Those who are inclined to language will find that the process of composition is itself ritual, a point of contact and congress.

THE MOON AND THE STARS

The method for timing the right moment to approach a star's power given in the *Picatrix* and many subsequent tomes is relatively simple when compared to the painstaking calculations necessary for planetary work. Find a moment when the Moon conjoins the star, and then wait for the two to reach the highest point in the sky together.

It is worth noting here that it is the Moon and not any other planet that is assigned the primary duty of carrying the stellar light down to earth. The Moon, of course, is not a planet in the modern definition of the term. It is the Earth's satellite, which puts it in a unique category among the 7 traditional planets.

The Moon has a special relationship to the stars. As Lady of the Night, the Moon is the luminary regent of the half of time when the stars' light is visible to those of us here on earth. Unlike the Sun, her light does not obscure the stars. Indeed, divine images of the Moon often see her either crowned with stars or draped in a sparkling stellar garment.

In addition to this visual association with the fixed stars, the Moon's power is also explicitly linked to one star in particular—the Sun. Indeed, there is no body in astrology whose effects are as contingent upon relationship to the Sun as the Moon. The Moon's power to absorb, reflect and transmit starlight is fundamental. The Moon fills and empties with light, governing the tides of generation and corruption that preside over all living things. Fueled by reflected star-power, beings awake and live, deprived, they sleep and die.

The unstated implication of the Moon's relationship to the Sun is that the Moon is the mediator of starlight down to Earth, which is attested to by the timing-method for stellar magic given in the *Picatrix* and by Agrippa. The Moon is the most influenceable of the planetary bodies, capable of being impregnated or seeded by any planet which she aspects. It is for this reason that the Moon's condition need be considered in any talismanic planetary working, no matter which sphere. It is thus to the Moon we look for what star-power is transmitted to Earth.

The relationship between the Moon and the stars also takes on a more formal relationship in the construction of the Lunar Mansions. The Lunar Mansions are a division of the Moon's path by the number of days it takes the Moon to return to the same position in the sky. Each day's worth of arc is then characterized by the brightest star or stars which the Moon encounters there. Though present in the Arabic phase of astrology and passed to Europe in the succeeding centuries, the Lunar Mansions are undoubtedly of a primarily Indian origin, and form a coherent and prominent part of Vedic astrology to this day.

The relationship between the Moon and the Lunar Mansion stars is conveyed quite nicely by means of myth. The Moon, seen as the male Chandra in the Indian traditions, possesses 27 star-wives, whose mansions he visits regularly, spreading himself among them equally. These visits are quite clearly conjugal, and their progeny is the effect of each day of the Moon's time for life on earth. The procreative duad here is the Moon and stars, although it is a bit odd that the Moon—changeable, receptive and reflective, the very essence of *yin*—is imagined as male, while the stars—radiant and nigh-immortal—are seen as the female 'wife' component of the generative duad. This is quite likely because in most strains of Vedic astrology, every planet is represented primarily by a male divinity. Although this conception may have some value, it seems more fitting to imagine the Moon visiting her 27 star-husbands regularly, as it is the Moon which receives and the stars which emit. Regardless of how, or even if, one imagines the sexual dynamics, the procreative pairing of the Moon and stars is paramount.

The Lunar Mansions are also one of the few vehicles for magical star power in traditional western astro-magical texts. The Arabic names for these mansions are often nothing more than star-names. Yet the brief entries which describe talismans for each lunar mansion are minimal, with the text seemingly cribbed from electional manuals rather than explicitly magical ones. The lunar mansion material given in the western texts is additionally problematized by the fact that the mansions, whose stars precess over time, are calculated from a tropical perspective, meaning that the Moon will be quite distant from the appropriate star when it is placed in the Arabic lunar mansion. This is in direct contradiction with the fixed star instructions, which state that the Moon must be conjoined the star to be approached. No matter how mangled in translation, lunar mansion lists and instructions are nonetheless a consistent feature of Arabic, Medieval and Renaissance astrological magic texts. If we follow the line of dissemination back to India, we find a lore which coordinates the power of the stars and the Moon in an often overtly occult manner, and which can be applied directly to practice. Multiple gods and spirits are associated with each mansion, and additionally, so is a particular magical power or 'shakti.' Furthermore, each mansion's god and spirit associations can provide another angle of approach to stars that comprise them.

FED BY THE ROOT

A group of 15 bright stars is the primary unit of astromagical star lore present in canonical sources, such as the *Picatrix* and Agrippa. These stars are referred to collectively as the Behenian stars. These lists provide each star with an accompanying plant and stone with which they are familiar, as well as a short description of their potencies. Agrippa, drawing from "Hermes on the 15 Fixed Stars," adds to this list a sigil for each star. The instructions are for the creation of magical rings using the stones and herbs of each star at a time when it is especially potent.

'Behenian' is a corruption of the Arabic *bahman*, which means 'root.' Period texts explain to us that these stars are the 'root' of celestial power in the sense that the power of the planets grows from them. Yet a root is not only an origin place, a root is also a feeding apparatus.

In this light, we would do well to re-evaluate the planets assigned to stars. The planets associated with a star, such as Mercury and Venus to Spica, appear only to provide a rough approximation of the stars' meaning using established planetary parameters.

Yet what is implied is that the star is capable of nourishing those planets, lending mere planets a quantum of starfire. This nurturer-nurtured relationship is interesting in both its astrological and magical implications.

First, it is in accord with our current knowledge of stars and planets to put stars in a place to nurture planets, and not vice versa. All planets are born from stars, in fact once being part of the same the material as the star, but spun out at a particular phase of solar system formation. Planets are thus quite literally the children of their parent stars, for they owe their bodies to them. Furthermore, planets are constantly fed by their parent stars. Planets are not, as they might appear from a distance, solid and inanimate balls. Each and every one is awhirl with motion. This motion might be perceived on its surface, but becomes even more dramatic when one penetrates beneath the skin. Our planet earth, for example, has but a thin solid skin, no thicker proportionally than the skin of our own limbs. Underneath lies increasingly active and mobile tissue, and the core itself is a white-hot electromagnetic furnace. Each of the planets within our solar system has such an anatomy.

Like children, the planets possess their own emanant cores. Yet also like children, they must be fed consistently or they will sicken and die. The Sun bathes each planet in a constant stream of particles and power. The light, heat and electromagnetism emanating from the Sun provide radiative nutrients for each planet necessary for their survival as the spheres they are.

It is clear that the Sun is the proper parent to each of the planetary children. Yet what is suggested by the traditional fixed star material is that the planets are also capable of being nurtured or fed by stars outside of our system. If the Sun is our parent, then other stars could be seen as our aunts and uncles, whose visits, gifts and advice impact the planetary children.

The idea of nurturing, edible starlight is not confined solely to astro-magical texts of an Eastern Mediterranean origin. It is, in fact, much more clearly defined and ubiquitous in the traditional sky-lore of China and other East Asian cultures.

In China, the stars are primarily sorted by their color, according to the 5 color *wu-xing* system. These 5 visible colors are used as a clue of what cosmological principle the chi of that star corresponds to. Red stars, for example, correspond to the power of fire. This simple system is further extended to the planets, of which there are, excepting the Sun and Moon, five visible. The colored light of the stars is matched to the phase of the *wu-xing* that the planet corresponds to.

These correspondences are mobilized in a wide variety of ways. Of particular relevance is the way in which esoteric Taoists do so. In one modern example of a widely exposited system of Taoist internal alchemy, the light of the red stars is harvested to feed the light of the red planet, Mars, which is then brought inward to nurture the appropriately fiery organ, the heart. The understanding of sequential levels of parent-child interactions are thus utilized to affect the part of the human being which exists as a link in this chain. What we have, then, is not a vague sort of 'association' or 'correspondence,' but an intimate cosmic animism, in which the stars are the *bahman*, or nourishing root from which further creation continues to spring.

STARS AND STONES

Although the example above is one of internal alchemy, in which the stellar and planetary power is used to feed an organ within the human body, the same principle is utilized in the creation of talismans, which do not use as their end point a human body, but one instead of metal or stone.

Here we loop back to the stones associated with each of the Behenian stars. Each of these stones represents a body capable of being nurtured by and housing the appropriate stellar power. Not only that, each of these stones is capable of being awakened by that stellar power. The star power brought into an organ does not awaken it—the organ is already alive and responsive. Yet by uniting a stone with an appropriate stellar power, the stone is awakened, like a sacred statue, and becomes a conduit for the expression of that particular stellar power. It is our power, as beings equally composed of living starfire and leaden earth, to act as the intermediary between the two, and to bring stellar light into the heart of sleeping stones. This is an archetypal vision of the magician—the one who talks to stars and stones, and presides over the consummation of their marriage.

The relationship between star and stone is an ancient one. Indeed, archaelogists studying long gone civilizations have little more to work with than immense stone megaliths and their alignment with stars. The preserved relationship between star and stone thus links back to eras of human history obscured by flood and fire alike. Though the priests no longer man the pyramids, star and stone remain together in the lore passed from one people to another. Dr. Aaron Cheak argues that much of the talismanic technology present in the Medieval *Picatrix* can be traced back to the stone temples of ancient Egypt, the methods a miniaturization of larger rites, the archetypal one being the 'Opening of the Mouth,' by which a stone statue was awakened with stellar power to house a god. Gnostic gemstones common during the Greco-Roman era, whose surfaces bear graven names and images, form an obvious intermediary step between the deep time of stone monuments, the temples of Egypt and the pages of Agrippa and the *Picatrix*.

The relationship between stars and stones is crucial for the construction of talismans. Though the Behenians also have herbs associated with them, it is not the plant matter that endures. Stone, like starlight, endures. Although occupying two ends of a spectrum, stones and stars both have a share of seeming immortality. There is no object floating in the cosmos that persists as itself for longer than the stars. Likewise, there is no substance on earth as enduring as stone. While metals bend and corrode, stone endures, unchanged, under all but the most titanic pressures. Even then, stone often becomes only more resolute. Some of the most precious stones, such as diamonds, are born only of such forces.

And here we find the core of the relationship between star and stones—gemstones. Most of the precious gems are also the hardest naturally occurring substances on planet earth. Though the diamond is legendary for this power, the other precious stones also share in it. Indeed, virtually all of the most valuable stones—diamond, sapphire, ruby, and emerald—rank well above a 7 on the Mohs scale of hardness, meaning that they cannot be scratched or abraded by wind–born minerals. Immune to environmental erosion, they are in many respects immortal within the confines of the terrestrial world.

Like the stars, not only are gems enduring, they are also luminous. Brilliant nodes, they reflect, capture and transmit light. While metals may be polished to brilliance, they do not take in light the way the way that a ruby can be seen to. Indeed, a backlit gemstone will glow with borrowed luminescence. The stars above and the gems below are thus mirrors of each other, unbreakable and brilliant.

HOLES IN A SHEET

If our ability to connect heaven to earth depends in part on our minds, then the ideas we hold about the nature of sky and space are of more than trivial importance. The predominant cosmological conception of the stars in Western thought for well over a thousand years placed them in the sphere of fixed stars, the concentric layer of the real which enclosed the earth and the orbits of all the planets. This model has been wholly discarded in astronomical circles, but many esoteric systems retain its use for mapping inner or initiatory space while jettisoning its physical truth claims.

Yet this model, long considered outdated, maps on to what we know about the structure of the solar system far better than it is currently considered to. Well beyond the orbits of Pluto, we reach the liminal zone between our world and the depths of interstellar space. The solar wind outpouring from our star races outward at speeds of 671 thousand to 1.79 million mph until it hits the termination shock. At that point, it impacts the interstellar medium, and slows down to below the speed of sound, a phenomenal reduction. At this point, the slowed solar wind mingles with the incoming interstellar medium. This region, called the heliosheath, extends further outward for many millions of miles. This, the layer of the world where the exuded potency of the Sun intermingles with the interstellar medium and radiation from other stars, is tantalizingly close to what is suggested by the archaic notion of the 'sphere of the fixed stars.' Furthermore, folkloric conceptions of the night sky often see it imagined as a dark sheet in which holes have been poked, allowing the light of the stars to shine through. Though it might seem absurd to take this metaphor seriously, when we consider the facts available to us, we know that the solar system is, in fact, surrounded by a sheath, and the light of these stars is, in fact, poking through it. The overwhelming majority of bright stars have maintained virtually the same position in relationship to our solar system for untold millennia. Precession, which changes the position of stars in Earth's sky, is a function of the Earth's wobble—it does not alter the relationship between the Sun and the many fixed stars.

Thus, the light from stars has had aeons to carve pathways through our solar system's outermost membrane. We can imagine these tunnels or rivers of energy by drawing lines between our Sun and the stars outside our system. Their light reaches us, and ours reaches them. There are thus tethers of intermingled light stretching between our star and many others. To the degree that there is a subtle physical component of stellar magic, it is undoubtedly these braided strands of stellar energy.

Such attempts to bridge ancient and contemporary conceptions are necessary, if sometimes awkward. For if this labor is neglected, the result is a constant and ongoing cognitive dissonance. The mind participates in magic, and to the degree that it is divided its potency is decreased.

The paradigm which astrological magic sits most comfortably in is certainly not materialism, for if the planets and stars are all without awareness, all dead, then there can be no astrological magic. Material facts must be reckoned with, but they cannot comprise the whole of our paradigm. The art can only take root in a world that is measured and weighed, but also alive.

An animistic approach to the heavens is fundamental to astrological magic. Why else address the planets and stars with lengthy conjurations? The planets and stars are host to intelligent power, and that intelligent power can be mediated in such a way that the world below is meaningfully changed. Astrological magic assumes that, like us, not only do planets and stars have bodies, but that those bodies are host to increasingly subtle layers of mind and spirit.

One's conception of the real must be voluminous enough to include both bodies and minds, measurable fact and subtle awareness. This is but another part of the celestial art, for the practice of astrological magic is the re-enactment of the marriage of heaven and earth. While one hand must reach upward to grasp empyreal fire, the other must reach low, into the depths of the earth, to set its mark upon stone. The marriage between heaven and earth is both mythic and immanent, eternal and ongoing, and by practicing this art we both come to comprehend it and participate in it more fully.

*   *

*

The Conjunction of Electional Astrology and Magic

J. Lee Lehman, PhD

THE THESIS THAT we present in this chapter is that major portions of electional methodology split between electional astrology and magic in the early period of the translation of Greek materials into Arabic. Possibly the needs of magic engendered a type of electional astrology, which, being specialized, never made it back into mainstream astrology. We will explore both of these alternative possibilities in this chapter.

To examine this idea, we will begin with the Greco-Roman world, and end in the magic and electional astrology of the 17th century. Along the way, we will discuss how electional was being used in magic, what methods were being done in electional astrology itself, who was practicing which, and whether the two types of electional practice were being done by the same, or different people. Then, we can examine how these two types became separate, and to what extent they can rejoin now.

ELECTIONAL ASTROLOGY AND MAGIC IN THE
GRECO-ROMAN WORLD

The world of the Roman Empire in the first century was a polyglot world, with many beliefs and practices. If you wanted to worship Isis, you did. If you preferred the Orphic mysteries, so be it. Yet within a couple of short centuries, this diversity and tolerance would vanish as monotheism would impose its beliefs on the Empire, and in the process, destroy whole swathes of knowledge on its way to dominance.

Pliny the Elder (Gaius Plinius Secundus; 23–79 CE) was one of the great compilers of the Roman world. His massive work, the *Natural History*, survived the end of the Western Roman Empire, becoming one of the major remnants of classical learning available throughout the early Medieval period. While we may quibble over many errors in the corpus, what Pliny stated as fact often became the beliefs of the following generations. Pliny believed that the origins of magic were incubated in Mesopotamia. He classified it as one of the three great arts, medicine, religion, and divination. He says:

> *That it first originated in medicine, no one entertains a doubt; or that, under the plausible guise of promoting health, it insinuated itself among mankind, as a higher and more holy branch of the medical art. Then...it has added all the resources of religion...Last of all, to complete its universal sway, it has incorporated with itself the astrological art; there being no man who is not desirous to know his future destiny, or who is not ready to believe that this knowledge may with the greatest certainty be obtained, by observing the face of the heavens. The senses of men being thus enthralled by a three–fold bond, the art of magic has attained an influence so mighty, that at the present day even, it holds sway throughout a great part of the world, and rules the kings of kings in the East.*[1]

Notice that by the 1st century CE, magic and astrology were linked in the minds of the literate public. Pliny's discussion of its origins is rather garbled, but he follows it from Mesopotamia to Greece.[2] Hellenistic astrology was still reasonably new in Pliny's own time, having emerged from Babylo-

---

1 Pliny the Elder, *The Natural History*. John Bostock, M.D., F.R.S. H. T. Riley, Esq., B. A. London. Taylor and Francis, Red Lion Court, Fleet Street. 1855, Book. XXX, Chapter 1.
2 Ibid., Book XXX, Chapter 2.

nian astrology only a couple of centuries earlier. Earlier still, although the Greeks had known of the existence of Babylonian astrology, they had neither learned the techniques themselves, nor begun the process of adapting astrology to their own culture.[3]

In *Magic of Electional Astrology*, I discuss how the origins of electional astrology in the Hellenistic Era have been obscured by an academic controversy which has developed over the question of whether electional astrology originated in the Hellenistic zone or in India.[4] One early author we possess is Serapio. While the use of Greek suggests an early CE date, his work is not referenced until the 4th century CE, so we cannot be sure. However, this very early electional text gives rules for the use of planetary hours, one of the systems that would achieve more popularity in magical works than in electional ones.[5]

Pliny spends many more words on magic than on astrology, which is perhaps indirect confirmation of the relatively recent familiarity with technical astrology, if not the descriptive aspects of it. He lists magical remedies in his long sections on medicine, which include both the use of ligatures, as well as casual references to the advice of magicians on the topic of healing.[6]

This discussion of magic with astrological medicine was a theme voiced by Frederick Cramer in his opus, *Astrology in Roman Law and Politics*. As Cramer notes, it is within the 1st century CE that we increasingly have the names of individual astrologers, but as he continues, "The character of iatromathematics [i.e., medical astrology] was truly astro-magical."[7]

Just following Pliny's work, we have the *Corpus Hermeticum*, which appears to have been variously written in the 2nd–3rd centuries CE. These

3 The dividing line appears to be Berossus (active 3rd century BCE). He wrote the *History of Babylonia*, and was said to found a school of astrology at Kos. He was sufficiently famous to have a statue erected to him in Athens, and to be mentioned by Pliny and others. Unfortunately, all astrological works from the last two centuries BCE are lost. See: Hand, Robert, and Robert Schmidt. *The Astrological Record of the Early Sages in Greek*. Cumberland, MD: The Golden Hind Press, 1995, pp 49–57.

4 J. Lee Lehman, *The Magic of Electional Astrology*. Atglen, PA: Schiffer Publishing, 2015, p. 14.

5 Robert Hand and Robert Schmidt. *The Astrological Record of the Early Sages in Greek*. Cumberland, MD: The Golden Hind Press, 1995, p. 45.

6 Pliny, Books XXXIV(54) and XXXII(24) as examples.

7 Frederick Henry Cramer, *Astrology in Roman Law and Politics*. Philadelphia,: American Philosophical Society, 1954, p. 188.

works combined magic, astrology, cosmology, medicine, and religious philosophy

The other major intersection of astrology and magic in the Greco-
Roman world related to the development of Neo-Platonism. Plotinus (c.
204–270 CE), the founder of this movement, was said to have remained
unharmed by astral magic that was directed against him. He allowed for
astrological effect, while maintaining the primacy of human free will.[8] It
is through his followers Porphyry and Iamblicus that we see criticisms of
magicians just as the Neoplatonists were promoting a system of theurgy.[9]

We can see that, in the ancient world, magic and astrology were each
well established, and the two fields talked to each other. Not all astrologers
were also magicians, or vice versa, but astrological timing of rituals was
common.

THE EARLY CHURCH FATHERS, ASTROLOGY
AND MAGIC

Christianity was hard on pagan learning. On the one hand, this religious
upheaval didn't disturb institutions: it disturbed people. Both magic and
astrology were present in Judaism—if not officially.[10] The beliefs of the
Christianity that emerged from Judaism looked magical, starting from its
insistence on worshipping a man who didn't die when he should have—
this smacked of magic. This, and the rituals of the mass seemed to a classical outsider (for instance the 2nd century philosopher Celsus) as if Jesus
was a sorcerer, and that his followers were frauds who were consorting
with demons. Celsus' original work is lost, but its arguments remain in the
refutation of it by Origen. The early Christians, having accepted the verac-
ity of the Old Testament, were forced to concede that demons existed, and
their approach was to condemn all demons as evil. In the Greek, *daemon*
was a spirit, and it was not necessarily either good or evil. Origen's contemporary, Tertullian, expanded upon these themes, claiming that magicians

---

8 Lynn Thorndike, *A History of Magic and Experimental Science*. 8 v. vols. New York,:
Macmillan, 1923, Volume 1: p 300–306.
9 Ibid., p. 312.
10 See, for example Lester John Ness, *Written in the Stars: Ancient Zodiac Mosaics*.
Warrenton, PA: Marco Polo Monographs, 1999.

could only produce results through demons.[11]

As for astrology, what value would this have to a people who believed that the End of the World was nigh, and that their Savior had just come to warn them to prepare? The eschatalogical urgency expressed by the early Church fathers precluded any interest in the more prosaic astrological or other divinatory practices. Nonetheless, they were certainly aware of the popularity of these practices with the masses. It is the contention of Chevalier that the early Christians deliberately encoded a form of pseudo-astrology into *Revelation* precisely for this purpose of capturing the lay imagination.[12]

Once Christianity became dominant in the Empire, the non-Christian scholars of the older forms of learning had only two viable choices: to submit to the New World Order, or to escape to where they could still practice the old ways. The Sassanian Empire, that old region of Mesopotamia, governed by rulers who were tolerant—and even welcoming—of scholars of medicine, astrology, and magic, was the refuge to which they fled. The old learning survived and thrived.

AUGUSTINE AND MEDIEVAL LATIN WRITERS
ON ASTROLOGY AND MAGIC

After the fall of Rome, technical astrology was very thin in the Latin West, because all the technical manuals of astrology were written in Greek. Since the 4th century, Christianity became the dominant religion, and it would push out all its rivals. At this stage, both astrology and magic were condemned.

The last word of early Medieval Christianity on both topics was that of Augustine of Hippo (354–430). His great work, *The City of God*, condemns all practices magical and astrological—and a host of other types as well. Being a former practitioner of many things sexual, occult, astrological, magical, and religious, he had the catalog of an insider, and so he knew exactly what he was against. Augustine can find no positive use to either magic or astrology. He adhered to the position that magic—and astral magic—were effective because they were performed by demons.

11 Thorndike, Vol.1, pp 462–463.
12 Jacques M. Chevalier, *A Postmodern Revelation: Signs of Astrology and the Apocalypse.* Toronto ; Buffalo: University of Toronto Press, 1997.

Augustine's approach to astrology was to restrict its use even more than his contemporaries, because, while he didn't outright ban the use of astrology for something like weather forecasting, he only tepidly admitted that it was possible. He also specifically criticized electional astrology, using the rather odd argument that, if the Nativity is supposed to show man's fate, then electional is interfering with the fate of the nativity. Notice that in this characterization of the natal chart, absolute predestination (i.e., the complete absence of free will) is assumed as the ground of being.[13]

However, though magic and astrology may have been proscribed, this is evidence of its continual practice! In fact, the culture in which Augustine lived still had all the so-called pagan attractions of Rome of a couple of centuries earlier. Julius Firmicus Maternus wrote a comprehensive work on astrology which continued, along with Pliny, to be available in Latin throughout the interval between the fall of Rome and the arrival of the Arabic translations of Greek works in the 12th century. Firmicus' work *Mathesis* is a good quality work on Hellenistic astrology. Later, he apparently converted to Christianity, and then wrote an apology.[14]

Contemporary authors who were neither magicians nor astrologers attest to the continued popularity of both. Thorndike lists the rhetorician Libanus (314–391) as one such witness.[15] In this period of the Late Roman Empire, or early Medieval period, both astrology and magic are being practiced, although some of the more technical aspects of astrology are being cut off in the West as fewer people read Greek. Both disciplines are under fire from Christian clerics. Both are officially unacceptable.

Based on the paucity of sources in Latin, and the fact that the vast majority of the technical sources on astrology to this point were in Greek, the belief was held until quite recently that only a popular form of non-technical astrology could have endured in the West prior to the 12th century translations. David Juste disproved this, by showing how *computus*, the Medieval system of calculating the correct date for Easter, could have been used to compute planetary positions as well, thus allowing for a more facile use of astrological indicators.[16]

---

13 Thorndike, Vol. 1, pp 504–518.
14 Julius Firmicus Maternus, *Ancient Astrology : Theory and Practice = Matheseos Libri Viii*. Park Ridge, NJ: Noyes Press, 1975.
15 Thorndike, Vol. 1, pp 538–540.
16 David Juste, "Neither Observation nor Astronomical Tables: An Alternate Way of Computing the Planetary Longitudes in the Early Western Middle Ages." in Pingree, David, and Charles Burnett. *Studies in the History of the Exact Sciences in Honour of David*

FROM INSIDE THE ROMAN EMPIRE TO
OUTSIDE OF IT: AGAIN

By the time of the splitting of the Roman Empire into Eastern and Western sections in the third century CE, the old land of Babylon had passed out of the influence of the Greco-Roman zone. The Sassanian Empire (224–651 CE) was the last Persian empire before the conquests of Islam. State support for Zoroastrianism meant that the strictures on astrology being developed by Christianity were not in force in this zone.

In ancient Mesopotamia, the physician (*asû*) might work hand-in-hand with the magician-exorcists (*āšipu*) on a single medical case. The involvement of magic in the healing process was seen as necessary, because of the high frequency with which ghosts were held to be the cause of disease.[17] Magic was properly invoked whenever a non-physical cause to an ailment was suspected.

By the Sassanian period, an astrological timing system for the practice of magic had been completely integrated, having been initiated in the Hellenistic period. We can see remnants of this era in the Mandean work *Sfar Malwašia*, which gives medical astrological remedies and their electional times.[18]

Some of the more interesting discoveries of the Sassanian period are the Mandaic magical incantation bowls. These clay bowls, of which there are thousands, contain inscriptions mostly in Aramaic, though some of them use the Mandaic script. They may include drawings of serpents, magical circles, and demons. There are some astrological referents in the inscriptions.[19]

But in the 7th century, the Sassanian Empire collapsed. In swept Islamic armies, establishing first the Umayyad Dynasty, and then the 'Abbāsids in turn conquered them. The 'Abbāsids found themselves in a land which

Pingree, Islamic Philosophy, Theology, and Science ; V. 54. Leiden ; Boston: Brill, 2004. 181–215.

17 See for example Jo Ann Scurlock, *Magico-Medical Means of Treating Ghost-Induced Illnesses in Ancient Mesopotamia*, Ancient Magic and Divination. Leiden ; Boston: Brill / Styx, 2006.

18 Maire Masco, *Mandaeans: Gnostic Astrology and Cultural Transmission*. Fluke Press,: Tacoma, WA, 2012.

19 Michael G. Morony, *Magic and Society in late Sasanian Iraq*, pp. 83–107 in Scott Noegel, Joel Walker and Brannon Wheeler, Editor. *Prayer, Magic and the Stars in the Ancient and Late Antique World*. University Park, PA: University of Pennsylvania Press, 2003.

was astrologically friendly, so they turned to the remaining Sassanian astrologers, and through their advice, founded the city of Baghdad at an astrologically propitious time. This regime saw the value in acquiring the ancient learning, and through a cadre of scholars—Persian, Christian and Jewish—created a translation movement that would bring the entire corpus of Greek learning into the Arabic language over the course of several centuries. They would then use the logic acquired to bolster their program for political aims, to convert people to Islam, and use the natural philosophy and astrology to improve their medical systems. Along the way, this multi–generational patronage would bring philosophy and the sciences to heights never before attained.[20]

ARABIC WRITERS ON MAGIC AND ASTROLOGY

The partial religious tolerance of the 'Abbāsid Dynasty resulted in a complex intellectual society, that further extended Hellenistic knowledge through debate, commentary, and observation. Among the relevant works that bridge the subjects of electional astrology and magic from this period are:

- *The Book of the Treasure of Alexander* is thought to be from Harran during the Sassanian period. This magical work is very sophisticated in its presentation, with specific astrological formulas for the production of all kinds of talismans, whether to promote the affairs of each of the planets, or to combat scorpions, or to force someone to fall in love with the talisman possessor.[21]

- *On the Stellar Rays* of al-Kindi (d. 850/873) gave the theory behind how electional could work.[22] Here we have a reference to the use of electional logic for the creation of talismans. He

20 Gutas, Dimitri. *Greek Thought, Arabic Culture: The Graeco–Arabic Translation Movement in Baghdad and Early 'Abbāsid Society (2nd–4th/8th–10th Centuries).* London: New York: Routledge, 1998.

21 Christopher Warnock. *Book of the Treasure of Alexander: Ancient Hermetic Alchemy & Astrology.* Translated by Nicholai de Mattos Frisvold. Charlotte, NC: lulu.com, 2010.

22 al-Kindi. *On the Stellar Rays.* Translated by Robert Zoller. Berkeley Springs, WV: Golden Hind Press, 1993, p 51.

also wrote a work, *The Choice of Days*, which treats the method of electing by the applying aspects of the Moon, with the sextile or trine preferred.[23] These elections do not involve a horoscope, and are thus general indicators.[24] This combination of works is suggestive of our thesis: al-Kindi's work *On the Stellar Rays* discusses a topic which, by this stage, was more in the magical realm, namely talisman electional. Then he also wrote a work of the simplified forms of electional.

· *De Imaginibus* of Thabit ibn Qurra (836–901): the purpose of this work was to give the method for creating astrological talismans; this included a sophisticated discussion of the electional rules. A Sabian, his work would be a major source for the later *Picatrix*; he emphasized astrology as the ground for all magical applications. What is most significant from our standpoint is that the electional astrology is complex: this was at a level of expertise of a master astrologer, not someone who was only familiar with Moon sign or planetary hour. This demonstrates the continued tight integration of magical and electional ideas through this period.[25] Thabit's works found their way into Latin readily in part because he also wrote *De motu octave sphere qui*, which was an important reference on planetary calculation.[26]

· The anonymous *Ghayat al-Hakim*, or *Picatrix*: the level of astrological knowledge which this book requires is immense. The lists of rulerships are as extensive as those found in any astrology text.[27] This work appeared in Spanish translation in 1256.

23 Benjamin N. Dykes, *Choices and Inceptions: Traditional Electional Astrology*. Minneapolis, MN: Cazimi Press, 2012, pp. 59–60.

24 Dykes, 2012, p. 39.

25 Thabit ibn Qurrah, al-Harrani, Christopher Warnock, and Nigel Jackson. *De Imaginibus: On Images: A Treatise on Astrological Talismans*. [United States]: Renaissance Astrology, 2008.

26 Boudet, Jean-Patrice. *Entre Science Et Negromance. Astrologie, Divination Et Magie Dans L'occident Medieval (XII–Xv Siecle)*. Paris: Sorbonne, 2006, p. 47.

27 Greer and Warnock, pp 31–51.

There were a number of other very detailed works on electional astrology, but not all books covered both fields. Still, we may note that the use of astrology in magic is extremely prominent at this time, and that much of the making of talismans and other remedial measures has passed into this field.

Islam is a monotheistic religion that rejected the trinitarian approach of Orthodox Christianity. Magic was officially banned, although it was energetically studied in this early period. Were the stars for Arabia, or not? The bifurcation of the more willful aspects of electional astrology into magic does not make it easy to answer this question. Even magic itself grades into something completely commonplace. As Canaan points out, the use of talismans is extremely old and common in the Middle East. They may be inscribed on paper, bone, stone, metal, glass, leather, or many other substances. Among the most popular such inscriptions are scriptural.[28] If these are seen to have power, then what is the difference between a phylactery and a magic square, or the angel of Mars?

The later 'Abbāsid Dynasty saw the development of a religious reaction against pagan philosophy, and so once again, the land would become unfriendly to the intellectual climate that had previously been nurturing. Yet again, the scholars would pack their manuscripts and go to centers where the corpus of knowledge—now extended by the remarkable scholars writing in Arabic—would now move into yet another language: Latin. Each of these two great transmissions moved words from one culture into a new language and circumstance, with each move accompanying a shift in religious perspective of the receiving region.

By the time these Arabic manuscripts were crossing the Latin barrier, a fundamental transformation had occurred. When the Hellenistic transmission occurred into Arabic, it would have been possible to skip the astrological material and not lose that large a piece of the science and philosophy. The reason for this is simple: the pre-Socratics, the Socratics, the Hippocratic tradition—all these great works of the Hellenistic Era were produced in the centuries before astrology transmitted out of Mesopotamia and into Hellenistic culture. The Hellenistic astrology works (apart from a small piece of Neoplatonism) were by separate authors, and could

---

28 Tewfik Canaan, "The Decipherment of Arabic Talismans", pp. 125–177 in Savage–Smith, Emilie. *Magic and Divination in Early Islam*, The Formation of the Classical Islamic World. Aldershot, Hants, Great Britain ; Burlington, VT, USA: Ashgate/Variorum, 2004.

be viewed as an epiphenomenon of Greek learning: interesting, but not at the heart of the system.

However, because the 'Abbāsid Empire had political reasons for elevating astrology by using the extant remnants of Persian astrology as practiced in the Sassanian Empire to justify the inevitability of 'Abbāsid conquest and dominance, astrology was not only a priority piece of the transmission of Greek language manuscripts, it was then systematically integrated into the works being produced in Arabic. Thus, by the time that the Arabic corpus was moving into Latin, there was no practical way to expunge the astrology from the sciences and philosophy: it had to be ingested along with the rest, and thus it had to accommodate to Christian theology. This accommodation also had to be a two-way street.

INTO THE LATIN WEST

As Jean–Patrice Boudet notes, the arrival of Arabic, Greek, and Hebrew texts into the Latin West forced a change in orientation toward both magic and astrology, because now both fields were practiced by those of the most profound learning. This was completely different from the more watered down folk versions of these arts, which were much easier to condemn. Old and Middle French lacked the noun form for magic, while possessing the adjective. This makes the point that while one could *perform* magic (presumably through the actions of a demon), there was no idea that there could be such a thing as a *theory* of magic.[29]

The first astrological transmissions occurred in Italy in the 10th century, and this included the lunar mansions. This fact is important, because the lunar mansions alone (i.e., without the background of formal chart calculation) represent a form of electional as well as a timing mechanism for astral magic.[30]

John of Salisbury (d. 1180) expanded upon the work of Isidore of Seville (560–636) whose early definitions concerning magic had held sway in the Latin West until the time when the Arabic language material was beginning to filter in. In his work *Policraticus*, John went beyond Isidore's classifi-

29 Jean-Patrice Boudet, *Entre Science Et Negromance. Astrologie, Divination Et Magie Dans L'occident Medieval (XII–XV Siècle)*. Paris: Sorbonne, 2006, pp. 18–20.
30 Juste, David. *Les Alchandreana Primitifs : Étude Sur Les Plus Anciens Traités Astrologiques Latins D'origine Arabe (Xe Siècle)*. Leiden: Brill, 2007, pp. 123–125.

cation of (demonic) divination by the four elements to include whole new categories: enchantment, making images, astrology, chiromancers, among others. He defined these all under the heading black magic, and stated that the biggest problem was with the clergy, not the laity. John's description was not that of someone attempting to define these matters theoretically, but that of someone who had knowledge of what was really going on. His personal experience as a young man was given in Book 2, Chapter 28.[31] He called attention to the tendency of these clerics to call upon saints, and to otherwise mimic legitimate Christian ways.[32] John followed the convention that, until the coming of Christ, astrology was legitimate, but afterwards, astrologers became false prophets.[33]

Adelard of Bath (c. 1080–c. 1152) has long been considered one of the major figures responsible for transmitting astrological and other Arabic knowledge into England—and the only non-cleric to do so. He would wander all over Europe, studying Arabic manuscripts, whether of astrology, or geometry—or the magical processes of creating talismans. The Arabic material was much richer in its use of astral magic than the indigenous folk magic of England.[34] Adelard dedicated his treatise on the astrolabe to the future Henry II (Plantagenet), and Henry employed another translator, Roger of Hereford, as his astrologer, who drew up the horoscope of Eleanor of Aquitaine.[35] He would also translate Thabit ibn Qurrah.[36]

Within these English and French courts, the frequency of magic themes in courtly romances is vast, and it appears that magic may have acquired a higher social reputation through its association with astrology.[37]

Michael Scot (1175–c. 1235) was astrologer to Frederick II, Holy Roman Emperor. Scot gave a couple of examples of interrogations in his *Le Liber introductorius*, although he did not specify the circumstances. However, it is clear that he was doing horaries and electionals for his client. This said, his work covered magic as well as astrology. His magical sources included Thabit and pseudo-Solomon. He elected for talismans. While Scot began

31 Boudet, p. 101.
32 Ibid., pp. 89–94.
33 Ibid., p. 96.
34 Ibid., pp. 157–162.
35 Ibid., p. 168.
36 Rondal Hutton, "Astral Magic: The Acceptable Face of Paganism," pp 10–24 in: Campion, Nicholas, Patrick Curry, and Michael York. *Astrology and the Academy*. Bristol: Cinnabar Books, 2004, p.12.
37 Boudet, pp. 170–164.

the work with the usual cautions, it appears according to a longer version of the *Introductorius* that he did invoke demons.[38]

Guido Bonatti's (1210?–1296?) astrological work was controversial enough for Dante to place him in the eighth circle of the *Inferno* for his attempt to see into the future. But what we do *not* see in Bonatti's work on electional is any hint for the magical side of the coin: the use of electional for creating talismans, or timing rituals.

The other great astrological compiler of this time period was Leopold of Austria. His *Compilatio*, which appeared about 1271, covered astrology, astronomy, and magic. Also, it became one of the few astrological texts in French before the 14th century, as its translation appeared before 1324. His work has been compared in scope to Haly Abenragel.[39]

However, their contemporary, Albertus Magnus (ca. 1200–1280) was still grappling with the boundaries of licit and illicit knowledge. Known both in his own right and as the teacher of Thomas Aquinas (1225–1274), Albert was more the natural philosopher, and Thomas the theologian. Albert's works are a trajectory toward a synthesis of Aristotle and Augustine: the Aristotle in question being the one inclusive of the spurious works.[40]

It was Thomas Aquinas who forged the new Christian understanding of astrology. Beginning with Aristotle's contention that the planets, as secondary causes could thus be understood as agents of God's will, Aquinas concluded that astrology was licit as long as it did not infringe upon the individual's freedom to make moral choices, nor God's complete power to create whatever future He willed. As long as astrology impacted only physical matters, such as meteorology, or the physical body, or mundane events, then astrology was acceptable.[41] Under this system, medical astrology would be fine, but electional was not. Aquinas discussed magic as well as astrology. Aquinas held to the common belief of his peers that demons could make magical works appear efficacious.[42]

Albert's own interests were not always neatly packaged within Thomas' revisionism. Albert was interested in occult virtues, a code word of acceptable magic, which also is found under the term natural magic. In his

38 Ibid., pp. 175, 182–185.

39 Francis J. Carmody, "Leopold of Austria, Li Compilacions De La Sciences Des Estoilles" Books I–III." *Univ. of CA Publ Modern Philology* 33, no. 2 (1947): i–iv + 35–102.

40 Thorndike, Vol. 2, pp. 530–531.

41 Paul Choisnard, Paul. *Saint Thomas D'aquin Et L'influence Des Astres*. Paris,: Librarie F. Alcan, 1926.

42 Thorndike, Vol. 2, p. 604.

theological writings, Albert condemns magic through demons, but leaves a place for magic devoid of demonic influence. Occult virtue falls in this latter category.[43] We can see these workings in *The Book of Secrets*, The abilities of the stones to accomplish feats do have the look of magic: "*If thou wilt have favour and honour,*" "*If thou wilt drive away fantasies and foolishness,*" "*If thou wilt judge the opinions and thoughts of others,*" "*If thou wilt have victory and amity*", "*If thou wilt that a man sleeping will tell to thee what he hath done.*"[44] Such a table of contents does not look significantly different from some magical spell books, nor some of the Medieval Arabic uses of magical electional astrology. Albert specifically discussed ligatures. He held that even the engraving of stones for this purpose falls more under the category of natural magic.[45] In *De Mineralibus et Rebus Metallicus*, Albert does not condemn electional astrology, even as he does champion free will, which includes the free will to elect.[46] He believes that the engraving of stones does not produce sigils of infinite duration, and distinguishes properties based on the latitude of the stone. Stones may be engraved to have virtues according to the constellations or the Triplicities.[47] This position is further elucidated in the *Speculum Astronomiae*, in which Albert not only mentions elections, but includes immediately thereafter a section on images, which he regards as the acme of astrology. He does acknowledge its association with necromancy—a reference to the precise overlap with magic that we have been discussing—and here he specifically references Thabit. One singular practice in the production of images that he condemns is suffumigations, the unquestionably magical practice of exposing talismans to incense. He discusses the effect of electing upon free will.[48]

Roger Bacon (ca. 1219–ca. 1292) also grappled with the relation between astrology and magic. He condemned magic absolutely.[49] However, he also reported on its prevalence, both in Roman times and his own.[50]

43 Ibid., 555–561.

44 Michael R. Best, Frank Brightman, and Albertus. *The Book of Secrets of Albertus Magnus of the Virtues of Herbs, Stones and Certain Beasts, Also a Book of the Marvels of the World.* Oxford [Eng.: Clarendon Press, 1973, pp. 40–41.

45 Thorndike, Vol. 2, p. 573.

46 Ibid., 587.

47 Evans, Joan. *Magical Jewels of the Middle Ages and the Renaissance, Particularly in England.* New York: Dover Publications, 1976, pp. 96–98.

48 Thorndike, Vol. 2, pp 697–700.

49 Ibid., 659–665.

50 Ibid., 660.

Even so, he supported the use of electional, and of engraved images for medical purposes that were produced using electional methods.[51] Thus, while he condemned magic, his realm for astrology definitely graded into the zone of magical practice.

One of the great astrologically inclined monarchs of this period was Alfonso X of Castile (1221–1284). He supported translations including Haly Abenragel, Ptolemy, Azarquiel (Abū Ishāq Ibrāhīm al–Zarqālī, 1029–1087, a contributor to the Toledan Tables) and al–Battâni. Such detailed work ultimately bore fruit as the Alfonsine Tables for computing planetary positions. He also supported the translation and production of magical and astral magical works, including the *Picatrix* and the *Liber Razielis*.[52]

THE CONDEMNATION OF 1277

In 1277, the Bishop of Paris Stephen Tempier condemned 219 propositions which may have been taught at the University of Paris. This was in part a reaction to the increased influence of pagan writings, especially Aristotle. There was also more than a tacit critique of Aquinas implied in the propositions chosen.

Eventually, the views of Aquinas would become orthodoxy. Some historians hold that the questioning of Aristotle done by the Bishop can be viewed as a marker for the birth of modern science; others are much more conservative in their conclusions.[53] What does seem clear is that, by this time, the criticisms of magic were achieving traction, resulting in magic becoming more restricted theologically than astrology.

The physician Arnald of Villanova (ca. 1240–1311), while condemning demonic magic, translated Costa ben Luca's *Incantations, Adjurations, and Suspensions from the Neck*, which itemizes the healing properties of stones, metals, and gems. Astrological properties are discussed, as well as the timing of the collection of medicines. He discusses the use of images for medicinal purposes.[54] There is a list of sigils that he developed made from metal only (no gem), representing the signs of the zodiac, and including

51　Ibid., 673.
52　Boudet, pp. 187–198.
53　For example, see Jason Gooch. "The Effects of the Condemnation of 1277" *The Hilltop Review* 2 (2006): 34–45.
54　Thorndike, Vol. 2, pp. 853–858.

not only electional information for their making, but the prayers to be said at the time, which include a mix of Christian, Jewish, and magic overlays to the talisman of the zodiacal sign.[55]

And then consider Andalò di Negro, who wrote *Introduction to Judgments of Astrology*, whose one dated work was from 1423. This work includes the lunar mansions. This already suggests that there may be a magic connection, because the lunar mansions were often used by magicians for what I have referred to elsewhere as quick and dirty electionals: ones using only a few astrological features when a precise electional was not deemed necessary.[56] His medical works emphasized horary and electional but because they concerned the diseases of the body, this would still be considered acceptable.[57]

Boudet has demonstrated that by far the biggest collector of astrological materials was Charles V (The Wise) of France (1338–1380).[58] Throughout his reign, he used medical and electional. During this period, astrological advice could be dispensed openly, but magical involvement is harder to find.

Antonio de Montulmo (fl. 1384–1390) wrote on both astrology and magic. His work, *On the Judgment of Nativities* was later expanded by Regiomontanus, and printed in the 16th century.[59] This work reads as a standard astrological work. But not so his treatise entitled *Liber intelligentiarum de occultis et manifestis,* which is a work on necromancy and spirit invocation. He proposes different astrological rules for magical work, and describes the fabrication of magical images. He mentions the use of electional astrology. He mentions Thabit.[60]

In Burgundy, the text *Traitié contre les devineurs*, composed in 1411 by Laurens Pignon, could be dismissed as a reworking of Aquinas, except that it also includes local events, and thus a picture of magic and astrology at the royal court. This work warned of the moral consequences of the

---

55 Evans, pp. 98–99.

56 Lehman,, 2015, Chapter 4.

57 Thorndike, Vol. 3, pp. 191–197.

58 Boudet, pp. 303–307.

59 A modern English translation is available:
Antonius de. Montulmo, *On the Judgment of Nativities. Part 1.* Translated by Robert Hand. Berkeley Springs, WV: Golden Hind Press, 1995.

60 Thorndike, Vol. 3, pp. 604–610.

excessive use of divination and its impact on all the social classes that were involved.[61]

In Catalonia, the *Tractat de prenostication de la vida dels hòmens* was produced sometime in the 15th century. This amazing work, a kind of a fortune-telling guide, is virtually unique. It contains astrology, astrological magic, astrological medicine, geomancy, numerology, and gematria. The Native is described by Sun sign, divided into male and female individuals. It includes the Faces, or decans. And further, this is clearly a manual for the less educated, being in the vernacular.[62]

Nicholas of Hungary (fl. ca. 1456) published *Liber anagliffarum astronimae*, a work in four books. The first three were standard astrology of the time, including medical astrology and electional, while the fourth contains magic, with references to both Albertus and Thabit.[63]

The Italian Renaissance has held scholars in its thrall for many decades. Among the figures in great esteem was Pico della Mirandola (1463–1494), who was rife with magical ideas. In the decades before Pico, there were a number of scholars, such as Barnard Basin, who were attempting to make the argument that the magical arts could actually be salutary toward salvation.[64] Pico's ideas were not well received by the Catholic establishment, and he was arrested for heresy. In his Apology issued in his defense, Pico makes the remarkable statement that no learning makes the case for Christ's divinity better than (natural) magic and the cabala![65] His apology was not accepted, and, chastened by this, he began to write against astrology.[66]

The reinvigoration of Platonic themes by the Renaissance translation movement, loosely under the aegis of Marsilio Ficino (1433–1499), did serve to increase interest in magic. Among this generation of scholars was Jacques Lefèvre (1455–1537), Johann Reuchlin (1455–1522), and Johannes

61 Jan R. Veenstra and Laurens Pignon, *Magic and Divination at the Courts of Burgundy and France : Text and Context of Laurens Pignon's Contre Les Devineurs (1411)*, Brill's Studies in Intellectual History,. Leiden ; New York: Brill, 1998.

62 John Scott Lucas, *Astrology and Numerology in Medieval and Early Modern Catalonia: The Tractat De Prenostication De La Vida Natural Dels HÃ²mens*, The Medieval and Early Modern Iberian World. Leiden ; Boston: Brill, 2003.

63 Thorndike, Vol. 4, pp. 247–250.

64 Ibid., 488–492.

65 Ibid., 493–499.

66 Ibid., 507–511.

Trithemius (1462–1516). Again, the disputations are concerning the limits of natural magic.[67]

Marsilio Ficino's *De Tripliciti Viti* discusses music and ritual which combine together into magical rituals—even if they were not labeled as such.[68] In *De vita coelitus comparanda*, Ficino discusses images, and he encourages the use of electional. His use of images was very creative; his use of electional was not especially.[69]

With Heinrich Cornelius Agrippa (1486–1535) we arrive at the most significant magical text since the *Picatrix*. But not only is Agrippa's work significant as a magical text: it is significant as an astrological one. Over the years, the study of ancient rulership definitions has been one of my areas of research. The early portion of this work was published as *The Book of Rulerships*.[70] I have continued to expand this work with additional authors. Table 1 gives a comparison of the number of rulership entries collected from three different sources: William Lilly's *Christian Astrology*, Culpeper's *Herbal*, and the *Three Books of Occult Philosophy* by Agrippa.

Table 1. NUMBER OF RULERSHIP ENTRIES FROM THREE DIFFERENT CLASSICAL SOURCES.[71]

Lilly	2,748	rulerships
Culpeper	378	rulerships
Agrippa	425	rulerships

What is easily observed is that Agrippa gave more astrological rulerships than Culpeper! Now, thinking about the relative numbers in this table is very useful. While these numbers are not an absolute count, they are a

67 Thorndike, Vol. 4, pp. 512–528.

68 Walker, D. P. *Spiritual and Demonic Magic : From Ficino to Campanella*. Notre Dame [Ind.]: University of Notre Dame Press, 1975, pp. 30–31.

69 Thorndike, Vol. 4, pp. 565–569.

70 J. Lee Lehman, *The Book of Rulerships*. Atglen, PA: Schiffer Press, 1992.

71 Lilly, William, and William Marshall. *Christian Astrology Modestly Treated of in Three Books. The First Containing the Use of an Ephemeris, the Erecting of a Scheam of Heaven; Nature of the Twelve Signes of the Zodiack, of the Planets; with a Most Easie Introduction to the Whole Art of Astrology...*, London, 1659.

Culpeper, Nicholas, David Potterton, and Michael Stringer. *Culpeper's Color Herbal*. New York: Sterling Pub. Co., 1992.

Heinrich Cornelius Agrippa von Nettesheim, (Donald Tyson, and James Freake, trans). *Three Books of Occult Philosophy*. Llewellyn's Sourcebook Series. 1st ed. St. Paul, MN, USA: Llewellyn, 1993.

good approximation of the content. Lilly's work, as one of the most comprehensive texts on horary astrology ever written would be expected to maximize the number of rulerships given for each planet, sign, and house.

But that Agrippa would have more keywords than Culpeper actually says a great deal. Culpeper's is a fine medicinal herbs reference, a text designed around rulership as a core concept. Agrippa's book is meant to be a book on magic, but Agrippa's contention is that magic is futile without astrology. Even so, the astrological knowledge is presented from a different perspective: one totally practical and focused.[72]

Paracelsus (Philippus Aureolus Theophrastus Bombastus von Hohenheim, 1493–1541) was a huge reformer of medicine. He is credited with many firsts in medicine, including the beginning of the use of chemical medicines. He had alchemical interests as well, placing three types of substances on an equal footing: "For Mercury is the spirit, Sulphur is the soul, and Salt is the body."[73] Some of Paracelsus' followers, such as Gerhard Dorn, were interested in applying Paracelsus' ideas on medicine through a magical overlay.[74]

As we enter the 16th century, our story becomes increasingly populated—but the general outlines are fully established by Agrippa's time. The great magicians of the Renaissance—whether Ficino, Agrippa, or later, John Dee (1527–1608) and Robert Fludd (1574–1637)—would know electional astrology well, even as astrologers were separating themselves from magic. Astrology was more enthusiastically taught in the medical departments of the university than elsewhere, and this allowed astrologers to more closely align with the profession of medicine, a much more religiously acceptable home.

Still, just as astrologers today often become enmeshed in tarot or other occult practices, so astrologers of the Renaissance and post-Renaissance periods often still dabbled with magic. However, magic in those years had a much edgier reputation than astrology was assuming. We can ascertain how little things changed in the intervening centuries by looking in at the 17th century, which was the last period of classical astrological method before a transmission break.

---

72 Agrippa, p. 359.
73 Paracelsus, *De Natura Rerum* (1537) cited in Paracelsus. *Paracelsus. Essential Readings.* Trans. Goodrick-Clarke. Berkeley: North Atlantic Books, 1999, p. 176.
74 Ibid., p. 192.

Historian Patrick Curry refers to this period in England as the halcyon days of astrology, the time of William Lilly, Nicholas Culpeper, John Gadbury, Henry Coley, John Goad, and William Ramesey—any one of whom individually would have made the period worth studying.[75] The breakdown in royal censorship during the English Civil War brought the publication of almanacs to new heights, as political astrological works, had not only changed the trajectory of almanacs, but placed them firmly on the road to permanent popularity.

William Lilly (1602–1681) was the poster child for this period. He is best known now for his fashionable horary and natal practice.[76] He studied astrology and other matters with John Evans, a cunning man—a term in use at the time for a local magic practitioner. Lilly tells the story that when he came to London, the husband of his mistress could only keep from committing suicide because of a sigil made for him by Simon Forman (1552–1611), who also allegedly was a teacher to Lilly.[77] Lilly's predictions were entertaining, pro-Parliament, and mostly correct. His practice was extensive, and he became one of the wealthiest astrologers of his day. He had also studied magic in the 1640s: the same decade in which he published *Christian Astrology*. He conjured spirits, but then he gave it up and burned his books. His great work does not contain electional, so we cannot see how his magical studies affected that branch of astrology.[78] As Thomas points out, the kind of magic of a cunning man or cunning woman had become virtually indispensable in England for an odd reason. When Henry VIII split from Rome and formed the Anglican Church, one of the reforms was to dispense with exorcism, and also with holy water and the sign of the cross. Many was the person in Catholic domains who relied on these as potent forces against witchcraft. Anglicanism unwittingly removed the only technologies they had against witchcraft—and so then the only protection one had against a spell was someone else's counter-spell.[79] However, Thomas also notes that the lines between religion and magic were never easy, because religion adopted magical forms, and magical practitioners prayed. What was the Church supposed to say about a cunning woman

75 Patrick Curry, *Prophecy and Power: Astrology in Early Modern England*. Princeton, NJ: Princeton University Press, 1989, chapter 2.

76 William Lilly, 1647.

77 Keith Thomas, *Religion and the Decline of Magic: Studies in Popular Beliefs in Sixteenth and Seventeenth Century England*. London,: Weidenfeld & Nicolson, 1971, p. 264.

78 Curry, pp. 27–31.

79 Thomas, p. 265.

who prayed over her sick neighbor? While the Church hierarchies might gnash their teeth, magicians and alchemists were often much more fervent in their beliefs than their ecclesiastical contemporaries—they simply did not toe the line of orthodoxy.[80]

Less visible but no less important, Elias Ashmole (1617–1692) was a patron of both the occult as well as emerging science in the form of the Royal Society. We might call him a reactionary occultist, with interests in astrology, alchemy, hermeticism, and natural magic. Ashmole referred to astrology as the key to natural magic.[81]

William Ramesey almost brought back the magical electional piece into regular electional astrology. His work, *Astrology Restored*, has many of the pieces typical of magical works: planetary hours, lunar mansions, and too much overlap in technique with Agrippa to be merely chance. But this is not done overtly. We are left to wonder, since the text otherwise reads like a conventional electional text.[82]

The restoration of Charles II in 1660 marked the end of this experiment in free speech. Now, the almanacs were censored again, and inappropriate political commentary by astrologers could result in jail time.[83] Astrology by now was viewed by the ruling elite as a very dangerous enterprise. So censorship begat ridicule, and from there, astrology was eclipsed.[84] Astrology would survive, but any chance of recombining with magic was lost for centuries.

HISTORICAL DISCUSSION

Boudet would note the irony of the position held by an anonymous astrologer in the time of Charles VII of France, who accepted the restrictions of Aquinas relating to free will when viewing nativities, and yet also enthusiastically accepted horaries and electionals, which imply a virtual absence

---

80 Ibid, pp. 267–279.
81 Elias Ashmole, *Theatrum Chemicum Britannicum. The First Part*. London: Printed by J. Grismond for Nathaniel Brooke, 165; cited by Curry, p. 36.
82 William Ramesey, *Astrologia Restaurata, or, Astrologie Restored Being an Introduction to the General and Chief Part of the Language of the Stars : In 4 Books … : With a Table of the Most Material Things Therein Contained*. London: Printed for Robert, 1654.
83 Curry, p. 47.
84 Ibid., pp. 49–51.

of free will.[85] This represents the extremely complex and not entirely consistent place occupied by astrology in the European mind after the 12th century renaissance.

What we have seen throughout this survey is that intellectual boundaries were very porous. The centuries-long toleration of scholarly magic meant that many of the individuals we have studied here maintained interests in both astrology and magic: and probably would not have seen a great deal of distinction. Further, since for much of the period dating from the 12th century, astrological magic might well be admissible as a form of natural magic, any association of magic with astrology could be seen as a way of passing off magical practice as licit.

It is also true that the overlaps really were extensive. Take medical applications. As mentioned previously, Lynn Bootes has traced the use of medical talismans from the Babylonian period to the Renaissance, and cross culturally into India as well. In the Babylonian period, suspensions (amulets) were used primarily by placing several herbs or other objects into a tuft of wool or other carrier, and placing it around the neck or some other portion of the body.[86] Is this magical, or simply medical? By the Hellenistic period, the situation had grown even more complex. As Bootes discussed, Franz Cumont had observed the complete overlap of astrological and magical medical practice in Egypt, complete with planetary invocations—the style we would call astral magic.[87] This idea has become standard in the history of medicine from that period: that Egyptians regularly chose between physicians, herbalists, and sorcerers as their medical practitioners.[88] The astrologers, practicing in the same temples, added auspicious times. Within this context, astrology and magic are working together in a way not easily distinguishable. James Evans has discussed the use of astrology in the temples of Serapis that extended beyond medical applications, so it is obvious that the astrology in question was not one particular magico–medical specialty.[89] Magicians and astrologers were working side

85 Boudet, p. 516.
86 Scurlock, 2006, p. 412.
87 Franz Cumont, L'Égypte des Astrologues (Bruxelles: Fondation Égyptologique Reine Élisabeth, 1937), 170, n. 3; as cited in Bootes, p. 46
88 Henry E. Sigerist, A History of Medicine. New York,: Oxford University Press, 1951, Vol. 1, p. 267.
89 James Evans, The History and Practice of Ancient Astronomy. New York: Oxford University Press, 1998.

by side to produce therapeutic results for their clients. So: what happened in the succeeding cultural eras?

The major and obvious change was that in the early Christian era, followed by the Islamic era, then the later period in the Latin West, there were no temples of Serapis where sorcerers and astrologers could work together! Further, monotheism emerging from the Hebraic tradition did not look kindly at the invocation of spirits. There are references to necromancy peppered through the *Tanakh,* most notably 1 Samuel 28, in which the Witch of Endor conjures the spirit of Samuel to appear before Saul. While these references forced Christians and later Muslims to accept the efficacy of spirits, even if they classified them demonic and malevolent. Any intercession against spirits would now be done by priests, not magicians. Meanwhile, astrology was being progressively defanged by declaring any kind of prediction apart from purely medical ones to be against free will, and only true because of demonic intercession.

Oddly, in both those first two centuries of the 'Abbāsid Dynasty, and in the later Medieval Christian era, scholars of magical exploration were tolerated. It is amazing that an author like Thabit ibn Qurra could continue to be quoted for centuries when the magical content of the work is so clear. Is it merely that the production of talismans had become so ingrained upon the Middle Eastern, and then European mind that this could somehow be mistaken for something else? This does stretch the imagination. But then, how different is this from wearing a crucifix, a Star of David, or a Hamsa as a pendant? Or what do we make of the observation of a modern jewelry designer, who has noted the embedding of herbs under precious stones in old jewelry settings? Surely here is a connection of seemingly secular gems to an older medico–magical practice.

Each of those religious societies went through a similar sequence. In the early phase of transmission, there was so much immediately useful and fascinating new material that both scholars and their patrons were completely entranced. We can see from these two societies that it takes a couple of centuries to digest such a corpus. Within the transmissions there are works on astrology, magic, and other portions of what we would now call the occult. However, they are wrapped up within their version of straight science. At first, no attempt is made to excise these less than politically correct pieces, because until the entire mass of learning is transmitted, there's no way to separate them. It is only after the scholars begin to digest the material that any sense of distinction is possible.

Following the initial translation, the next phase is digestion. The quality of translation is improved as multiple copies can result in a primitive critical edition, and the translations themselves can be improved upon as the vocabulary in the new language is created. It is in this phase that the astrology and magic begin to be assimilated.

The pathway was somewhat different between our two examples. When the 'Abbāsids took over in the 8th century CE, not only was their dynasty new, but so was Islam. As Gutas noted, they were anxious for the astrologers of the old Sassanian Empire to declare the inevitability and desirability of their dynasty. Thus, in the early years of Islam, the rulers became trapped: clerics would go on to strongly condemn both magic and astrology for Muslims, and yet, for over three hundred years, it was eagerly used. This happened both because one portion of their new empire had a strong astrological base, plus the pairing of astrology with medicine was a very useful practice.

It was in the time of Averroes ('Abū l-Walīd Muammad Ibn 'Ahmad Ibn Rušd, 1136–1189) that this philosophical inquiry reached it height, and then very rapidly crashed. Averroes' work was attacked by al-Ghazali ('Abū Hāmid Muammad ibn Muhammad al-Ghazālī, c. 1058–1111). Al-Ghazali was seen within Muslim society as a renewer of the faith in challenging the foreign philosophy and all that was associated with it. It is from this point onward that the spirit of intellectual openness that allowed the flowering of both astrological and magical ideas was crushed. As a result of this attack on the emerging Muslim Neoplatonism, intellectual pursuits snap back into religious legalism, and those who preferred to continue in the earlier spirit of inquiry would have to find homes and patronage elsewhere.

Magical texts had developed the methods of planetary hours, Faces, and lunar mansions as satisfactory means for doing elections, while the astrological texts continued to elaborate the more formalized system of electional astrology that was based on the same edifice of rules as horary astrology. There was considerable overlap between those practicing magic and astrology, so it's possible that they either didn't even notice this subtle differentiation, or they move so effortlessly between the two models that there was no need to think much about it.

Our subject was touched upon in an interesting way by the translator Benjamin Dykes. In *Choices and Inceptions*, Dykes cites the neoclassical astrologer Deborah Houlding, who had contrasted the less complete forms of electional with the later, more complex ones.[90] Then, the sources he gives for these allegedly more primitive types are two Arabic sources, plus the unknown source Bethen, whom Dykes believed was from the Medieval Latin period, because his work seems composed of material derived from Sahl plus a section on planetary hours. Actually, all this demonstrates is that Bethen could be anywhere from the Arabic period up to the Medieval Latin period.

But I think that sequencing misses an important point, and also demonstrates insufficient appreciation for the complexity of doing formal electional as it had developed. Electional is by far the most difficult type of astrology to do. The iteration of multiple criteria for any particular type of electional makes it extremely unlikely that a time which meets all the conditions will be found within given season, let alone a week! The supposedly primitive electional methods may be understood as a way to short–circuit the 'ephemeris fatigue' that is so likely to infect someone who regularly does elections. The simpler methods, or as I would say, specialized methods, give hope that an electional within a relatively short time interval is possible. Someone like Thabit was not 'primitive' in his thinking at all.

Why then, should Western astrology so lovingly preserve a method of electional which is in fact so difficult to do, while works on magic preserved the simpler methods? There is a very interesting insight made by Robert Hand in his PhD thesis relating to the astrology of warfare. Hand focuses on the great Medieval Latin astrologer Guido Bonatti, for whom there is ample historical evidence of his actual military horaries and electionals.

Hand, in his thesis, seeks to demonstrate that one of the ways to examine whether a technique is actually being used is to look for modifications in the technique from one author to the next. The idea is that, if a field, such as astrology, is sufficiently broad it would be next to impossible to actually use all of the methods, then the tendency of any one author would be to tweak the methods that he or she personally uses, and then to transmit the unused methods in a way which simply reproduces one's sources. So, for example, if I do a lot of real estate electionals, I will have the chance to develop my own ideas about what works best, but then if I am asked to elect something that I have never done before, like a time for putting on apparel, I will simply follow the ancient rules as precisely as I can.

Now here is the interesting point: when Hand examined Bonatti's work, he found the section on election for warfare to be completely derivative

90 Dykes, 2012, p 1.

except on one point, whereas Bonatti's material on horary showed great originality.[91] The obvious question is this: Bonatti was doing both horary and electional. That being the case, why would only the horary part show much originality?

In thinking this through, there actually is a plausible hypothesis. For many centuries, most electional astrologers have subscribed to the premise that if a moment in which the answer to a horary of the nature of the electional would be 'yes,' then that would be a good electional moment. In other words, by whatever method you create the electional, if you now examine that proposed time as if it were a horary, and if you get a 'yes,' it's therefore a good time.

So it is entirely likely that Bonatti could have started with one of Thabit's methods of creating an electional, and then used his horary method to check the moment. Accordingly, there would be no need to really work out a separate electional method.

When I began to think about this topic, it was because I had observed in the works on horary no general methodology of electing for a whole class of obvious events, which are electing for improving the condition of the Querent. It is precisely this sort of topic we see in the magical works, where the purpose of creating a talisman is exactly to create an advantage for the Querent. Why is such an obvious point missing from conventional astrological references?

Up through William Lilly, it was extremely common for astrologers to have also studied magic, or at least some of the Arabic sources about magic, such as Thabit. As a result, they already had the method for such electionals. All they had to do was to switch over to a magical work, and they could go about their business and create the desired election. Whether the fact that none of these astrologers did much to present these matters (except Ramesey, who did present some materials from Agrippa) may be seen either as conservation of written style, or deliberate obfuscation of method. In the end, we will never know which.

---

91 Robert Hand, "The Use of Military Astrology in Late Medieval Italy: The Textual Evidence." Catholic University, 2014, pp. 170–182.

SOME IDEAS FROM PRACTICE

Magical works are replete with ideas for how to create talismans for all sorts of functions, many of which translate directly to potential electional topics. Thus, one could make an image of Jupiter that would result in prosperity and free the Native from enemies—or one can create an electional for an appropriate event of that nature to begin at the time designed for the creation of the talisman.[92] It was this insight that I have been investigating in my own electional practice over the years.

In practice, all the astrologer really has to do to apply these ideas is to acquire the magical references to talisman-making, and then to carefully read the astrological indicators for creating an appropriate talisman for the electional subject at hand. So the real barrier is not technological, it is mental: the astrologer has to expand her or his horizons to include otherwise unknown references, and to think in an entirely different way about problem-solving.

Reading the lists of talismans by planet compared to the lists of elections by house, the magical options are often wilder than the electional ones. For example, one might create a talisman to inflame love, but the electional rules are for electing for a marriage to be fertile. The magical methods definitely include the possibility of attempting to affect another's will, changing that other person's behavior toward the possessor of the talisman. The elections generally do not. Contrast presenting your intended with flowers compared to dosing her with a predator drug, and you get the idea.

The magical versions directly address the agenda that is often left unstated in the electional materials: they relate to having the power to fulfill one's desires. Electional astrology has repeated a mantra since the Arabic period: that you cannot elect what the natal chart denies. This statement implies a degree of fate or predestination that precludes the possibility of free will. The question is: did all electional astrologers believe this historically—and did all magicians?

There is little point to learning and practicing magic if one believes there is no free will, because then, why bother to cultivate will at all? So it is unlikely that there have been many magicians who rejected free will entirely. However, astrology is technically agnostic with respect to free will. In the time of Marcus Aurelius, when Stoicism was the preferred philoso-

---

92 Agrippa (Tyson), p. 383.

phy, astrology could simply be understood as a means to examine one's fate. The presumed absence of free will had no bearing on astrology at all.

However, as we have seen, astrology went through considerable elaboration during the Christian era. Christianity—and specifically Catholicism before the Reformation—not merely accepted free will, but mandated it as a prerequisite to choosing the path to salvation. Within this assumption of free will, magic could operate—and then astrology shows tendencies, not inevitabilities.

Thus, we may return to the electional mantra. *It is only with an assumption of the absence of free will that the statement that you cannot elect what the natal chart denies is true.* Otherwise, the assumption might well be that, without electing or some other activity that removed the Native from his or her normal procedures, that the Native is unlikely to achieve something denied in the natal chart.

Speaking in a more modern parlance, the acceptance of the existence of free will sets up the assumption of an intentionally probabilistic Cosmos, which is considerably different from the *pronoia* assumed by many neoclassical philosophical texts. In this system, the nativity expresses the tendencies of the Native. Free will represents deviation from those tendencies—or *habits*. And further, magic operates by applying the will to the application of energy in order to effect a particular result. This view of the Cosmos hinges on the assumption that there is such a thing as choice. It does not necessarily make any assumptions about how frequently any particular individual will exercise it.

Within this understanding, electional astrology actually becomes a form of magic, because it is an application of will, expressed as deliberate timing, applied to the desired situation at hand. In our current, somewhat more secular society, this can be easy to understand; within certain eras in which dogma was less kind to magic, this understanding was deliberately suppressed.

Like most electional astrologers of the last two millennia, I first cut my teeth on horary before moving on to electional. Horary is the branch of astrology devoted to answering specific questions. Its methodology is extremely similar to electional, but learning it is somewhat simpler, hence the sequencing. One may well ask how horary could operate at all in the presence of free will. The ability to predict the future assumes that the future is in some way fixed. As I worked with this over time, I realized that horary works well precisely because individuals don't actually exercise free will very often—but in any moment, they can. Thus, if somebody asks if they'll have a relationship with Amelia, and the chart says no, then what is actually being said is that it would require more free will than either party is likely to engage in order for a different outcome to occur.

There is historical precedence for this idea. In William Lilly's horary concerning some stolen fish, the chart clearly indicated that he wouldn't be able to get the fish back—or mostly so. But Lilly could be a stubborn man. And so he gives the story of how he reverse–engineered his horary and found the thieves, who had eaten most of his fish, although he recovered his fish bag![93]

I came to understand horary questions as beginning with the unspoken phrase, "If things continue as they are now, then..." If we understand the matrix of fate and free will in our lives, then we can begin to appreciate that an electional *can* be a moment of the application of will—the same as would be exercised in any conventional magical practice. However, this moment could (and sometimes has) been understood as a prayer: an opening to the possibility implied by the moment. May we dare to conclude that the choice of path is given to the person who executes the electional?

✳ ✳
✳

---

93 Lilly, pp. 397–399.

Planetary Magic Among the Harranian Sabians

Benjamin N. Dykes, PhD

NUMEROUS MEDIEVAL ARABIC and Latin manuscripts contain instructions for magical practices, whether for the use of precious stones, or astrological talismans, or invocatory rituals. Some texts assign a legendary pedigree and author for their material, such as Hermes, while others have more reliable backgrounds. In this article I will give examples of three types of magical texts, translated by me from Latin sources. These should give readers a sense of some of the magic practiced between late antiquity and the High Middle Ages, apart from what we find in large grimoires (although we will have occasion to mention the *Picatrix*).

One very simple kind of text can be found in Paris BN lat. 16204, which contains many important works in traditional astrology translated from Arabic authors into Latin. Pages 500–507 contain a long list of different magical rings and their uses, all with stones bearing the sculptures of astronomical symbols or images. Some entries name the precious or semi-precious stone to be used (such as chrysolite or hematite), while others are more generic. Some of the generic examples read as follows (pp. 505–06):

If you produced[1] a stone in which Saturn is sculpted, having a sickle in his right hand, this stone renders the one bearing it powerful, whose authority always grows while he wears it.

In whatever stone you produced a sculpted sigil in which there is a winged horse (who is called Pegasus), it is the best for those who are soldiering and marching across land to war, for he will show courage and speed, and it is even said to free horses bearing this stone about themselves, from confusion and from the rest of infirmities...

If you produced a stone in which there is Aquila, which is above Capricorn, that stone will preserve ancient honors for you, and you will acquire new ones.

This text is formally attributed to Sahl b. Bishr, a famous Jewish–Persian astrologer of the late 700s—early 800s AD, calling him *Zehel*. But we should keep in mind that the Arabic word for Saturn is *Zuḥal*,[2] so not all attributions to Sahl—especially if they are magical—should be taken at face value. In the opening lines however, the author claims to be named Theel, and to have crossed the Red Sea with the biblical Exodus from Egypt: "I, Theel, one of the sons of the children of Israel,[3] who, after the crossing of the Red Sea ate of manna in the desert..." Apart from the Arabic giveaway in his opening statement (see footnote), Theel's identity is unknown to me and it is unclear where these kinds of lists come from. There are no ritual instructions, and the text does not seem to use magical words on the rings and gems, only images.

Luckily, we can trace other important and explicitly ritual practices to the city of Harrān and the so–called Sābians, and in the rest of this article

---

1 *Inveneris*, which normally means "discover, find" (Ar. *wajada*). But the Latin can also mean "invent," and probably translates the variation on the Arabic, *awjada*, which means 'produce.'

2 Arabic normally omits the short vowels in script and has more than one *h*, so this word could easily be transliterated into Latin as *Zehel* and be mistaken by someone for Sahl.

3 This construction is common in Arabic, and should be understood simply as "one of the children of Israel."

I will discuss two important sources: a work on talismans by the Harrānian astronomer and astrologer Thābit b. Qurra, and a Latin translation of a report of Sābian planetary rituals by the astrologer ʿUmar al-Tabarī. First, let me introduce this city and its people.

The Harrānian Sābians have a long and illustrious reputation in the realms of astrology and astrological magic. Located a few miles from the Turkish–Syrian border and about 25 miles southeast of Edessa (modern Şanlıurfa), Harrān sits at the juncture between ancient Anatolia, the Levant, and the Middle East—and therefore along important travel and trade routes. It featured in the Jewish Bible as one of Abraham's settling places before heading to Canaan (Gen. 11:31–12:4), and was already known anciently as a city dedicated to the Akkadian Moon god Sin, just as other Mesopotamian cities were consecrated to other gods who had special planets as their manifestations (such as Marduk-Jupiter).[4]

Harrān was also an important place for Hellenistic astrology, as its geographical position allowed easy interactions between the Hellenistic Levant and Near East, and Babylon. Indeed, Greek-language astrology was already present there in the 3rd Century AD, as evidenced by a nativity described in a book by Zaradusht (pseudo-Zoroaster), which can be dated to April, 232 AD in Harrān. When the Sasanian Dynasty of Persia overthrew the Asacid (or Parthian) empire in 224 AD, the Persians quickly expanded throughout the region, entering even into modern Turkey: and the Sasanians were known to be interested in astrology and other intellectual disciplines, which they also connected with Harrān. For one thing, it was in the Sasanian court that early Greek editions of the astrologers Dorotheus and Vettius Valens were studied and translated into the Persian language. Again, the 232 nativity in the book attributed to Zoroaster was based on Greek methods, and was itself revised in the 6th Century in the reign of Khusrō Anōshirwān. Some Zoroastrians also believed that Zoroaster had received his first inspirations in Harrān, and so were anxious to preserve its culture. And a few centuries later, when scholars fled Athens after Emperor Justinian's closure of the philosophical schools in 529 AD, they went first to the court of Khusrō Anōshirwān but in about 533 some (in particular the Neoplatonist Simplicius) stayed in Harrān.

---

4 For this and the next few paragraphs, see the nice summary in David Pingree, "The Sābians of Harrān and the Classical Tradition," *International Journal of the Classical Tradition* Vol. 9, No. 1, pp. 8–12.

Simplicius is important for the topic of Sābian astronomy, astrology, and magic, for two reasons. First, he was known to have brought key astronomical texts with him, such as Ptolemy's *Almagest*. Second, Neoplatonism itself was already, and would continue to be, the chief philosophical system that helped justify and explain astrological magic: how it works, and how astrological magic and theurgy can play a role in the salvation and enlightenment of the soul.[5] This is not to say that earlier Neoplatonists had not made an impact in Harrān, but Simplicius is a notable and verifiable figure whose activity there coincided with and contributed to many other philosophical and astrological developments at the time. Some centuries later, the astronomer Thābit b. Qurra studied the Arabic version of Ptolemy's *Planetary Hypotheses* in Harrān, which must have been translated from the copy brought by Simplicius (more on Thābit below). And the Christian astrologer Theophilus of Edessa (8th Century AD) wrote that he preferred the classicist intellectual atmosphere of Harrān to his native, ascetic Edessa.

This provides a thumbnail sketch of the city of Harrān, and of its geographical and cultural role in the region. Most people identify the city and its inhabitants with the religion of Sābianism, a syncretic religion only adopted by some Harrānians at some indeterminate time before the city's conquest by the Arabs in 639–40 AD. Based on their intellectual past, the Sābians were proud of their sciences and religious practices, and believed that they had provided an indispensable cosmopolitan and civilizing influence to the world.[6] They were first and foremost star and planet worshippers, engaging in both philosophical-spiritual and magical approaches to their deities: this included talismanic magic and statue-animation (perhaps using actual human bodies), the latter already being familiar as an Egyptian practice through the Hermetic *Asclepius*. Temples to different planets had different geometric shapes in their architecture (such as a triangular temple for Jupiter), and included special oratories and doors towards the east (facing the rising Sun). Extensive suffumigations with planetary incenses and animal sacrifices were important both ritually and for smoke divination, and are described in several contemporary sources. As for their philosophy, the Sābians believed that we should try to escape

5 An excellent source on Neoplatonism and theurgy, but focusing on Iamblichus, is Gregory Shaw, *Theurgy and the Soul: The Neoplatonism of Iamblichus*. The Pennsylvania State University Press, 1995.
6 Pingree 2002, p. 35.

this world of elemental change (to the extent that is possible) by worshipping the planets, which act as mediators between us and higher realities. By following magical procedures and the general teachings of Hermes, we may rise through the celestial spheres to union with the One.

The role of Hermes as the particular prophet of the Sābians is worth dwelling on for a moment, because in point of fact the title 'Sābian' was consciously adopted for political purposes, at the point of the sword as it were. As one of the subject peoples of Islam, it was in the end necessary to identify themselves both with one of the good peoples mentioned in the Qur'ān and to name which (Islamically acceptable) prophet they followed. Since the Qur'ān mentions people called 'Sābians'[7] and identifies Hermes with Idris-Enoch,[8] they formally adopted these associations and enjoyed many centuries of intellectual influence in astronomy, astrology, and magic. They were finally deported by the invading Mongols in 1271.

One of the most famous Harrānians was Thābit b. Qurra, an astronomer, mathematician, and scientist who wrote on all manner of topics, including astrological talismans. Born in 836, he spent the most important part of his career in Baghdad and died in 901. As for his work on talismans, an important one has come down to us in two Latin translations (or perhaps two versions of the same translation), at least one by John of Spain: *De Imaginibus*, "On Images." This text gives instructions for several types of talismans: for making scorpions flee an area, to destroy or harm a geographical region, to seek money, have a successful business, to be in charge of a city or region, to be on good terms with a king, for love, and so on. Below I translate several paragraphs from one of the versions edited by Carmody (1960, pp. 183–85), on recovering money.[9]

Thābit's method combines either natal or question charts with an astrologically chosen or 'elected' time for making the talisman. In this example, Thābit requires first that the client have a successful question or 'horary' chart. Questions are one branch of traditional astrology, in which an astrologer casts and interprets a chart for the time a client asks about a pressing need and whether or not it will be successful, or at least what will happen: for instance, whether one will marry so-and-so, or where one's

---

7 Qur'ān 2:62, 5:69, 22:17.
8 Ibid., 19:57 and 21:85.
9 This material was used in other medieval texts, and appears in Leopold of Austria's *Compilation* (translation by Dykes, 2015).

lost wedding ring is, and so on.[10] Here, we need a chart whose question is something like, "will I be able to get my money back?" The answer must be 'yes.' Once we have this chart, the astrologer-magician must begin to create the metal talisman at a time when that same Ascendant arises, but also timed so that the lord of the Ascendant and the lord of the second (the house of money) are joined appropriately at that moment (19). For example, let the Ascendant of the question be Pisces (ruled by Jupiter),[11] and the second house Aries (ruled by Mars): we would want there to be a sextile or trine between Jupiter and Mars at the time of making the talisman, at a time when Pisces is also arising. Thābit adds further conditions that strengthen the planets, and warns us not to let the planets be harmed, such as through retrogradation (moving backwards), being burned (within 15° of the Sun, or perhaps less than about 7.5° from him) or being cadent (in the third, sixth, ninth, or twelfth) (21).[12] Although Thābit does not say so here, the talisman should be engraved with the names of the key planets, and probably the chart itself (modern magicians would probably add sigils and Divine Names).

Then, the second talisman must be created during a time when the appropriate house of the question is rising. That is, if the money is sought from some authority figure (a tenth-house person), then the second talisman must be made when the tenth house of the question is rising (22–23). In our example above, the tenth house would be Sagittarius: so, Sagittarius would have to be rising when the second talisman is made. Likewise, the time must be chosen so that the planets in this chart are in a good condition (24). Obviously, these are not the kinds of talismans one may simply whip up at a moment's notice. Finally, the talismans are joined, wrapped, and put in an appropriate place or carried on one's person (27–28)—but they must also be buried at an astrologically appropriate time, too (27).

18 *If you wanted to make an image*[13] *for a man who seeks assets which were taken from him (or denied or prohibited), and he wanted that they be returned to him, make the image for him out of gold or silver or copper, or*

10 A classic medieval book on questions, still popular in the Renaissance, has been translated and published by me as *Bonatti on Horary*, The Cazimi Press, 2010.
11 In this kind of astrology, it is best to use traditional rulerships: Jupiter rules Pisces, Mars rules Scorpio, and Saturn rules Aquarius.
12 I discuss many of these conditions in my essay on magical elections, in Dykes and Gibson (2012); see also Dykes 2010.
13 That is, a talisman.

whichever of these one pleases. **19** *You should begin to operate under the Ascendant of his interrogation, and make the lord of the house of assets be joined with the lord of the Ascendant, and let there be reception between them, and let their conjunction be from the trine or sextile aspect.* **20** *And if it was appropriate for the lord of the house of assets to be in the obeying signs, and the lord of the Ascendant in commanding signs, this will be even more powerful (and the obeying signs are the crooked ones, and the commanding ones are the straight ones).*[14] **21** *And you will make the Ascendant and its lord fortunate, and beware lest the lord of the Ascendant be retrograde or burned up or cadent or in the house of its own opposition (that is, the seventh from its own house), or impeded by the bad ones*[15]*—but let it be strong, in an angle; and you will make the Ascendant and its lord fortune, and the lord of the house of assets, and the Moon, and when you have done that according to this arrangement, preserve it.*

22 *Then, on the other hand you should make another image which will be the significator of the one with whom the assets are [now]: if it was with the king, you should begin the second image under the tenth from the Ascendant of the first.* **23** *And if it was with a partner or friend or thief or someone against [him] or others of this kind, you should begin the second image under such an Ascendant as pertains to the one from whom the money is hoped for: that is, if it was with the son, you should begin under the fifth; if with the father under the fourth, likewise under the rest of the signs according to how it pertains to him.* **24** *And you should make each strong and fortunate, without impediment, and make there be a conjunction of the one with the other from a trine or sextile aspect.* **25** *And you will make the significator of the one for whom you make it (that is, the significator of the second image) be joined with the lord of the Ascendant of the first one, and let him receive him. 26 And you will make all bad ones be cadent from him,*[16] *and you will make the tenth and the fourth be fortunate (or one of them), if you could.*

14 In the northern hemisphere, the commanding signs (according to Thābit, these are also the straight signs) are from the beginning of Cancer to the end of Sagittarius, and the rest are obeying or crooked. In the southern hemisphere, these labels are reversed. Thābit probably prefers that the planets be in the commanding and obeying signs that mirror each other across this axis: Sagittarius-Capricorn, Scorpio-Aquarius, Libra-Pisces, Virgo-Aries, Leo-Taurus, Cancer-Gemini.

15 That is, the malefic planets (Mars and Saturn). This would especially be by a square or opposition to them, even if only by sign.

16 This means that the malefic planets should be in signs that are "in aversion to" the

*27 And if the second image was completed along with the first, put the face of
the one against the face of the other, and wrap both in a clean cloth. And bury
[them] in the middle of the house of the one seeking [the assets], under a fortunate sign with a strong fortune, and turn the face of the image towards that
direction*[17] *when you bury it. 28 But if the one seeking it is one who walks
a lot (that is, if he is moved frequently from place to place) and he would be
joined to the one with whom the assets were, you put both images with each
other so that he might bring them with him wherever he went. 29 And know
that if you did this and wisely worked the image according to what I told you
before, you will find what you seek and make profit.*

As they stand, these astrological talismans suggest that the engraving of
the chart and names themselves is the magical act. First, the election of
an appropriate time is meant to channel the authority and influence of
the planets directly into the talisman. It may or may not require belief in
the causal power of the planets themselves; perhaps the planets are only
visible indicators for the true spiritual powers that are being channeled.
Second, it is the old idea that writing and drawing are themselves magical
acts. However, the instructions do not really require any special or trained
intentionality, or notion of a sacred alphabet, or spiritual beings of any
kind. There is no intelligent negotiation or intercourse between the en-
graver and what the talismans are being imbued with. To my mind there is
something disappointingly mechanical about this, as though working with
talismans is simply like getting across town in a large city by navigating
various timetables for buses, subways, and taxis. We know when the bus
comes, so just be at the right corner and the driver will take care of the
rest; we know when Sagittarius rises, so just write the name 'Jupiter' at that
hour and don't worry about the rest. Or we might think of it as a kind of
primitive medicine: mix a bit of this and that, and make the patient drink
it, without worrying about how or why it works. Of course, Thābit might
have omitted the other magical and spiritual requirements for an effective

lord of the Ascendant. In traditional astrology, there are no so-called "minor" aspects
such as a semi-sextile (30°), so planets in certain signs cannot aspect or see each other:
this means that they are unconnected and have little to no influence on each other. The
four places in aversion from any position are always the adjacent signs, and the sixth and
eighth signs from it. So for example, if the lord of the Ascendant was in Gemini, then
the malefics should be in any adjacent sign (Taurus or Cancer), or in the sixth or eighth
from Gemini (Scorpio, Capricorn).

17 Reading with version A for *septentrionem* ("the north").

talisman, but we do know from other grimoires that this kind of mechanical procedure is common enough for the time.

Of a very different and more sophisticated character are certain Sābian planetary invocations (or evocations) which have been preserved in several sources, including *Picatrix* III.7.[18] In this chapter, the author provides two versions of most of the planetary rituals, including incense recipes and sample invocations. One primary difference between the two types of ritual is that one includes animal sacrifices while the other does not. But the two rituals are sometimes mixed together or other material is introduced. Luckily, a Latin manuscript edited by David Pingree[19] translates an Arabic work by the 8th Century astrologer 'Umar al-Tabarī, who relates all seven of the non–sacrificial rituals, with slightly different incense ingredients and speeches, and with instructions for electing a proper time to perform them (similar to the version in the *Picatrix*). Below I translate all of the rituals, sometimes offering corrections or alternate readings based on the Arabic, German,[20] or Latin versions of the *Picatrix*. A modern English translation by Green and Warnock (GW) is also available. Before moving directly to the rituals, it is worth making some comments about them:

(1) *The magician.* In this Latin version, the magician is called the Agent or Actor, or 'performer' or 'doer' (*agens*). This is an intriguing title both because certain aspects of the rituals are definitely a performance (such as the cultural costumes involved), and because even in modern magic we speak of a ritual as a "working" or "operation." The Agent's attitude must explicitly be devotional and humble (Ch. 1, 4). Moreover, the initial information on Saturn (Ch. 1, 11) and less clearly Jupiter (Ch. 1, 13) suggest that each planetary spirit should be sought for, or may provide, some kind of moral or intellectual benefit: teaching in the case of Saturn, and something unclear about being pleasing in the case of Jupiter.

(2) *Types of beings.* The rituals explicitly mention three types of entities: the Creator, the planets, and the planetary spirits, and after the invocations

---

18 The Latin edition does not acknowledge that the rituals are S bian, but the Arabic does.

19 David Pingree, "Al-Tabarī on the Prayers to the Planets," *Bulletin d'Études Orientales*, Tome XLIV 1993 (Année 1992), pp. 105–17. The manuscript is listed by him as Florence, *Biblioteca Nazionale* Lat. II. Iii. 214, ff. 31–33.

20 The German edition (1962) is a translation of Ritter's Arabic edition (1933).

the planetary spirit is supposed to appear in an appropriate guise. But no spirits are mentioned by name, as we normally have in later or even earlier angelic hierarchies. Instead, it is implied that each planet is the outer appearance of a single planetary spirit or angel (Ch. 1, 3–4) bearing the name of the planet itself, with no other hierarchy implied (such as subordinate angels, intelligences, and spirits). No doubt the Sābians would have been familiar with elaborate spiritual hierarchies through their exposure to Neoplatonism, if not through other earlier sources. But none appear here.[21]

Speaking of influences, note that each planetary spirit is addressed using planetary epithets that belong to Ptolemaic astrology. That is, Ptolemy (but not always other early astrologers) said that Mars was excessively heating and drying, Venus warming and moistening, and so on—this is because Ptolemy treated astrology naturalistically, trying to tie astrological interpretations to combinations of elemental qualities. So these rituals, even if they predate the Arab invasions in the 630s AD, reflect a Ptolemaic influence that may well be due to Simplicius and his teaching. But I do note that the rituals treat Venus as being *cold* (rather than warm), which is typical of Persian and Arabic astrology (Ch. 6, 8): this suggests that the Harrānians might have treated her this way early on, rather than it being a late misread of Ptolemy by Persian and Arabic-speaking astrologers when making the initial translations of astrological works into Arabic in the 8th Century.

(3) *The election for the ritual.* In Ch. 2, 1–5, 'Umar presents five conditions for choosing the best time to perform the Saturn ritual.[22] The first condition is being in its own dignity: this includes being in the sign or signs it rules by 'house' or domicile (such as Mars being Aries and Scorpio, or the Sun being in Leo), or exaltation (such as Mars being in Capricorn or the Sun in Aries). It also includes three lesser dignities which are common in traditional astrology but hardly known in modern astrology: triplicity, bound or term, and face or decan. Without explaining them here,[23] in the case of Mars that would include being in the earthy or watery signs, or in certain

---

21 In the ritual for Venus (10), she is asked to send "one angel," but without any identification or distinction between this angel and the angel of Venus itself.

22 For more on these conditions, see Dykes and Gibson 2012. Mercury (11) adds the planetary day and hour, possibly also implied in Saturn (19).

23 See Dykes, *Introductions to Traditional Astrology: Abū Ma'shar & al-Qabisi*, for tables of these dignities.

degrees such as 17° 00'–24° 00' Gemini, or in his face in the first 10° of Aries or the last 10° of Pisces.

The second condition involves a classification of the astrological houses called the 'busy' or 'advantageous' or 'profitable' or even 'good' places, of which there were two types. The version here uses the "eight-place" system: the four angles and four succeedents. So, a planet in the Ascendant, tenth, seventh or fourth (the angles) or the second, eleventh, eighth, or fifth (the succeedents) would be very strengthened and stimulated. The author mentions that he prefers the eastern quadrant between the Ascendant and Midheaven (Ch. 2, 2), but omits the fact that the twelfth house or place is expressly *not* a good place even though it falls in this region. It should be avoided.

The third and fourth conditions are rather straightforward: that the planet be moving forward in the zodiac rather than being retrograde (Ch. 2, 5), and in a sign of its own gender or perhaps its own sect (Ch. 2, 3). In traditional astrology, planets are divided into two groups or sects: a diurnal or day sect, and a nocturnal or night sect. Diurnal planets (the Sun, Jupiter, Saturn) act in a more supportive and balanced way during the day and in daytime charts, while the nocturnal planets (the Moon, Venus, Mars) do so during the night and in nighttime charts.[24] So since Saturn is diurnal and masculine, he should be in the fiery or airy signs (which are all diurnal and masculine); we might add that he is better invoked during the day as well. Likewise, since Venus is nocturnal and feminine, she should be in the earthy or watery signs (which are all nocturnal and feminine), and probably better invoked at night. Mars is always the odd planet here, because he is masculine but nocturnal: so he would probably prefer a masculine sign, but a ritual performed at night.

Finally, the planet must be unharmed (Ch. 2, 4–5), which traditionally can cover many things, but here emphasizes the planets' relationships to the malefics. 'Umar al-Tabarī would have understood this to mean any malefic being in the same sign as the invoked planet, or squaring or opposing it by sign. For example, in an invocation of Venus (let her be in Taurus), neither Mars nor Saturn should be in Taurus, or squaring Taurus from Leo

---

24 Mercury is variable. Typically, when Mercury is in an earlier degree than the Sun (i.e., so as to rise before him in the morning), he is considered diurnal; but when he is in a later degree than the Sun (i.e., so as to set after him in the evening), he is considered nocturnal. He is normally considered masculine, but in the end rather neutral or hermaphroditic.

or Aquarius, or opposing Taurus from Scorpio. 'Umar would also not have wanted the invoked planet to be within 15° on either side of the Sun.

(4) *Incense*. The incense ingredients here should be considered more reliable than those in the GW edition of the *Picatrix*, since they come from a separate source and well match other Arabic lists.[25] Most of the ingredients should be available through a good occult bookstore or other herb source, except for some of the special liquids associated with each planet. Goat urine (Saturn) could be gotten from a farmer I suppose, wine (Jupiter) or blood (Mars) should be easy enough, and dew water (Venus) would be tedious but a fun experience—but what are we to make of wolf's milk (Moon)? Perhaps that is a euphemism for something else. Unfortunately, the liquid for Mercury is missing. Each roll of incense should be burned in a censer of the appropriate metal, accompanied by a ring of that same metal (which does not always match our modern associations). Finally, let me mention the word 'integumen,' an accurate but unfortunate Latin word Pingree uses to translate the equivalent in Arabic: this word means the shell, rind, or husk of something, and is used for certain herbs and plants. Your herbalist should be able to tell whether it really means a rind or husk or peel or whatever, as the case may be.

(5) *Dress*. One unfamiliar feature of the rituals is the use of cultural costumes to help the Agent adopt the appropriate planetary identity: black or Jewish clothing for Saturn, a bespangled woman for Venus, and even an armed Christian for Jupiter—reflecting the role of Byzantine soldiers in the Near East. According to Pingree, this practice comes from the Indian tradition (2002, p. 22). Obviously one might expand this list to draw on other significations of the planets. But the use of contemporary imagery (such as an armed Christian) suggests that perhaps one should draw on one's own cultural milieu for the images, rather than adopting imagery from the past. For example, Jupiter signifies notable people, leaders of society, the wealthy: perhaps one could do a Jupiter ritual while wearing an elegant modern suit or dress?

---

25 Pingree, "Al-Tabarī on the Prayers to the Planets," pp. 108–11, 116–17.

With these preliminary remarks, let us now turn to the rituals themselves:

The *Book on Speaking with the Spirits of the Planets,* begins:

[Chapter 1: Significations of the planets][26]

2 Abū Hafs ['Umar b. Farrukhān] al-Tabarī,[27] a certain philosopher and astrologer, spoke about what he found in the books of the ancients. **3** At the beginning of this book, let us speak about the praise of the seven spirits of the seven planets. **4** Whoever therefore wished to speak with any of the seven spirits so that he might demand or ask anything of it, should not act carelessly but in a devotional way, neither by testing nor with respect to any stupid or cavalier matter, but only concerning what he wanted to accomplish for a great work.[28] **5** Without that, [the spirit] will not listen to the words of the one intending [the action], nor will it respect his actions, but perhaps it will worry him with a serious infirmity.[29]

6 And since fumigations are necessary for this book and for the rest of divine things, we will speak about them first. **7** If therefore necessity loomed over anyone to such a degree that he was very much hurt by it,[30] in the first place it is necessary to inspect the nature of the planet he wanted, and [see] whether the present chart agrees with the nature of the planet.[31] **8** But then, he should hold his mind fixed on what he proposes, so that he may be filled with the assistance of divinity.

9 First then, let us speak about the matters pertaining to Saturn. **10** And so, all old men and things pertaining to them, and supervisors,[32] and laborers of lands and cultivators, and seeds, and the beginnings of things

---

26 This corresponds to *Picatrix,* Ar. pp. 190–97, Ger. 206–09, Lat. 112–13, GW 156–57.

27 *Abuelabec Altanarani.*

28 This could also be read as, "for *the* Great Work" (*pro magno opere*), which sounds like good advice to me.

29 This is probably meant in a physical sense, but I suggest that such a magician might be afflicted by spiritual and life imbalances and problems of the very planetary sort he treats so cavalierly.

30 This seems to mean that the situation is an emergency or is truly a problem for the magician's life.

31 That is, make sure the elected time is appropriate for that planet.

32 Reading *praefecti* for Pingree's *perfecti* ('perfect'), and more in line with the Ar. and Ger.

and obstacles,[33] malice, and the like, are attributed to Saturn. **11** And these are entreated from him so that afterwards he will be taught; without that, the effect will not follow.

12 To Jupiter pertain governors,[34] sages, and the powerful, and likewise masters of rulership[35] and counsels, or laws or wisdom or arts; the good, arms, buying, profit, wisdom, and the like. **13** The things pertaining to Jupiter should be sought by one who is pleasing to every spirit.[36]

14 Mars should be asked about wars, quarrels, murders, burnings, and every shedding of blood, and similar things pertaining to Mars. 15 And it must be noted that every evil which is introduced by Mars, is restored by the benevolence of Venus.[37]

16 The Sun should be asked with the greatest devotion concerning kings, dukes,[38] and other powerful people, and the greatest matters.

17 Venus is asked about every womanly and female matter, and the ornamentation of women, and singing and games and laughing, and the taking care of clothing, and delight, and feasting and drinking, and the like. **18** And for those things in which Venus agrees with Mars (or another [planet]), let them both be asked together.[39]

19 Mercury [should be asked] for philosophy and every science, and wisdom, and teachings and disciplines, and all books, for writings, paintings and sculptures, and eloquence.

20 The Moon should be asked for legates and messengers, and the bearers of papers and commands and instructions, and [for] roads and journeys and moving, and movable things, and concerning rivers and mills and wheels and ships, for nourishing children and nurses.

---

33 *Detenti.* That is, things which hold something back or occupy one so that activities do not move forward.

34 Again, reading *viri praefecti* for *viri perfecti*, again in line with the sense of the Ar. and Ger.

35 Reading rather broadly for Pingree's guess at *dominie*; the Ar. and Ger. list 'authority figures' here (Ger. *Obrigkeitspersonen*).

36 *Omni spiritui placet.* Meaning unclear; it could be that one's own character or at least attitude should be Jovial and pleasing.

37 This comes from the *Fifty Aphorisms* (or *Judgments*) of the astrologer Sahl b. Bishr (see Bibliography). Aphorism 34 says that while Jupiter breaks or loosens the evil of Saturn, Venus breaks or loosens the evil of Mars.

38 Or more simply, 'leaders' (*ducibus*).

39 This seems to refer to romantic matters, as Venus and Mars together imply eroticism and sexuality.

[Chapter 2: Rituals of Saturn][40]

1 Whoever desires to speak with Saturn, it is necessary for [Saturn] first to be in his exaltation,[41] namely in the [twenty-first] degree of Libra,[42] or in the sign[43] of his joy in Aquarius,[44] or in Capricorn, but certainly[45] at least in his bound or triplicity or face. **2** And he should not do this, nor should it happen, unless Saturn was established in the aforesaid places, from the Hour–marker[46] up to the Midheaven, or at least in one of the four pivots, or in a sign following in front of a pivot.[47] **3** Let him even be direct, in a masculine triplicity if it can be so. **4** Let him even be benevolent, not impeded. **5** Let him even be powerful and moving forward, free of every misfortune, with Mars in no way looking at him from a square or the opposition, and apart from every dejection and slavery.[48]

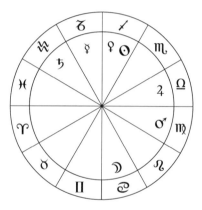

Figure 1: A possible election for Saturn (Dykes)[49]

40 This corresponds to Ar. 202–04, Ger. 213–15, Lat. 117–18, GW 161–62.
41 Reading the singular.
42 Typically, it is enough for Saturn to simply be in the sign of Libra; the text should probably be read as "in the *sign* [*signo*] of Libra."
43 Reading *signo* for *gradu*, as there is no degree of his joy.
44 I have reversed the order of Capricorn and Aquarius along with the Ar., as Saturn does rejoice in Aquarius. See Dykes 2010, §I.10.7.
45 Reading somewhat uncertainly for *pro notatis* (Pingree's reading for *pro notata*).
46 That is, the Ascendant.
47 A 'pivot' is an angle, such as the angle of the Midheaven; so, Saturn should be in an angular or succeedent place.
48 This would include being in detriment (in Cancer or Leo) or in fall (in Aries).
49 In this figure, Saturn is in a sign he rules (Aquarius), between the Ascendant and Midheaven in the eleventh (a very good, succeedent house), in his own triplicity and a

6 And if Saturn was placed thusly, let the Agent advance to the fore-seen and most clean place, being dressed in a black or grey vestment, with blackish slippers[50] on the feet,[51] in the manner of a woman.[52] **7** And before he asks anything of him, let him adore the Creator with devotion in the aforesaid place, prostrate, with the greatest devotion and humbleness and religion—but let him be dressed in the manner of a Jew praying in the synagogue, for Saturn is attributed to the Hebrews. **8** And in his right hand he should have an iron ring, and in that same hand he should hold a spade made of iron, with coals laid on it so that his suffumigation may happen.

9 Now the fumigations attributed to Saturn are: opium, storax,[53] pome-granate blossoms, saffron, plantago,[54] wild cumin,[55] integumen of iris,[56] frankincense, dirt from wool,[57] tamarisk seed, pulp of colocynth.[58] **10** Let as much [as you want] be taken, but in equal amounts, and let it be put on the coals on the spade, mixed together in a single mass with this added: goat's urine. **11** And let the mass be long like a taper, and thrown on top of the coals. **12** And when it smokes, this oration should not be kept silent:

13 "O gleaming spirit of this star whose name is great, whose reign is also the greatest,[59] appearing in the degree of your exaltation! **14** And O you, Saturn, cold and dry, and deceitful and malefic, and speaking the truth in every matter,[60] you who are above all virtues, moving slowly! **15** And you

sign of his own gender, not aspecting Mars by any classical aspect, configured to both benefics by good aspects, moving direct, and in a diurnal chart (as he is a diurnal planet).

50 Reading *subtalaribus* (a medieval word) for *substellaribus*.

51 *Calciatus*, which is a bit redundant and also refers to footwear.

52 The Ar. here refers to one's attitude, being humble and even a bit sorrowful: per-haps like a woman in mourning?

53 *Al-asturak*, which differs from the storax mentioned for Jupiter (5) and the Sun (5), *may'ab*. I do not know the difference between them.

54 Lit. "lamb's/ram's tongue" (Ar. *lisān al-hamal*), probably because of the shape of the leaves.

55 Ar. *qurdamānā*, which suggests rather 'cardamom,' as the German translates it (*Kardamom*).

56 Perhaps the covering of the iris fruit.

57 This must be something other than normal dirt; the German translates this as "wool fat/grease" (*Wollenfett*).

58 A viny plant with bitter roots and seeds.

59 This refers to the lesser years of Saturn (30), an important astronomical cycle close-ly related to the "Saturn return."

60 Traditionally, Saturn is something of an enigmatic planet, as he is attributed both many good qualities (wisdom, deep counsel, authority, *etc.*) and many bad ones (de-ceit, obstacles, *etc.*). These differences may be due to sect and condition: namely, by

are the one attributing to every man every evil to the extent as is the power of your nature, from whom every delight and joy is taken away. **16** You, cunning even and respectably wise, old man and laboring in every malice, granting good to the good and evil to the evil, however this may be according to the quality of your existence. **17** I pray you, great father, through the great name of your Creator, and through your eagerness, that you come to me and show me the truth of all things which I will ask."

18 These things being stated,[61] let the Agent fall down upon his face, adoring the Creator, and immediately there will appear to him the image as though of an old man, complying in all things which he wanted. **19** But according to what he had asked before,[62] all of these things will come to pass on the day of Saturn and his hour.[63]

[Chapter 3: Rituals of Jupiter][64]

1 If someone wanted to ask Jupiter about something, in the first place let him be dressed in white or bright[65] clothing. **2** But on a finger of his right hand let him wear a ring, and let him wear a cape.[66] **3** With these things being so prepared, let him be fitted in the manner of a Christian leaving for war (that is, armed).[67] **4** And let him have a censer filled with fire for making the fumigation.

---

day (where the Sun is above the horizon) or when he is in his own dignities and a good place, he exhibits more favorable qualities; but by night or when he is not in his own dignities, or in a bad place, he exhibits the opposite. Saturn has these contrasts more so than the other planets.

61 Reading for *interdictis*, which refers to forbidding things from happening; perhaps the scribe meant *introductis*, "these things being introduced," or stated "by way of introduction."

62 This seems to mean simply, "the things which were stated earlier."

63 The Ar. says that the ritual itself should be done during his day and hour, which makes sense; but the Latin here makes it seem as though the effect will, or will *also*, come to pass at some later time during his day or hour.

64 This corresponds to Ar. 204–05, Ger. 215–17, Lat. 119.

65 *Glaucis*, which also has connotations of greyness.

66 The Ar. has a burnoose, a kind of hooded cloak.

67 This is not the Christian of the Crusades, but the Byzantine, Orthodox Christian whom the Muslims had conquered in Syria and along the Levant—that is, the Christian representing the power of Constantinople, or as the defender of its faith and customs. We might also suggest other typical Christian clothing, such as a monastic type of robe.

5 The fumigations of Jupiter [are]: liquid storax,[68] sandarac,[69] bugloss,[70] a fish of the Euphrates,[71] calamus,[72] gum,[73] pine resin, juniper seed. **6** Of these drugs,[74] let it be taken according to your wish, but in equal amounts. **7** And let all of these be mixed as one, along with wine, into a long mass.

8 And let Jupiter be placed in good places as we said regarding Saturn.

9 And at the fumigation this oration should be stated: **10** "O blessed lord, hot and moist, temperate, handsome, wise, lord of truth and faith, whom it is necessary to fear, whose will is grand, you who puts all things in right order, who even bestows and lavishes upon all things abundantly what is necessary for them, who even aids perseveringly in all things, whose good nature endures in faith [and] stability! **11** I pray you father, through your good natures and your accomplished goods that you respond rationally to me, without doubt, to whatever I ask of you."

12 These things being completed, let him fall down upon his face while adoring the Creator, and there will appear an image of Jupiter responding to the one asking.

[Chapter 4: Rituals of Mars][75]

1 If someone wanted to ask Mars, let him be dressed in majestic, red fabrics, and on a finger of his right hand let him have a ring made of lead.[76] **2** And let him be armed in the likeness of one doing battle, according to his ability. **3** Let him even be equipped in accordance with those wearing togas who are always eager for battle and adore idols, for Mars rules these

---

68 But the Latin writer also adds "that is, mastic" (*masticum*).

69 A somewhat aromatic tree resin.

70 This refers broadly to plants of the borage family.

71 This seems odd to me.

72 Or, 'sweet flag' (*acorus calamus*). The Ar. has simply "a fragrant reed," while the German interprets this as calamus (*Kalmus*). The leaves and roots have been used as fragrances (among other things) for many centuries.

73 Or, 'gum Arabic' (al-Razi, in Pingree 1993).

74 *Speciebus*, which can also mean simply 'types,' but in the Middle Ages also came to mean medicines or drugs, which seems more appropriate here.

75 This corresponds to Ar. 211–12, Ger. 222–23, Lat. 124, GW 168–69.

76 The Arabic *Picatrix* has 'copper,' perhaps because copper is a reddish metal. Normal astrological attributions would make the Saturnian ring lead and the Martial ring iron, but note that the Saturnian instrument for fumigations is an iron spade, which correctly links Saturn to agriculture.

people. **4** Afterwards, let him go to the extremely clean place which he wants, with the fumigations, having a leaden censer.

5 The fumigations are: aloe wood, peppergrass,[77] willow seeds,[78] flowers of palmarosa,[79] euphorbia,[80] long pepper,[81] aloe,[82] and amber. **6** Of these, let there be taken as much as one wants, but in equal amounts, and let it be drawn out in a long mass, with blood, in the manner of wax. **7** And let it be fumigated in the censer, saying:

8 "O good lord, dry and hot, [you] who are filled with all boldness and even pours out blood, who fills every approaching male with victory,[83] who is the master of all evil and evildoing and killing, who performs every lie and evil, who even seeks arms and is much feared! **9** I entreat you father, through the goodness of your nature, that you do truthfully for me what I want to ask of you."

10 Then let the Agent adore God as has been stated, and there will appear an image of Mars responding.

[Chapter 5: Rituals of the Sun][84]

1 Let him who wished to speak with the Sun be dressed in the clothing of kings, but bright. **2** On his head he should wear a golden helmet, on his finger a golden ring. **3** Then, let him be equipped in the manner of priests and bishops and guardians of the Church, according to his ability: for the Sun is the lord of all of these people. **4** But in his hand he should have a golden censer for fumigating.

5 The fumigations are: crocus, storax, olibanum, pomegranate blossoms, Indian aloe, raisins, talc. **6** Take as much of each as you want, but

---

77 The plant family is *lepidium*.

78 Other sources have laurel seed, or the seed of European musk.

79 *Andropogon* (or *Cymbopogon*) *schoenanthus*, an aromatic relative of lemongrass.

80 A common plant, unfortunately without any more specifying detail. Pingree's Hermetic source has: iris.

81 A flowering vine with a spicy fruit.

82 I am not sure how this differs from the aloe wood mentioned above.

83 Reading *victoria* (following the Ar.) for *doctrina*, 'teaching.' The Arabic Picatrix reads, "the *masculine*, the overpowering, the *victorious*...". Unless 'Umar's Arabic read rather differently, the Latin translator blended the 'masculine' with the 'victorious,' turning them into a power that Mars gives to individual men (rather than a descriptor of Mars himself).

84 This corresponds to Ar. 217–18, Ger. 228–29, Lat. 129, GW 174–75.

equally, and let it be rubbed together[85] and processed along with milk so that it becomes a mass, and let it be fumigated in the censer with this oration:

7 "O Lord, hot and dry, offering every light to the world, who are benign in all things and as though a modest woman and queen,[86] handsome, and most clean and most wise, who holds every faith, whose reign even shall always last, to whom all the other stars, once they have elongated from you they immediately return, [and] even before they approach you, you burn them in your light. **8** Being situated in the middle, you make all six[87] circles gleam with the great light of the spirits. **9** You even, as a lady and queen in all things, overcome other spirits with your light. **10** And when you regard anyone, you aid his spirit, but when one is conjoined to you, you harm him; the greatness of whose circle cannot be comprehended by the human mind."

11 Then the Agent should adore God as was stated, and seek what he ought to, and he will obtain it.

[Chapter 6: Rituals of Venus][88]

1 If someone wanted to ask Venus, let him be clothed in the manner of a woman, adorned with the cleanest fabrics. **2** And about his temples[89] let him wear a circlet of silk inlaid with precious stones in the manner of a crown, [and] he should have a ring made of any precious stone on the finger of his right hand. **3** And let him be adorned as much as he can in the likeness of a bride, for Venus is in charge of women. **4** And let him have a censer of gold or silver or white copper or another beautiful metal, in which the fumigation will take place.

---

85 *Tritum.*
86 'Sun' is a feminine word in Arabic, which helps explain the feminine language; but perhaps the Ḥarrānians were also drawing upon older mythologies with feminine Sun deities. This use of the feminine (such as 'queen') is explicit in the Arabic *Picatrix* too, but was changed to masculine terms in the Latin.
87 Reading for *quinque* ('five'). The Sun is in the middle of the planetary hierarchy, with the superior planets (Saturn, Jupiter, Mars) above him, and the inferior ones (Venus, Mercury, Moon) below him.
88 This corresponds to Ar. 219–20, Ger. 230–31, Lat. 130–31, GW 176–77.
89 *Tympora*, a medieval spelling (sing. *tympus, tempus*).

5 [To Venus are attributed:] raw aloe, musk, costus,[90] labdanum, mastic, integumen of poppy, willow foliage, root of white lily. **6** One part therefore of each (that is, in equal [amounts]) should be taken. **7** And being rubbed together it should be prepared with dew water so that it becomes a mass, to be burned until smoking in the censer, with this oration:

8 O tender lady, cold and temperate, whose gleaming none can discern[91] fully, who is even good and well created among the rest of the spirits, who is even the laughing mistress of all beauty, namely gold and every precious thing, and all delight and games and singing! **9** You are even the mistress of all truth and all concord and delight, whose proper quality is to cultivate wine and desire, and you rejoice in every game. **10** Send to me one angel to this place, not frightening me, but one openly revealing whatever I shall ask that pertains to your nature."

11 Then, prostrate, let him adore the Creator, and an image of Venus will appear, speaking with him.

[Chapter 7: Rituals of Mercury][92]

1 If someone wanted to ask Mercury, let him be dressed as much as he can be in the manner of a writer, and let him be fitted to that likeness in all things, body and behavior. **2** Let him wear a ring (but leaden)[93] on a finger of the right hand. **3** And let him enter the place for asking, very quickly, and let the foreseen place be according to your desire, [and] extremely clean. **4** And let him have a leaden censer filled with fire, in which the fumigation may come to be.

5 [Attributed to Mercury are:] moss, cumin of Kirmān,[94] mountain basil, sweet basil, basil,[95] Scotch thistle,[96] the shells of bitter almonds, tamarisk seed, grapevine. **6** Let as much as you want of each be taken, but equally, and let them be mixed and fumigated in the censer[97] with this oration:

---

90 *Sausurrea costus*, a kind of aromatic thistle used in perfume.

91 Reading *perspicere* for *prospicere*.

92 This corresponds to Ar. 221–23, Ger. 232–35, Lat. 132–34, GW 178–80.

93 The Ar. has "fixed quicksilver" (*al-zi'baq al-ma'qūd*), which makes more sense.

94 A province in modern Iran.

95 These three basils are *habaq jabaliyy*, *hamāhim*, and *rayhān*. Pingree treats the second one as *Ocimum basilicum*, which is a general name for sweet basil or Thai basil. I am unsure how exactly these differ.

96 *Onopordum (onopordon) acanthium*.

97 Note that the text omits a liquid to mix it with.

7 "O lord, well eloquent and wise, and bringing all things to completion, understanding all things which pertain to knowledge or writing, who even—being most wise—speaks on all things which are contained from the upper heaven down to the earth, and who rarely rejoices, and who does not always benefit everyone wanting to acquire money, but you desire more to harm, and you harm merchants![98] **8** You, lord of all knowledge and as though cunning in it, whose nature human reason is never able to conceive nor explain in words because you operate good with good spirits and evil with evil ones, being male with males, female with females, diurnal with diurnal ones, nocturnal with nocturnal ones, blending your nature with all those wanting to know your nature, you introduce what is unerring[99] in the reason of the mind, and for those with whom you are mixed, you operate according to their nature. **9** Be here with me, and pleased, so that whenever I ask you with devotion as a friend, you respond to me with gentle visage and be present to me, favorable, helper and defender and guide (after God), and giving to me from God. **10** And may you respond to me always in every question of mine, and satisfy me most quickly and truly."

11 Let these things come to be on the day of Mercury and his hour, with him being placed well in some dignity of his own, free from the bad ones. **12** And let him adore God the Creator, prone on the ground, and it will come as was said.

[Chapter 8: Rituals of the Moon][100]

1 If someone wanted to ask the Moon, let him be clothed in the manner of a youth or adolescent prepared for running,[101] in white clothing not excessively long. **2** In his hand let him hold a silver censer, on his finger a ring of silver, and fire in the censer, and let him enter a suitable[102] place.

3 The fumigation of the Moon: the seed of the ben tree, *aristalqawāj*

---

98 The *Picatrix* is much more positive here, not speaking of Mercury harming.
99 Reading *inerrorem* for *in errorem*.
100 This corresponds to Ar. 223–24, Ger. 235–36, Lat. 134, GW 180.
101 This is probably in order to imitate the Moon's fast movement. Perhaps one could simply wear loose-fitting and comfortable clothes to move in.
102 *Idoneum*, which in its Greek form also has connotations of cleanliness and reverence (as was stated for the other rituals).

(that is, the seed of the sweet *citrolus*),[103] aloe of [*missing*], gum,[104] carob seed, integumen of the palm tree's flower-sheath, daisy flowers, cloves. 4 Let it be taken at will, but in equal amounts. 5 And let them be ground into small bits and mixed with wolf milk, and let it be a long mass like a taper. 6 And let it be burned with this oration:

7 "O lady[105] of knowledge, and soft, temperate, most shapely queen, and always steady in faith, whose nature does not despise delight and joy! 8 You, lady, to whom every command and the messenger of the command is subject, teacher of counsels, maintaining concord and rectitude among the seven spirits, whose interposition obscures the light of all spirits, but your conjunction with any of them takes away the malice of a malefic and increases the benevolence of a benefic—since therefore you are first among all of them, I ask you humbly, with the whole devotion of my mind, that whatever I ask you, you will not keep from speaking openly to me."

9 And let him adore God, prostrate, and it will come.

* *
*

---

103 *Citrolus* is perhaps a kind of citrus fruit, though that does not mean the Latin translator understood the Arabic. The transliteration *etherttallin* is (Pingree suggests) the same as the unknown *aristalqawāj* mentioned in the Hermes manuscript.
104 Perhaps gum Arabic?
105 The Latin reads in the masculine, as the Moon is grammatically masculine in Arabic.

Thessalos of Tralles: On the Virtues of Herbs

Astral-Herbal Magic in an Early Greek Botanical

Demetra George

ON THE VIRTUES OF HERBS is one of the earliest extant astrological herbals and it dates to about the 1st century CE.[1] This treatise details the medicinal plants that are associated with each of the twelve zodiacal signs and seven visible planets. It explains the plants' medicinal properties and gives precise formulas for combining the juice or roots of the plants with other ingredients to make pills, potions, ointments, salves, and plasters. Instructions are given concerning how and when to take the medicines. And most important for our interests in this paper, the Herbal includes instructions about astrologically propitious times and places to harvest the plants and make and administer the medicines. Prayers and invocations to increase the herbs' potency are also included.

There are several manuscript traditions for this text. They attribute authorship variously to a Thessalos, a Harpocration (author of the alchemical *Kyrannides*), Hermes Trismigestos, and a king Alexander. The Thessalos/ Harpocration manuscripts open with a letter from Thessalos, who de-

---

1 There are two Greek and three Latin manuscript traditions for this text, all of which have been edited and published by H.-V. Friedrich, *Thessalos von Tralles, griechisch und lateinisch*, Beitrage zur Klassischen Philogie 28, Meisenheim am Glan, 1968.

scribes himself as a young Greek student from Asia Minor. The letter is
written to Caesar Augustus (either Claudius or Nero) and claims its author
has successfully accomplished an incredible feat known only to a precious
few. Thessalos describes his miraculous journey to obtain secret healing
knowledge while communing with the god Asclepius during a vision revelation experience in an Egyptian temple.[2] The astrological herbal is the
transmission of that visionary experience.[3]

This Thessalos prooemium to *On the Virtues of Herbs* places the text in
the genre of revelations texts in the hermetic mystery traditions centered
in Egypt at the turn of the millennium. Since the first publication of the
text in 1878, historians and scholars of religion have recognized it as an
important document for understanding the religious life of late antiquity.[4]
However, this is the first paper to focus on the astrological timing that underlies the efficacy of the medicines and to publish the translations from
the Greek (my own) of the relevant passages. This paper will examine the
herbal lore in this text within the context of the fusion of Hermetic astrology, and alchemy and magic in the early centuries CE. It will also discuss
several examples of the magical uses of these plants through invocations
to the planetary gods.

2 For the Greek text and English translation of the Thessalos letter, see Philip A. Harland, "Journeys in Pursuit of Divine Wisdom: Thessalos and Other Seekers", in Philip A.
Harland, ed., *Travel and Religion in Antiquity*, Studies in Christianity and Judaism, Vol.
21, Wilfried Laurier University Press, 2011.
3 The Thessalos/Harpocration manuscript tradition contains the Thessalos letter
and the first four entries of the zodiacal herbal, but it breaks off in the middle of the
sign Cancer. A second Greek manuscript tradition of the same text ascribed to Hermes
Trismegistus replicates the zodiacal herbal of the Harpocration version and completes
all the passages for the remaining 8 zodiacal signs, includes the planetary herbal, and an
epilogue; but omits most of the prefatory letter from Thessalos. However it does contain
the final section of Thessalos' revelation where Ascelpius gives the instructions for the
proper times and places to gather the plants and make the medicine. See David Pingree,
"Thessalus Astrologer," in F. Edward Crantz, ed. *Catalogus Translationum Et Commen-
tariorum: Medieval and Renaissance Latin Translations and Commentaries: Annotated Lists
and Guides*, Vol. 3, The Catholic University of America Press, 1976.
4 Jonathan Z. Smith, "The Temple and the Magician," pp. 172–189 in *Map is not Ter-
ritory: Studies in History of Religions, Studies in Judaism in Late Antiquity*, 23. Leiden: E.
J. Brill; and Ian Moyer, "Thessalos of Tralles and Cultural Exchange, pp. 39–56 in Scott
Noegel, Joel Walker, and Brannon wheeler, eds., in *Prayer, Magic, and the Stars in the Ancient and Late Antique World*, Pennsylvania State University Press, 2003.

Thessalos relates that he is a distinguished student with financial means who travels to Alexandria to pursue his studies and specialize in medical training. At the completion of his studies, as he is gathering medical materials from the libraries in preparation for his return home, he discovers a book of Nechepso dealing with twenty–four medical treatments for every condition according to the zodiacal signs through both stones and plants. In his enthusiasm he immediately writes to his parents making extravagant claims as to his newly acquired healing powers, but when he actually attempts the solar cures, he is dismayed to find out that they do not work. Humiliated in front of his colleagues and ashamed to return home empty–handed, he wanders around Egypt, desperate to find some teachings of value, praying to the gods to grant him a vision in a dream or by a divine spirit, with thoughts of suicide as his alternative option.

He arrives in Diopolis (i.e., Thebes), the city of gods, full of temples, and develops friendships with various scholarly high priests and elders; he petitions them for information on magical healing powers. However most of them strongly protest against his rash expectations. One elderly priest who professes to have the ability to perceive divine visions in a dish of water, offers to help Thessalos and commands him to keep pure for three days. Thessalos is then led into a pure room which has been prepared, and without the priest's knowledge, secretes a papyrus roll and black ink to record the revelation. He requests a private audience with the god Asclepius, which is reluctantly granted. He is led to a seat opposite the god's throne and instructed in the chanting of the god's secret names. Thessalos is awed by the incredible nature of the spectacle that appears before him where the god Asclepius reaches out his right hand to bless Thessalos and tells him how he will be worshipped as a god when his successes become known.

Asclepius asks what he desires to know, and Thessalos inquires as to why Nechepso's prescriptions failed. The god's response is that while King Nechepso was knowledgeable in the sympathy of stones and plants with the stars, he did not receive his knowledge from the utterance of a god and therefore did not know the correct times and places to pick the plants. Asclepius then prefaces his transmission of the essential teachings with the comment, "that the produce of every season grows and withers under the influence of the stars and that divine spirit which pervades throughout all substance is most concentrated in the places where the influences of the stars are produced upon the cosmic foundation."

Before proceeding with the astrological directives, let us first consider this treatise within the context of the hermetic tradition. The *Hermetica* is a body of writings that emerged from Hellenistic Egypt. It is attributed to the Greco-Egyptian legendary sage Hermes Trismegistos, and discusses astrology, alchemy, magic and philosophy. The tenets of Hermetic world view, especially as pertaining to the technical hermetica, hold that the cosmos is alive, permeated by divine and semi-divine spirits. These divine energies emanate from God, flow through the stars and planets, and operate on bodies, divine or mortal, animate or inanimate. A cosmic sympathy, an invisible link between all parts of nature that connects celestial and terrestrial entities, establishes a chain of orders whereby the human body parts, plants, metals, stones, animals, colors, scents all correspond to a particular god, planet, zodiacal sign, star, or decan. This view provided the theoretical rationale for astrological medicine and astral magic.[5]

Claudius Ptolemy in the introduction to his *Tetrabiblos* classes astrological medicine among the benefits of the science of the stars and credits the Egyptians with uniting medicine with astrology through their *iatromathematical* systems. He cites their astronomical skill in prognostication of impending illness and knowledge of the sympathetic and antipathetic remedies to prevent and prescribe treatment for disease.[6]

One of the fundamental principles of astrological medicine is the doctrine of *melothesia* which is a system of correspondences between zodiacal signs, planets, and the parts of the human body. It is fully explicated in the opening to the *Iatromathematika—From Hermes to Ammon the Egyptian*[7]

Ammon, the wise men say that man is the world, because he is similar to the nature of the world. For at the moment of the emission of human sperm, rays were cast from the seven planets upon each part of man. In a similar manner, also at the moment of birth, rays were cast upon each part of man according to the position of the twelve zodiacal signs. Thus, the Ram (Aries) is called the head. The sense organs of the head have been divided among the seven planets. The right eye is assigned to the Sun, the left eye to the Moon, hearing to Kronos, the brain to Zeus, the tongue and throat to Hermes, the sense of

---

5 Garth Fowden, *The Egyptian Hermes: A Historical Approach to the Late Pagan Mind*, Cambridge: Cambridge University Press, 1986, p. 75–78.

6 Claudius Ptolemy, *Tetrabiblos*, I.3

7 'Iatromathematika—From Hermes to Ammon the Egyptian', J. L. Idler, ed., *Physici et Medici gracci minors*, Vol. 1, Berlin, 1841, pp. 387–396; pp. 430–440.

smell and taste to Aphrodite, as many parts that are engorged with blood to Ares. If a certain planet happens to be in a malefic condition at the moment of birth or conception, an affliction occurs in the part of the body associated with that planet.

This passage recalls an ancient Egyptian inscription from the *Pyramid Texts* where each organ of the body was identified with a particular god:

Your head is Horus of the Underworld, your face is Mekhenty-Irty, your ears and your eyes are the Twin Children Atum, your nose is the Jackal, your teeth are Sopd, your hands are Hapi and Duamutef...

These correspondences assist the astrologer in identifying the part of the body that may be vulnerable to illness and also to suggest possible remedies. For example, if the malefic planet Mars is casting a destructive ray to the Moon in Aries, the left eye in the head may be subject to affliction and the herbs linked to the Moon or to the zodiacal sign Aries may be used to treat the ailment.

Nechepso and Asclepius are mentioned by Thessalos as sources of astrological wisdom in the realm of healing. Whether they were historical persons or legendary figures, they both played critical roles in the early history of Hellenistic and Hermetic astrology. A clarification of their spheres of influence sheds light on the positioning, implications and subtleties of this text as well as of other astrological botanical texts from this period.[8]

Many of the ancient astro–herbals begin with the heading "From Hermes Trismegistus to Asclepius".[9] These two figures are considered the fountainhead of astrology as a revealed wisdom teaching during the Ptolemaic Era in Egypt. The lineage recorded by Firmicus Maternus, a Roman astrologer writing in Latin during the 4th century CE, credits one Hermes Trismegistus with the founding of the Hellenistic astrological tradition,

8 The *CCAG* contains a wealth of other botanical texts that discuss the relationships of plants to zodiacal signs, planets, stars, and decans. Many give alternates systems of classifications of plant and celestial body correlations. See Andre-Jean Festugiere, *La Revelation d'Hermes Trismegiste: l'astrologie et les sciences occultes*, Paris: J. Gabalda, 1950, pp. 137–186.

9 *The Sacred Book of Hermes to Asclepius* concerning the plants and amulets for the 36 decans, pp. 247–277, in C.-E. Ruelle, ed., *Revue de Philologie*, Oct. 1908.

which he handed down to Asclepius, and which Petosiris and Nechepso explicated...[10]

In the religious syncretism that occurred in Greco–Egyptian culture of Ptolemaic Egypt, the learned Greek god Hermes (whose grandfather Atlas was credited with the knowledge of astronomy and astrology) was fused with the Egyptian Thoth, god of time, astronomy, and magical incantations into the composite Hermes Trismegistos. The Greek healing god Asclepius found his counterpart in the Egyptian god of healing Imhotep. Both Asclepius and Imhotep facilitated oracular dream incubations for healing purposes in temple settings. Imhotep was also associated with astrological knowledge, as an inscription from Hathor's temple in Denderah states, "Imhotep—he who makes known the course of the stars." Here we see the background for why Thessalos might have requested a visitation with Asclepius/Imhotep who was already linked with both astrological and medical knowledge that came through oracular visions and divine transmission.

Nechepso and Petosiris, cited as the explicators of the Hermetic astrological tradition, have their own complicated histories. They were attributed as the authors of a comprehensive textbook of astrology written in the second century BCE, which while no longer extant, is cited and quoted by almost every subsequent Hellenistic astrologer. Nechepso is the name of a king whom Manetho included in the twenty-sixth Egyptian dynasty (ca. 600 BC); and the most famous Petosiris was the high priest of Thoth (ca. 300 BC). It is unlikely that these two were the actual authors of the astrological manual. However, the attribution to King Nechepso (or Necho) may have served to link him to the members of his family dynasty who had diplomatic relations with the Assyrians. In the 7th century BCE these Egyptians traveled to Nineveh to meet the Assyrian kings Esarhaddon and Ashurbanipal, who were well-known advocates of priestly astrological guidance for political objectives.

The astronomer priest's role of interpreting celestial omens from planetary gods and conveying the gods' intentions to the king date to the earliest period of Babylonian astrology during 2nd millennium BCE. It continues for the next two thousand years through successive empires in Mesopotamia, where even Alexander the Great was contacted and warned by the Chaldean astrologers as his army approached the city walls of Babylon. The symbolism of Nechepso and Petosiris, as a king and high priest,

---

10 Julius Firmicus Maternus, *Mathesis*, IV. Preface.

represents an ancient tradition in the history of Mesopotamian astrology. The attribution of their names in the astrological textbook points to the attempt to establish the cultural primacy of a native Egyptian priestly tradition that preceded the Hellenistic astrological tradition of Hermes Trismegistos' revelation, one that connected it even further back into the Assyrian and Babylonian periods.

The implications of Thessalos' revelation suggest that the authority of Nechepso as an author of medical treatises according to the zodiacal signs and planets through both stones and plants is superseded by the superior version of Asclepius that includes the necessary timing for the efficacy of the treatments.[11] This comparison hints at the existence of two different astrological traditions in Roman Egypt during the time of Thessalos' visit. Or at least, in the process of explicating the revelation of Hermes Trismegistos, Nechepso and Petosiris followers developed and taught some alternate doctrines. Antiochus reports differences between Nechepso and Hermes in the classifications of advantageous (*chrematizo*) and un-advantageous houses and Thrasyllus lists differing significations for each of the houses between these two main proponents of astrological teachings.[12]

Thessalos' visit to Thebes, hoping for a vision revelation to clarify the Nechepso material, places him on a well-trodden path during the Roman era. Thebes was the spiritual center of the old Pharaonic Egypt and the seat of the great god Amun (Ammon), euhemeristically regarded by some as one of the country's early kings.[13] The medical text known as the *Iatromathematica*, which describes the influence of lunar motion in the diagnosis of illness, begins by describing the transmission of this doctrine from Hermes Trismegistos to Ammon the Egyptian.

At the time of Thessalos' visit, there were two temples at which it would have been likely and possible for him to receive his vision. One was a joint shrine of Amenhotep together with Imhotep that functioned as a dream incubation center for pilgrims seeking healing. But it also contained in-

---

11 Cumont traces the Nechepso treatise mentioned by Thessalos to the first book of the alchemical *Cyrannides* authored by Harpocration where indeed there are 24 medical treatments each consisting correspondences between the properties a plant, bird, stone, and fish, but they are organized by the 24 letters of the alphabet, not zodiacal signs and planets. See Franz Cumont, "Ecrits hermetiques: II. Le medecin Thessalus et les plantes astrales d'Hermes Trismegiste", *Revue de Philologie* 42, 1918, p. 103.

12 Antiochus, *Introductory Matters*, 19, CCAG 8.3:111–119; Thrasyllus, *The Tablet to Hierocles*, CCAG 8, 3; 99–101.

13 Fowden, *The Egyptian Hermes*, p. 32.

scriptions documenting the visits of a number of doctors seeking medical knowledge.[14] Another temple, now called Qasr el-Asuz, just south-east of Medinet Habu, was a joint temple for Thoth, Imhotep, and Amenhotep. This is of special interest in that it was built by Ptolemy VIII (145–116 BCE), a Greek king who supported the Egyptian priesthood, and it was during his reign that Hellenistic astrology proliferated. A cache of demotic horoscopes were found near this temple attesting to the presence of both astrological and medical knowledge.[15] This places Upper Egypt as a locus where the hermetic iatromathematical teachings were being passed on by the Egyptian priesthood.

Thessalos, having been honored as a recipient of divine knowledge from the Hermes/Asclepius lineage, albeit by some trickery, displaces Nechepso's authority on the subject. Thessalos then transmits this wisdom to his own king, placing him in the archetypal role of priest conveying astrological wisdom to the king, equal and even superior to Petosiris and Nechepso, in a tradition that goes back to earliest stratum of celestial divination.

Now we are ready to look at the astrological portion of the herbal. The following excerpts are my own translations and they come from the Hermes manuscript version. Here we pick up from the unpublished part of Asclepius' exposition on the proper times and places to pick the plants.

...I will set forth from one of them as a cause for believing the explanations that remain. This is the so-called hemlock plant. This plant seems to have originated from the effluence of Ares. This happened just when it was casting its rays into the cosmic foundation, to be precise into Scorpio. (In any case, it struck hemlock in the portions of Italy for the clime of Italy happened to lie underneath Scorpio). And so this plant has more of the divine effluence. For having drawn forth a greater amount of the divine effluence, if eaten by a quadruped or human, kills immediately. But also certain people who because of the vapor of the plant, after having laid down next to it in remote places, by drawing in the power of the plant through inhalations, they perish. And Crete lies under the clime of the Archer. And there Zeus happened to be cast-

14 Ian Moyer, *Egypt and the Limits of Hellenism*, Cambridge: Cambridge University Press, 2011, p. 250.

15 Otto Neugebauer, "Demotic Horoscopes", Journal of the American Oriental Society, 1 April 1943, Vol. 63 (2), pp. 115–127.

ing his ray on the cosmic foundation into Crete. And so there, the men eat this hemlock plant which is sweeter than any garden herb. Thus the effluences of the gods are able to injure or help according to the places and the times.

In this first section concerned with location, Asclepius discusses hemlock as a prototype example that is deadly when found in Italy, but beneficent when found in Crete. The background for understanding his reasoning is that the known world was divided into zones called *klimes*, each under the rulership of the various astrological signs. The hemlock plant originates from the effluences of the planet Ares (Mars), and at the moment of creation when Mars was in its home sign of Scorpio, Italy in the cosmic foundation (that is on the earth) lay under the portion of the zodiac designated by the sign Scorpio. Mars was considered to be a malefic destructive planet and thus the hemlock in Italy is fatal when humans or animals eat it or breathe in its vapors. However, because the island of Crete lies under the section of the Archer (Sagittarius), this zodiacal sign's planetary lord is the benefic Zeus (Jupiter), and there the hemlock plant is a sweet garden herb. The conclusion is that the planetary gods can injure or help the plants that are sacred to them in accordance with the regions of the earth where they have dominion.

The correlation of zodiacal signs with geographic locations was a well-established doctrine at the time of Thesallos' letter, and most Hellenistic astrologers included these listings in their discussions of the significations of the zodiacal signs.[16] This material was often utilized in mundane astrology, for general indications of politics, weather, and crops for different countries or regions.

In the Epilogue of the Hermes text, there is another section addressing the optimal places to gather the plants.

The plants that are useful for the needs mentioned before are from Egypt and Arabia and Syria and Asia, and even still Italy. For these climes are hotter than the other warm ones. For nothing is able to increase upon land that is open and in the midst of wind. And so in the colder of the climes when the passageways are dense in the plants and because of the thick opening are not able to have strength the plants are set down as diminished in power, in the previously mentioned climes through the greater thinness in themselves they

16 Paul of Alexandria, *Introductory Matters*, 2 lists Italy under the rulership of Scorpio and Crete under that of Sagittarius.

draw forth the lively air, with the result that they have more active power.

We can take at face value the reasoning that the hotter climates produce more powerful plants because the warmth contributes to the open porous quality of their cells allowing more absorption of the vital force in the air. But we can also consider that the author of this text was more familiar with the plants of the regions mentioned, and in fact these are the regions where the majority of Hellenistic astrologers originated or practiced. Discussions concerning the identity of Thessalos and whether he was the physician Thessalos of Tralles point to this passage concerning the role of pores which was one of the contributions of his medical sect, the Methodists.[17]

Asclepius now goes on to discuss the optimal timing to gather the plants.

> *And so it is absolutely clear that the king of all the stars is the Sun; for when it is in the Ram it is exalted and takes the greatest power in the zodiacal sign the Ram. And so the plants have the greatest power, not only on account of the Sun, but also because this zodiacal sign is most common to all the gods. For as I said before, the Ram is the exaltation of the Sun, the depression (fall) of Saturn, the domicile of Mars, and the trigon of Jupiter. In any case the fore-mentioned sign has these powers. And so when the Sun is in this zodiacal sign, collect the plants which will be mentioned, extract the juice, without boiling it, for they (the plants) are altered by fire. Chop them, extract the juice, and put one cup of honey into each measure of juice. For it gives a good healthy permanence to the juices themselves, for as many years as you wish to preserve it. When you have made this, put it in a glass vessel and let it set for 60 days. And in this way you arrive at the proper use of the plant. After these things, prepare each as follows.*

In the second paragraph of his instructions regarding the optimal time to pick the plants, Asclepius' advice is that the plants have the greatest power when the Sun is in the sign of the Ram (Aries, March 21–April 20). The vital force of medicinal plants peak and are most concentrated when they first emerge after winter's hibernation. Astrologically this is connected to the various systems of zodiacal rulerships where planets are especially

---

17 Alan Scott, 'Ps.-Thessalus of Tralles and Galen's De Methodo Medendi', *Sudhoff's Archiv*, Bd. 75, H. 1 (1991), p. 107.

strong and powerful in certain zodiacal signs. The Sun's power is exalted, or occupies a place of primacy and honor when located in the sign of Aries. Aries is also the trigon dominion of the great benefic Jupiter and the domicile of Mars, who is not only the god of war but also rules the emission of sperm in the sexual act which generates the creative life force.

This section alludes to knowledge of the *thema mundi*, the chart of the creation of the world that was discussed in astrological and philosophical literature from the Hellenistic era through to the Renaissance.[18] The *thema mundi* demonstrated the theoretical rationale behind many of the core principles of astrological postulates. The placement of planets in certain signs on the day of creation, timed to the Egyptian New Year and the helical rising of the star Sirius heralding the flood of the Nile River, indicated the signs in which the planets had the greatest power. This chart had Cancer as the rising sign which places Aries at the Midheaven, or peak of the chart. When we apply the doctrine of *melothesia* to this proto-type chart, Aries represents the head of the cosmos and the head of upright man. It is here in Aries that the diurnal motion of the Sun reaches its highest elevation overhead at noon on the day of creation. Aries thus represents the peak of the Sun's power.

There are additional sections on timing in the Hermes manuscripts. In the introduction to the zodiacal botanical in the Hermes text, there is a listing of plants associated with each zodiacal sign.[19] It is followed by a set of timing instructions concerning when to gather the plants and make the medicines so they are most effective.

An abridged medical book of Hermes Trismegistos according to the astrological science and physical emanations of the stars which have been given to the disciple Asklepios

18 Firmicus Maternus tells us that no one believed that this was the chart of the actual creation of the world, but it was a quasi–nativity constructed by wise men as a teaching device. *Mathesis*, III. 8–10.

19 See John Scarborough's discussion concerning the difficulty in identifying the Greek plant names with their English counterparts due to the many false nomenclatures in LSJ Greek lexicon supplied by William Thiselton-Dyer's less-than-skillful botany. Scarborough supplies a listing of more reliable sources. "The Pharmacology of Sacred Plants, Herbs, and Roots" p.163–4, footnote 2, in Christopher A. Faraone and Dirk Obbink, eds., *Magika Hiera: Ancient Greek Magic and Religion*. Oxford: Oxford University Press, 1997.

The plant of the Ram (Aries)—sage (elelisphakos)
The plant of the Bull (Taurus)—upright verbena (peristereon orthos)
The plant of the Twins (Gemini)—supine verbena (peristereon uptios)
The plant of the Crab (Cancer)—comfrey (sumfuton)
The plant of the Lion (Leo)—cyclamen (kuklamion)
The plant of the Virgin (Virgo)—catmint (kalaminthe)
The plant of the Yoke (Libra)—grand heliotrope (skorpiouros)
The plant of the Scorpion (Scorpio)—wormwood (artemisia)
The plant of the Archer (Sagittarius)—pimpernel (anagallis purra and
kuane)
*The plant of the Goat (Capricorn)—monk's rhubarb, water sorrel, water
dock* (lapathon)
The plant of the Water Pourer (Aquarius)—dragonwort (drakontion)
The plant of the Fishes (Pisces)—birthwort (aristoloxeia)

*It is necessary to gather these plants and make then into a tincture when the
Sun enters into the Ram, but also more precisely whenever it enters into each
zodiacal sign of one of the plants, or even when the Moon enters into the trigon of the Sun or into the* Horoskopos. *Let it also be the day and hour of the*
oikodespotes/lord of the sign. *And so you will prosper by the influences of
the stars and nature, as the teacher says.*

Let's take an example to better explicate these instructions. One plant
associated with the sign Taurus is upright verbena. While the potency of
the plant is especially strong when the Sun is in the zodiacal sign of Aries
in the springtime, it is also potent when the Sun passes through Taurus
(April 20–May 21).

However an herbalist might need it at some other time of the year, so
when the Moon transits through Taurus (for several days each month), this
plant can be safely gathered; as well as when the Moon passes through
the other signs that have a trigon/trine relationship to Taurus, which are
Virgo and Capricorn. Yet an even better time is when the Moon in Taurus
rises over the Ascendant (*Horoskopos*). Finally since Venus is the lord/ruler
of the sign Taurus, upright vervain has the most power on the day sacred
to Venus which is a Friday, and best on the first hour of that day which is
Venus' hour on a Friday.

In the Hermes manuscript tradition, the planetary herbal follows the
zodiacal herbal.

And so having explained to you the plants in accordance with each zodiacal sign and their powers, it is necessary to transmit the efficacies and conditions associated with each of the seven planets.

Several manuscripts of this tradition are attributed to a 'king Alexander' and contain an introduction that summarizes the plants connected with each planet. Additional instructions are given for timing the harvesting the plants. This entry also includes a prayer to say when picking the plants, making, and administering the medicines.

From Hermes Trismegistos to Asclepius concerning the Plants of the Seven Planets

If however you do not have a supply of the plants from these climes, you must go to take what is necessary from other places, watch to get each of them on one of the seven days of the week, is the one of each star, it is not the plant, but also in accordance with the hour of that day, that belongs to the star, just as been set forth here by us. Pulling it up, select this plant from the earth and that has been wrapped in prayer and with the taking, throw a seed of grain or barley into the pit in which the plant was found.

These are the days of the planets:

Day 1, verily the lord of the Sun and the first hour, its plants are chicory (kichorion) *and* (polygonon) *multi-fruit knot grass*

Day 2, first hour, Selene/Moon, peony (aglaophanton) *and wild rose* (kunobate)

Day 3, first hour, Ares/Mars, sulpherwort (peucedanum) *and large plantain* (arnoglosson)

Day 4, first hour, Hermes/Mercury, mullein (phlomos) *and cinquefoil* (pentaphullon)

Day 5, first hour, Zeus/Jupiter, sugar (sagcharonion) *and agrimony* (eupatorion)

Day 6, first hour, Aphrodite, all-heal (panacea) *and vervain* (peristereon)

Day 7, first hour, Kronos/Saturn, houseleek (aeizoon) and asphodelos (as-phodelos)

For these things, let it be also when the Moon is full or when it passes through the zodiacal sign of the day of the planet.

Here we see more timing instructions concerning the potency of plants on the planetary days and hours when their corresponding planet has dominion. This order follows the days of the week: Sunday for the Sun, Monday for the Moon, Tuesday for Mars, Wednesday for Mercury, Thursday for Jupiter, Friday for Venus, and Saturday for Saturn. The first hour after sunrise on each of days is ruled by the planet associated with that day and is the most potent time on that day for the efficacy of the plant. Thus for Jupiter's plant agrimony, the best time to gather it is during the first hour after sunrise on a Thursday. The text instructs that one could also gather this plant when the Moon passes through the zodiacal sign that Jupiter rules, which is Sagittarius.

Following this listing is the text of the prayer to recite when picking the plant. The herbalist is instructed to place a seed of that plant in the hole from which it was taken to ensure the continued growth of that plant in that place.

PRAYER TO RECITE AT THE MOMENT OF HARVESTING EACH PLANT

Lord, master of the universe, master of all creation invisible and visible, you who as far as the visible creation has made certain parts naturally allied in agreement with one another so that they possessed the same power in these things that came into being from the created things that were born from them, and who also made the other things in turn not sympathetic and not in agreement except in this condition, in regard to their joining and union, in a mixture well-tempered and these are things which proclaim from afar your majesty so you at this moment when I called the plant here XX which you have made sympathetic with the planet XX, consent that this plant will be strong and full of power and full of efficacy for the use of medicines which one has aimed against the maladies which afflict mortal creatures, with the assistance of the same star which obeys your command, because your name is blessed and glorified into the ages, amen.

Say the same prayer also when you employ the use in the treatment of the malady and also when you prepare it.[20]

There are several phrases in this prayer that date it. Phrases found in astrological doctrines in the 1700s—such as "lord pantocrator" (lord, master of the universe) and "in the aeons and aeons, amen"—suggest composition at a later date than the original Greek during the first century.[21] But the author or scribe/copyist is retaining the essence of the hermetic notion that the efficacy of the plants as medicine comes from their celestial counterpart. He adds that behind the power of the stars stands the power of God who is the ultimate source of the beneficence.

In this passage we see the continuity of the belief in the divine power of drugs and the tradition of acknowledging the gods who stand at the head of the chain of orders that flows down through the stars into the vegetal, animal, mineral and human kingdoms below.

The zodiacal herbals in the Thessalos and Hermes texts focus exclusively on the plants, the remedies, and the treatments from a precise medical point of view. They are devoid of any magical uses. This may be due to the religious bias of medieval scribes who deliberately excluded pagan references in certain manuscript traditions, or to the existence in Egypt of two different rival Greco–Roman schools of herbalism. One school was more committed to the pharmacological properties of the medicinal plants while the other was turned entirely toward their magical uses.[22] The emphasis on the magical uses of astrological herbalism is found in the botanical texts attributed to Solomon. While these are vague in terms of providing precise prescriptions for medical preparations and treatments, they abound in indications for their use in magic and in the construction of amulets and charms to ward off disease and other misfortunes.

However, it is in the planetary herbal of the Hermes text that we see several instances of the magical uses of the plants, and invocations to the gods associated with the plants and planets.[23] In the hermetic world view the rationale behind invocations is the supposition that not only is there

---

20 My translation from Festuigere's translation of the Greek into French. Andre–Jean Festugiere 'L'experience religieuse du medecin Thessalos', p. 69 in *Hermetisme et mystique paienne*, Paris: Aubier-Montaigne, 1967.

21 Ibid.

22 Festugiere, *La Revelation d'Hermes Trismegiste*, p. 153

23 The *CCAG* version which is in the Codex Parisinus Graecus 2256 manuscript shows the names of Helios and Hermes in the text ; in the manuscripts used in the Friedrich

a chain of correspondences downward linking celestial bodies to the human and terrestrial realm; but in turn it is also moves upward whereby it is possible for humans to influence the planetary gods through invocations and rituals employing the special attributes of that chain– such as roses to Venus Aphrodite at astrologically determined times when that planetary deity has dominion, such as a Venus hour on a Friday.

According to this text, the plant of the Sun is chicory. Its uses include treatment for heart conditions, linking the Sun's rulership of the zodiacal sign Leo with its correspondence to the heart in the human body. Instructions are given for preparing an ointment as well as pills with specified amounts of other ingredients. The text advises to face the sunrise and anoint one's face with the plant to gain the god's good will. It suggests that the medicine made from the plant picked at sunrise be especially efficacious for his own ailments.

In the entry on the plant of the Moon, which is peony, we are told that the power of the plant develops in a similar manner to the Moon, increasing when the Moon is increasing in light and decreasing when the Moon is decreasing in light. For most conditions—such as reducing tumors and other swellings of the flesh—the plant is useful when decreasing. The magical uses involve fumigation with the decreasing root—this will drive away demons and halt a storm at sea.

The plant called the good staff (caduceus) of Hermes (Mercury) is mullein. In general its indications are good for relief of pain and strengthening the limbs when walking or competing in running races. Hermes was the patron god of travelers (on foot) and of the athletic competitions such as the Olympic Games. He was also the god of words and eloquent speech, and the text instructs:

> If someone who is fasting should drink down this juice and summon the god Hermes, he will be most prepared in speaking and will be greatly believed.

By ingesting the juice from the plant while in a state of spiritual and physical purification, a person can channel the persuasive eloquence of Hermes' nature for his or her own intentions. The planetary herbal concludes with an epilogue that exhorts the reader to guard and protect this teaching on forbidden things.

---

edition B Codex Parisinus Graecus 2502 and Vindobonensis med. Gr. 23, a copyist inserted a literary cryptograph into the text instead of the god's name.

You have in brief a collection of teachings that has been handed over to you of all the remedies for all the illnesses. And so what remains is for you to construct and also the things that have been written previously and to guard this doctrine for me, so that this writing is never handed over to ignorant man...

These final statements firmly place this text in the category of mystery teachings and secret initiatory knowledge gained through revelation. This was a standard for the spiritualizing philosophies of late antiquity. It reflects the hermetic view that stands behind astrological thinking: "As Above, So Below." The celestial realm that is teaming with divine spiritual energies finds its earthly manifestation in the human and terrestrial realms below.

⋆　⋆
⋆

Sources of Power in Medieval and Modern Magic

John Michael Greer

SEVERAL YEARS AGO, traditional astrologer Christopher Warnock and I prepared the first English translation of the Latin edition of the *Picatrix*, the most important medieval handbook of astrological magic.[1] That was an immensely educational project for me, in more than the obvious ways. I came to the *Picatrix* expecting to encounter a great deal of magical lore I hadn't previously encountered, and that expectation was more than fulfilled. What I was not expecting, though in retrospect I realized I should have been, was a completely different way of understanding magic, and in particular, the sources of magical power.

To judge by the baffled reaction the translation got once it was published, I was not the only person taken aback by this. A surprisingly large fraction of the occult community these days seems to believe that the kinds of magic practiced nowadays are the only magic there is, and have been practiced in identical form since the Paleolithic, if not the Paleozoic. This isn't simply a habit of the clueless; as important a magician and occult theorist as Dion Fortune was apparently convinced that the rituals

1 John Michael Greer, and Christopher Warnock, trans., *The Picatrix*, Adocentyn Press, 2010.

practiced by her Fraternity of the Inner Light differed only in small details from the rites performed in the Sun Temples of ancient Atlantis more than ten thousand years ago.[2]

The same thinking pervades the occult community these days. It has not been that long since two books titled *Celtic Magic* and *Norse Magic* respectively, by an author who will remain nameless here, could be found on the shelves of most occult bookstores. Any of my readers who happened to read them both will have noticed that large parts of the text differ only because the author ran a search-and-replace, swapping out Irish words and deities with their alleged Norse equivalents. Inevitably, the theory of magic, the practices, and the spells in both books were neither Irish nor Norse, but generic twentieth century pop Neopaganism dolled up in Norse or Irish decor.

This flattening out of cultural and magical differences is part and parcel of a broader bad habit that pervades contemporary culture. All too often nowadays, when people think about the past, the result is simply a projection of their own desires, hopes and fears onto a collection of random details pulled out of context and edited to make them look a lot more familiar to us than they actually are. When modern people think about people in the past, they tend to imagine themselves in exotic clothing in a world that's basically the same as the one they know. They have been encouraged to do that by generations of historical novels and movies that portray ancient people as though they had the same hopes, fears, and outlook on life as modern people do. Yet that habit of thinking completely falsifies the difference between present and past. The past is a foreign country; not only do they talk funny there, and wear strange clothes, and do things in ways that don't make sense, they didn't experience the universe in the same way we do. In a very real sense, they didn't live in the same universe we do.

Oswald Spengler, whose extensive study of the cycles of history has been languishing in the memory hole of contemporary culture for too long, offered a remarkably crisp example of the difference between the universes of the past and the one modern people inhabit. He notes that none of the languages of the western world in ancient or medieval times had a word for our concept of space—that is, space as an infinite void in which everything floats around.[3] *Spatium*, the Latin word from which

---

2 Dion Fortune, *Esoteric Orders and their Work*, Aquarian Press, 1987.
3 Oswald Spengler, *The Decline of the West*. Vol. 1, trans. Charles Francis Atkinson, Knopf, 1926, p. 83.

our word 'space' comes, meant the gap between two objects, and that gap was always filled by something, because nature abhors a vacuum. The concept of infinite space did not exist for people in the ancient and medieval worlds; it never occurred to them that such a thing could be. Yet that concept is fundamental to our modern way of thinking.

What color is the universe, by the way? To the modern mind, it's black: an infinite empty night reaching away into eternal darkness in all directions. To people in the western world from ancient times through the end of the Renaissance, the universe was a solid transparent body full of light. The reason the night sky looks black, they believed, was that the Earth's shadow darkened the small portion of it into which we look at night. The difference between the universe as a black void and the universe as a solid body full of light is one measure of how the universe changed at the birth of the modern world.

*

Changes of the sort just outlined, between different ways of understanding the universe, affect magic as well. Such changes take their time, though, because magic is remarkably conservative. For a working magician, what's important about magic is that it works, and the most popular way to be sure that your spell will work is to copy something that's been used successfully for a long, long time. That's why medieval German Cabalistic incantations are still common in twentieth century Pennsylvania Dutch pow-wow magic,[4] and why Renaissance sorcerers scrounged so many of their incantations from classical Greek sources such as the Orphic hymns and the Corpus Hermeticum.[5] It's also why you find the medieval cosmos, with the earth at the center of the planetary spheres reaching up to the Primum Mobile, in the version of the Cabalistic Tree of Life used by most ceremonial magicians today, even though nearly all of these same mages also believe that the earth moves around the sun and the stars are scattered through infinite space.

Everything in magic is thus affected by the interplay of shifts in cosmology with ideas from earlier understandings of the universe, which are preserved like flies in amber by the essential conservatism of magical tra-

4 *The Sixth and Seventh Books of Moses*, Ibis Press, 2008.
5 Frances Yates, *Giordano Bruno and the Hermetic Tradition*. University of Chicago, 1964.

dition. Ideas about the sources of magical power are no exception to this rule. Such ideas are worth close study, because their changes over the centuries have much to say about the nature of magic and its relation to the theories used to understand it.

A survey of all the different places from which mages have drawn power around the world and across the millennia would fill a book larger than the one in which this essay appears. The subset of the western world's magical history that extends from ancient Greece to the modern world will be sufficient for present purposes.

That trajectory begins with the *goetes* and *magoi* of ancient Greece. *Goetes* practiced a homegrown Greek form of magic, while *magoi* claimed imported wisdom: *magos* had almost exactly the same connotation in fifth-century Greece that "swami" had in twentieth-century America. We know something about the practices of classical *goeteia* because *goetes* liked to write incantations on pieces of lead and dropping them into open graves and shrines of underworld deities, thus preserving them for today's archeologists.[6]

One of the things revealed by this practice is where the *goetes* believed magical power came from: from their perspective, it came from the deities of the Greek underworld, who could be induced to put a curse on somebody if you made the right offerings. With appropriate apologies to the deities in question, this might be called the Marlon Brando theory of magic: you go to the Godfather, and in this case the Godmother as well, and if you ask nicely and make it worth their while, they send a couple of toughs to have a little talk with the guy who's been giving you trouble. This is a very widespread theory of magic in polytheistic societies, and tends to be the default option until philosophers get into the act, which they invariably do sooner or later.

In ancient Greece, the philosophers got into the act in the fourth century BCE, as intellectuals started having trouble making sense of traditional Greek religion. That's a common difficulty faced by intellectuals in every literate society at one point or another in its history, but the ancient Greek examples of the species found an ingenious way around it. It so happened that just at that time, the starlore of the ancient societies of Mesopotamia was in the process of mutating into something close to the kind of astrology we practice today. Astrology in those days was understood as

---

6 See, for a good collection, John G. Gager, ed., *Curse Tablets and Binding Spells from the Ancient World*, Oxford University Press, 1992.

the practical side of astronomy, and so it had no shortage of intellectual respectability even among philosophers. Thus it was easy, even inevitable, for Greek intellectuals to end up thinking of astrological influences as the reality behind religion, and also the source of magical power.

For the next two thousand years, that was the answer that mattered. It was, among other things, the answer that shaped the magic of *Picatrix*, and it still underlies so much of modern magical practice that it's worth taking a moment to try to think through how it works. That starts with a universe very different from the one most people imagine themselves inhabiting today. Imagine for a moment that you're sitting outside on a starry night, looking up at the sky. From the old perspective, you're not looking out into an abyss of black emptiness with lumps of rock and blobs of incandescent hydrogen scattered across the face of the void. In fact, you're not looking out at all. You're looking up; what's more, you're looking up at a structure—and you're looking at it from the inside.

High up above you, and surrounding you on every side, is the second biggest thing that has ever existed or will ever exist: the sphere of the fixed stars. It's so far away that if you could go there and look down, the Earth would be smaller than a pinpoint; even if you could walk more than forty miles a day straight up, the medieval *South English Legendary* notes, you wouldn't yet have reached the sphere of the fixed stars after eight thousand years of walking.[7] The only thing bigger than the sphere of the fixed stars is the sphere just outside it, the Primum Mobile or sphere of first motion. Both those spheres, and everything else from there down to the orbit of the Moon, are made of a kind of matter that only exists in the flasks of alchemists here on Earth: the quintessence or fifth element, perfectly transparent, perfectly solid, brighter than fire and subtler than air.

The planets, like the spheres they move in, are made of the quintessence. More precisely, the bodies of the planets are made of the quintessence. The planets themselves are conscious living beings, and they're smarter than you are, by the way. In the great chain of being that reaches from matter right up to the throne of Deity, they rank below the angels, above the spirits, and a very long way above humanity. If you're a Pagan, they're the younger generation of gods; you know which ones, since they still have the same names. If you're a Christian, a Muslim or a Jew, they're mighty spiritual beings created by God and given charge over parts of the cosmos.

7 Quoted in C. S. Lewis, C. S., *The Discarded Image*, Cambridge University Press, 1964.

Below the circle of the Moon, things are different. This is the realm of the four elements. Fire is outermost, reaching from the top of the atmosphere up to the Moon's orbit. This is pure fire, not the muddled, impure fire we see down here, and it's transparent, luminous and formless. The reason fire down here always rises upwards is that it's trying to return to its proper place in the universe. Earth falls, water flows downwards, and air bubbles up for the same reason: each thing has its assigned place, and though things are all jumbled here below the Moon by the great mixmaster of the planets, the elements are always trying to sort themselves out.

Below the element of Earth, at the very bottom of creation, is something that shouldn't exist, didn't have to exist, and won't exist after a certain point in the future. The universe is all there is, and there's nowhere outside it, so when certain parts of creation went completely awry, a place had to be found for them inside the great structure. That's Hell: the trash can of creation, tucked away at the very bottom of existence at the center of the earth. Fallen angels end up there, and so do fallen humans. Pagans in the Middle Ages and Renaissance believed in Hell just as much as Muslims, Christians and Jews: the Chaldean Oracles, one of the most popular works of Greek Pagan spirituality in the Renaissance, mentions it,[8] and older Pagan writings about Hades got reinterpreted along the same lines. Sooner or later, everyone agrees, the trash will be disposed of, but until then, the apple of the world has a worm at its center. Things occasionally creep out from the depths to make trouble, and have to be sent back there.

The world is round, by the way. You learned that in grammar school, and if you go on to college you can listen to learned professors explain the evidence that proves it.[9] They'll also prove to you that the Moon is smaller than the Earth, that the Sun is much, much larger, and the stars are so far away you can't even imagine the distance. They can explain how eclipses happen, and they're right. They can tell you how big the earth is, too, and their figure is within a few hundred miles of the right one; that's why every geographer in Europe knew that Christopher Columbus was nuts when he said he could sail across the ocean to the Indies. They were right, too; he and all his crew would have starved to death months before

---

8 W. Wynn Westcott, *The Chaldean Oracles of Zoroaster*, Aquarian, 1983, p.56.

9 See, for example, Lynn Thorndyke, *The Sphere of Sacrobosco and its Commentators*. University of Chicago Press, 1949. The common modern claim that people in the Middle Ages thought the world was flat is a barefaced lie that will not stand up to fifteen minutes of impartial research.

they could have reached China. It's just that neither the professors, nor Columbus, nor anybody else except a few bedraggled Vikings in Iceland had any clue that there were a couple of unknown continents in the way.[10]

Those same professors can tell you quite a bit more. They'll explain to you that humanity isn't the pinnacle of existence by a long shot. We occupy the middle rung on the great ladder of creation. Below us are animals, plants, stones, elements, and raw unformed matter itself. Above us are spirits, intelligences, and the nine choirs of angels rising up rank on rank to the foot of the divine throne. They may get into an argument with one another if you ask them about faeries; everybody knows that those exist, along with fauns, satyrs, dwarves, and the like. Some scholars argue that they are a distinct order of being all their own, either slightly above or slightly below humanity; others have other opinions, but their exact place in the great chain of being is a matter of lively debate.[11]

Nobody doubts that they have a place, though, because everything does. Nothing in the universe is random, and nothing is outside, since there is no outside. Whether you're Pagan, Christian, Muslim, or Jew, you know that the universe didn't just happen. It was created. It's an artifact, and was shaped by powers that are so far beyond merely superhuman the word's hardly worth saying. You've read Plato's *Timaeus*—everybody who could read at all read Plato's *Timaeus*, or Calcidius' commentary on it, which was the standard text before the *Timaeus* itself was translated into Latin—and so you know that the divine power that made the universe made it as perfect as anything made of matter can possibly be.

Whether you're Pagan, Christian, Muslim or Jew, you believe that sometime in the distant past the whole elemental realm below the Moon was purified with water; you call that the Flood, whether you think of Noah or Deucalion as the guy who survived it. You also believe that sometime in the future everything below the Moon will be consecrated with fire and transmuted into something new and even more perfect; Pagans call that by the fine old Stoic term *ekpyrosis*, Christians refer to the Second Coming, and so on, but nobody doubts that it's going to happen one of these days. Above the Moon, no such changes have ever happened or will ever happen; the planets and the sphere of the stars turn in their everlasting cycles. Beyond that is—what? Not space; space in our sense of the word doesn't exist in that universe, the universe before ours; the entire cosmos is a single

---

10 See Jeffrey Burton Russell, *Inventing the Flat Earth*. Praeger, 1991.
11 Lewis, *The Discarded Image*, pp. 122–138.

body of matter without a bit of empty space in it anywhere. Beyond it is the Empyrean, the realm of pure spirit, in which there is no space and no time: the realm of the divine unity and the angels.

That's where the power and wisdom that guide the whole vast structure comes from. They don't come all in a lump, though. There are specific currents that descend from the Empyrean; the technical term is "influences." That word has been watered down into perfect vagueness in English, but in Latin it's still visibly derived from *in-fluere*, flowing inward, like great waterfalls of force cascading down from the Empyrean through the spheres, pushed this way and that by the planets, and finally pouring down into the realm of the elements. Everything here below the Moon exists because some influence makes it happen. Everybody knows that, and most people use it in little ways, making charms and medicines out of particular herbs and stones to cure an illness or bring a blessing, because those herbs and stones participate in some current of influence.

The adepts who wielded the *Picatrix* weren't limited to little ways. They studied the influences that descend through the heavens from the timeless and spaceless light of the Empyrean. They knew that the movements of the planets against the backdrop of the stars reveal the way those influences ebb and flow, harmonize and struggle, create and destroy. They knew that particular material things receive and collect different influences; that particular colors, shapes, musical modes, geometrical patterns, words and names resonate with each influence. They knew that magic is just our name for the process that creates and sustains the entire cosmos, and their books tell you how to step into the flow of that process, shape the dance of creative power, and accomplish wonders in the world.

*

In the minds of those who practiced the old astrological magic, there was nothing supernatural at all about their art. The descent of influences from the Empyrean to the sphere of the elements was entirely natural, and magic was just a matter of knowing what the influences are, how they're affected by the movements and relative positions of the planets, and what substances down here on Earth will absorb and hold any influence you happen to want. Notice that this implies that people don't have magical power; the universe has the power, and doing magic is purely a matter of knowing how to tap into the power as it flows from heaven to earth.

That makes it sound simple. In practice, it became enormously complex as the tradition matured and flourished. There were, broadly speaking, three ways to tap into the flow. You could simply gather together material substances that naturally stored and radiated an influence you wanted; that was called natural magic. You could fashion an object so that its form and the symbols on it would resonate with the influence you wanted, and make it at the right moment, when that influence was particularly strong and unhindered by contrary forces; that was called mathematical magic (in Roman times, the word *mathematicus* meant "astrologer"). You could also use ceremonies and incantations to get into contact with the intelligences of the planets, who were vast, cool, but by no means unsympathetic, and would work with you under certain conditions; that was called ceremonial magic.

Mages could also combine any two of these, or all three of them. What's more, the planetary intelligences weren't the only sources of influences that could be invoked in working. Each sign of the zodiac had its own spiritual powers and influences; so did each of the twenty-eight mansions of the Moon, the stations through which the Moon moves night by night against the stars; so did each of the thirty-six decans, or divisions of ten degrees, into which the sky was also divided.[12] The one drawback to this profusion of powers was that their influences waxed and waned on a time-table defined by the heavens, not by the mage. If you wanted to summon a spirit of Saturn, or consecrate a talisman of the third decan of Virgo, or even make an amulet using natural magic, you had to wait until the stars were favorable. Depending on the arrangement of the heavens, that could require quite a bit of waiting.

This was one of the reasons why a very different kind of magic had its adherents during the Middle Ages as well. The Marlon Brando magic of the ancient Greek *goetes* had equivalents all through ancient Europe, and cutting deals with the underworld stayed an option even when the powers of the underworld were redefined, dressed in red, and made to wear a set of horns surreptitiously borrowed from the great god Pan. Some of what later got defined as witchcraft had its roots in those practices, but these same workings also moved in a different direction, thanks to the Catholic

12 See, for example, *The Picatrix*, pp. 122–125 for the signs of the Zodiac, pp. 32–38 and 290–296 for the mansions of the Moon, and pp. 113–121 for the decans.

Church's enthusiastic practice of exorcism.

As the Middle Ages ripened, manuals of practice for exorcists proliferated, teaching them how to command demons to depart by means of the holy names of God. There were also Jewish manuals that had similar material in them, and some of these ended up in the hands of the church through various more or less brutal means. Over time, material from these Jewish sources found its way into the exorcist's manuals. Combine that with the folk magic already mentioned, and in due time, you inevitably got exorcists who decided that, since they could command demons, maybe they could get the demons to do something other than depart.

That's where the magic of the grimoires came from: a fusion of Christian exorcism, Jewish lore about demons and the names of God, and native European folk magic, in which the symbolism of Jewish and Christian faith was put to use extorting favors from the minions of Satan. (The word grimoire, by the way, is an old French version of "grammar;" grimoires typically presented themselves as grammar books, or as we'd say now, ABCs of the art of magic.) The writers and users of the grimoires had no doubt where magical power came from; it consisted of what demons could do for you, whether you got them to do that by commanding them using the mighty names of God, or by signing one of those friendly little contracts with them—the latter was considered the easier approach, though everyone knew about its eventual drawbacks.

Even so, the grimoire tradition might have remained a footnote in the history of magic, except for Nicolaus Copernicus. Even those modern thinkers who use Copernicus as an icon for the greater glory of science rarely realize just now much of a shock rippled through the western world when the heliocentric position elbowed the old, elegant Ptolemaic geocentric system out of the way.[13] The disproof of some scientific theory today wouldn't begin to have the same effect—by this time, most people are used to hearing that this or that theory has been disproved. If astrophysicists announced tomorrow that the Big Bang never happened, there would be some fluttering in intellectual dovecotes, but even among the scientifically literate, most people would read the article, chat about it with colleagues, and go on with their lives.

Imagine instead that something kicks down the foundations of science as a whole. Let's say, for example, that it turns out that the Sun and

13 See particularly Alexandre Koyre, *From the Closed World to the Infinite Universe.* Johns Hopkins University Press, 1957.

the planets are actually intelligent beings, as the old astrological mages thought, and there are no laws of astrophysics, just the habitual behavior of heavenly bodies who might just change their minds without warning and do something different. That's the kind of vertigo-inducing jolt the Copernican revolution imposed on the European world, except in the other direction. Everyone had been used to living in a solid, structured, meaningful world full of intelligent beings, and suddenly they found themselves precariously perched on a lump of rock in the midst of an infinite black void.

While it was a shock to everyone, the heliocentric theory of the solar system delivered a particularly devastating body blow to the old astrological magic, since the whole theory of that end of magic depended on the belief that everything that happens on Earth is controlled by what happens in the heavens. Once the Earth was yanked out of its position just above the bottom of creation and sent spinning through the void, the entire theoretical scheme fell apart. Mind you, the magic still worked, and there were people who kept on practicing it straight through the Copernican revolution and out the other side, but the sense of intellectual respectability that had once given the tradition validity in the popular imagination went right out the window.

That cleared the way for an explosion of interest in the grimoire tradition. Disbelief in the planetary spheres and their intelligences didn't require disbelief in God, Satan, and their respective servants—quite the contrary, the absence of the familiar spheres made people cling all the more tightly to the Bible and the teachings of religion. While the location of Heaven was a matter of some perplexity after Copernicus, furthermore, no one doubted that Hell was where it always had been. (Go into a deep mine and the further down you go, the hotter it gets; this was considered evidence in early modern Europe for the location of Satan and his pals.) The invention of printing also helped feed interest in the grimoires, as printers found they could rake in money hand over fist by churning out manuals of demon–summoning for fun and profit.

Grimoires duly appeared on the shelves of booksellers. Some of them were authentic magical manuals; others were pretty clearly cooked up for sale by enterprising promoters.[14] When the legend of Johann Faust became popular in Germany, for example, boatloads of books hit the stands

---

14 Butler, E. M., *Ritual Magic*. Cambridge University Press, 1949, has a helpful survey of the European grimoire tradition, including its more absurd and meretricious aspects.

claiming to be the authentic manual Faust had used to summon up Mephistopheles, and nearly all of them were focused with the exactness of a well–tuned laser on the fantasy of getting rich quickly by metaphysical means—Rhonda Byrne's heavily marketed opus *The Secret* is part of a long tradition, though she somehow didn't get around to telling her readers how to sell their souls to Satan. (I think she assumed they'd just go ahead and hand them over without any additional encouragement.)

Like *The Secret*, the published grimoires of the early modern period were a mass market phenomenon. Like most mass market phenomena, they were dismissed by the cognoscenti as vulgar impostures, and to be quite honest, most of them deserved that accolade. Still, the way the grimoire literature understood the sources of magical power became standard in popular culture all through Europe and the European diaspora. Until quite recently, even among many occultists, magic was by definition the art and science of getting spiritual beings to do things for you.[15]

Not all the beings in question were evil ones. There's a rich tradition of Christian magic in the western world, and the age of grimoire magic saw no shortage of that in print. An example that comes to mind is *The Long Lost Friend*, one of the few very widely used American grimoires.[16] It was written and published in 1840 by Johann Georg Hohman, a *braucher* or folk magician of Pennsylvania Dutch (i.e., Pennsylvania *Deutsch*, a descendant of German immigrants) extraction. It's a collection of charms, spells, and household hints, just the kind of thing you want if you're a small town farmer in 1840s Pennsylvania.

The charms and spells in *The Long Lost Friend* are resolutely Christian, both in symbolism and in intention. What hoodoo doctors call "bad work" does not feature there, nor does any trafficking with devils. The good Christian wizards of nineteenth century America wrote charms on paper invoking the blessings of Christ and the saints, recited specific Psalms to heal this disease or protect against that evil influence. Where their opposite numbers were taking copies of *The Sixth and Seventh Books of Moses* out to the crossroads at midnight to command the obedience of Mephistopheles—yes, he's one of the spirits in there[17]—those who followed the counsel of *The Long Lost Friend* weren't commanding anybody. Like their

---

15 See, for example, Hall. Manly P., *The Secret Teachings of All Ages*. Philosophical Research Society, 1928, pp. 101–104.

16 John George Hohman, *The Long Lost Friend*. Llewellyn, 2012.

17 *Sixth and Seventh Books*, p. 130.

more conventionally devout neighbors, they were counting on the blessings promised by the Bible to those who love God and pray to him.

Despite the theological and moral differences separating them, these forms of magic had a crucial point in common: they started from the presupposition that human beings don't have magical powers of their own. Only spiritual beings, whether good or evil, had such powers, and the only way human beings could arrange for magic to be used on their behalf was to make some kind of arrangement with those beings. That's still a common belief among many people today, and it was all but universal until the modern era of magic began. Not coincidentally, the same basic assumption—that human beings have no magical powers of their own—was also central to the astrological magic discussed above.

In the Middle Ages, scholars talked knowledgeably about *goetia* and *magia*, which were the respective Latin terms for these two approaches. You'll find the same distinction in modern scholarly writings such as D. P. Walker's *Spiritual and Demonic Magic from Ficino to Campanella*—Walker here meant 'spiritual' and 'demonic' in their precise Renaissance Latin senses, with *spiritus* meaning the descending influences of the heavens, and *daemon* any disembodied being who wasn't either a ghost or a god. It's almost impossible to make sense of the older works of magical philosophy unless you keep the distinction in mind: is magic a natural process that simply works with the flows of energy that sustain the world anyway, or is it a supernatural process that cajoles or coerces nonhuman intelligences into serving as your labor force? Depending on the specific book you're reading, it could be either or both.

In the first half of the nineteenth century, certainly, both these approaches remained in common use all over the Western world. Now of course most people insisted loudly that magic couldn't possibly work, that astrology was an exploded superstition, and as for angels, demons, and the like, whatever the Bible said about them—and of course it says a great deal on those subjects—they couldn't possibly have the least bit of relevance to life in progressive, modern, up-to-date Europe and America. Yet it's a matter of record that magic, astrology, and traditional ways of dealing with angels and demons were practiced all over progressive, modern, up-to-date Europe and America in those years. Magic is like sex; what's socially acceptable to say about it need not have anything in common with what people actually do.

The main influence that a lack of public respectability has on magic is that fewer people talk about why it works. The Renaissance was one of the great eras of occult philosophy because the broad acceptance of astrology and astrological magic among intellectuals encouraged people to wonder about why, for example, planting vegetables in the Moon's first quarter, with the Moon in a watery or earthy Zodiacal sign and applying to a trine aspect with Venus, and free from hostile aspects with the malefic planets, would give you a great harvest three or four months later. The early nineteenth century was a barren period for occult philosophy because most intellectuals weren't talking about such things; people just kept on watching the Moon through her phases and signs, and getting the bumper crops of vegetables as a result.

*

That's roughly where magic was when one of the great figures of the occult tradition put in an appearance. His name was Alphonse Louis Constant, but most of my readers will know him better by his magical nom de plume, Eliphas Lévi.

Lévi, as we might as well call him, was a remarkable and many–sided thinker, but that's a subject for another day. What matters here is the revolution in occult philosophy he launched with his first and most important book on magic, *Dogme et Rituel de la Haute Magie* (*Doctrine and Ritual of High Magic*).[18] In that book, Lévi showed that it was possible to take the philosophy of astrological magic and make it work in a Copernican universe.

What's more, he did it by an act of decentering that more or less paralleled the one Einstein carried out in physics half a century later. In Lévi's theory of magic, the currents of creative force don't move in a single direction, cascading down from the throne of God past stars and planets and the circle of the Moon to yank things here on Earth about like so many puppets on celestial strings. The Astral Light, the unseen continuum that unites all things, communicates influences from everything to everything else—from the Earth to the planets and stars just as much as the other way around—and that was, in Lévi's view, the basis on which magic rests.

One implication of this shift in focus deserves special attention. The ways of thinking about the sources of magical power that were in circulation before the dawn of modern magic assumed, as already noted, that human beings didn't have magical powers. If you wanted to practice magic,

---

18 Eliphas Lévi, *Doctrine and Ritual of High Magic*, trans. John Michael Greer and Mark Mikituk, Tarcher Perigee, 2017.

you either had to figure out how to direct and concentrate the powers of the stars, or you had to figure out how to obtain help from, or mastery over, spiritual beings. For Lévi, by contrast, human beings were capable of magical action in their own right. The Astral Light, the universal medium of magic, could be shaped directly by the power of human will guided by the human imagination, without any need to call on other forces.

To Lévi, in turn, that was how magic worked. The operative mage was an exceptional human being who developed the faculties of will and imagination beyond the norm, and could therefore set the Astral Light in motion to accomplish marvelous effects. Lévi didn't talk much about gods or spirits except as symbols through which the imagination could be directed; what interested him was the training of the individual human being.

In that orientation toward the individual, Lévi was very much a man of his time. It's indicative that he was born in 1810, three years before Arthur Schopenhauer wrote the first of his philosophical treatises, and died in 1875, three years after Friedrich Nietzsche did the same thing. Both these philosophers had the same focus as Lévi; what set them apart from their predecessors and most of their contemporaries was precisely that they rejected abstract theories about the cosmos in order to place human experience and the human condition, with all their paradoxes intact, at the center of the philosophical project. Both of them, in turn, came to see the unique, self-creating human individual as the only answer to the world's perplexities that mattered—and so did Lévi.

In the process, he took a familiar trope from the traditions of occultism and reframed it in a new and explosive way. From ancient times on, occult lore had included colorful tales about masters of the secret arts who pushed straight past the boundaries of ordinary humanity to wield marvelous powers. From Pythagoras and Apollonius of Tyana to the secretive adepts of Renaissance alchemy and the Unknown Superiors of the eighteenth–century Masonic fringe, such figures have always been popular. What made Lévi's work revolutionary is that he set out to explain to his readers how they could become such a figure themselves.

For more than a century after *Dogme et Rituel de la Haute Magie* first saw print, as a direct result, that was what occultism was about: becoming such a figure. All across the Western world, people who were dissatisfied with the mainstream culture of their time flung themselves into the quest to become occult adepts. The law of supply and demand being what it is, schools claiming to offer the necessary training popped up like mushrooms after a rainstorm. Some of those schools were utterly forgettable, and have been duly forgotten; others were epic flops, and we'll be talking about some of those down the road a bit; but a respectable number of them succeeded in putting together a workable collection of occult practices, infused the set with some variant of Lévi's basic approach, and proceeded to turn out competent occultists, astrologers, operative mages, or what have you.

One of those schools has gotten almost all the press in recent decades: the Hermetic Order of the Golden Dawn, which was founded in 1887, blew itself to smithereens in a series of pointless political quarrels between 1900 and 1902, and managed to create the modern world's most influential system of operative magic in the interval.[19] The way the Golden Dawn understood the sources of magical power is crucial to the trajectory explored in this essay, because that understanding and Lévi's became the two standard theories of magic across most of the Western world during most of the twentieth century.

The core of the Golden Dawn approach was a return to something like the astrological theory of magic, but with a crucial difference. Where the old astrological mages had understood the different realms of being as separate in space—the elemental world below the Moon, the planetary realm above the Moon but below the stars, the Empyrean beyond the stars—the Golden Dawn interpreted them as planes or modes of being that were simultaneously present in every corner of space. In the order's Cabalistic jargon, you've got the divine realm of Atziluth, the archangelic realm of Briah, the angelic realm of Yetzirah, and the material realm of Assiah; the latter is the only one human beings normally perceive, but all are present at every point in space and time.

Golden Dawn initiates thus didn't need to direct their attention to a distant realm beyond the stars, or wait for the planets to come around to favorable positions, in order to work magic. Instead, they had to open up contact with more exalted planes of being, using ornate ceremonial and an assortment of more or less intricate psychophysical techniques. They weren't using their own wills and imaginations to transform the world directly; they were, like the astrological mages of old, tapping into the cre-

---

19 Israel Regardie, *The Golden Dawn*, Llewellyn, 1971 is the standard collection of the Golden Dawn's teachings; Ellic Howe, *The Magicians of the Golden Dawn*, Routledge & Kegan Paul, 1972 is a reliable if waspish history.

ative process that brought the world into being—but they were doing it in a way that wasn't inconvenienced by the Copernican cosmos or dependent on the cycles of the heavens. Notice also that the Golden Dawn model gives a more important role to the individual mage than the old astrological magic did; a Golden Dawn adept didn't simply wait patiently for the influences to descend, he or she tore open the walls of the sky to summon down the influences needed for a particular working.

As the twentieth century got under way, therefore, operative mages in the Western world had access to two coherent theories of where magic gets its power. As a very rough generalization, mages in the English-speaking world used some variant of the Golden Dawn theory, while mages in continental Europe used some variant of Lévi's theory; there were always exceptions, and plenty of people who combined the two in an assortment of ways. Still, a third approach was about to appear, courtesy of the intellectual earthquake being set in motion at the twentieth century's dawn by a Viennese physician named Sigmund Freud.

The depth psychology revolution has transformed the Western world's collective imagination so drastically over the last century or so, and become so much a part of our ordinary notions of ourselves, that it's hard for many people to grasp just how explosive it was when it first emerged. In 1900 most psychologists believed that the phrase 'unconscious thinking' was a contradiction in terms. The idea that people's thoughts and perceptions could be distorted without their knowledge by the lingering aftermath of emotional trauma was profoundly unsettling to cultures that had spent centuries treating thought and perception as simple, straightforward, and rational by definition. As Freud and his followers broke through into the buried vaults of the unconscious mind, though, their discoveries upended millennium-old certainties—and, in the process, provided operative mages with another way to understand their art.

Central to the depth psychology revolution was the discovery that the deeper strata of the mind think in symbols and symbolic relationships, rather than logical categories and logical relationships. Though Freud himself tried to turn his theories into a bulwark against occult ideas, plenty of his students and even more of the people who read his books weren't anything like so squeamish.[20] If the unconscious mind thought in symbolic terms, the reasoning went, and a very large part of magical practice

---

20 See Carl Jung, *Memories, Dreams, Reflections*, for an account of Jung's quarrel with Freud over occultism.

makes use of symbols and symbolic actions, might that mean that magic was simply a richly developed and sophisticated way of working with the unconscious mind?

That's why some of the leading lights of early twentieth century occultism were depth psychologists. Violet Firth, better known by her magical pen name Dion Fortune, was a Freudian lay therapist, and Israel Regardie was a Reichian therapist. Then there's the most successful figure of the lot, who managed to become one of the century's most influential occult philosophers while convincing nearly everyone that he really, truly was just a working physician—yes, that would be Carl Jung.[21] The best way to describe the relation between these figures may be to point out that it was more or less a matter of happenstance, rather than any real difference of approach, that Violet Firth and Israel Regardie didn't become famous as the founders of Firthian psychology, a cutting-edge but more or less respectable school of post–Freudian psychotherapy, and Carl Jung and Hermann Hesse didn't win lasting fame in occult circles as the leading adepts of that famous European magical order, the Ordo Peregrini Orientem.

By 1950, three theories of how magic worked were in common circulation in the Western world. There was Lévi's theory of the Astral Light, a subtle continuum that unites all things and can be shaped by the will and imagination; there was the Golden Dawn theory of higher planes of being from which currents of force could be drawn down by magical techniques; and there was the psychological theory of unconscious forces in the psyche that could be influenced by symbols and symbolic action. You'll notice that it's not actually that hard to restate any one of these in terms of any of the others: to redefine the Astral Light as one of the higher planes of being or as the unconscious mind, to redefine the higher planes of being as modalities of the Astral Light or the unconscious, or to redefine the unconscious as a function of the Astral Light or one of those higher levels of being.

This sort of intellectual promiscuity was extremely common in occult circles all through the century. Dion Fortune herself made room for both the Astral Light and depth psychology in her own theory of magic.[22]

---

21 Richard Noll's *The Jung Cult*, Princeton University Press, 1994, and *The Aryan Christ*, Random House, 1997, explore Jung's occult connections in the process of denouncing Jung and all his works.

22 See, for example Dion Fortune and Gareth Knight, *The Circuit of Force* (Thoth, 1998), which describes magic throughout as an interaction between the Astral Light and the psychological technique of autosuggestion.

She had plenty of company, some of whom took the process a good deal further than she did. It became widely recognized in occult circles in the 1960s and 1970s that all three of these descriptions could be seen as ways of talking about the same thing, and a great many intellectuals—not all of them part of the occult community—began probing the possibility that the other ways of thinking about the sources of magical power might also be ways of talking about that same thing.

It's an unfortunate fact of the history of ideas that when such exercises get going, they almost always end up with a reductionist bias. The most restrictive of the models generally becomes the default option, and if any of the other models permit possibilities that go beyond what the most restrictive model will justify, those possibilities get ignored when they don't get denounced or derided. That's more or less what happened in the present case. Psychology, as the most restrictive model for magical practice, turned into the default model in many circles, and models that embraced other options came in for the usual treatment.

The reductionist bias in modern magic reached its peak during the heyday of Chaos magic in the late twentieth century. While the Chaos magic movement was nothing if not diverse, it tended to default to some version of the psychological model in practice, defining the entire panoply of gods and goddesses, spirits, demons, planes of being, celestial influences, and the Astral Light as constructs of the human mind with no reality of their own.[23] In many ways, Chaos magic can be seen as the logical endpoint of the revolution kicked into motion by Eliphas Lévi: the French mage's then–revolutionary idea of magical power as something inherent in the human individual became, in the eyes of many Chaos magicians, an insistence that magical powers existed *only* in human beings, and the rest of the cosmos was for all practical purposes a blank slate on which the mage could scrawl whatever he or she willed.

It's not accidental that Chaos magic became popular just as the New Age movement, with its insistence that "you create your own reality," also hit the big time—nor is it an accident that Chaos magic began to wane in popularity around the time that the New Age began to collapse under the weight of its own unfulfilled promises. Both were cultural products of a particular period in Western culture, an era when the cult of the untrammelled individual ego reached its zenith under the influence of the

23 Peter Carroll, *Liber Null and Psychonaut*, Weiser, 1978 is a good example of this approach.

revolution of nihilism that swept the industrial world during the Reagan–Thatcher era.[24] Both have lessons of value to teach, but those lessons arguably need to be incorporated into a wider context if they're to provide useful guidance to the operative mages of the future.

*

There are many other ways to think about the sources of magical power, to be sure. These days, as the orthodoxies of the recent past lose their grip on the magical community and mages begin to get a clearer sense of the sheer wild diversity of magics that have been practiced around the world and across the centuries, it's hard to think off hand of anything that hasn't been seen as a source of magical power! There's much to learn from considering these other options, but for the purpose of this essay, enough ground has been covered to make the points I want to discuss.

The first of those points is simple and straightforward, and flies straight in the face of one of the most deeply rooted prejudices of contemporary occult thought. The prejudice in question is the belief that there has to be one and only one true occult philosophy that all real initiates have taught since the dawn of time. I'm thinking here particularly, though by no means only, of the Traditionalist movement, which has been having one of its periodic revivals of popularity in recent years. Traditionalist philosophers such as Julius Evola claim that all valid spirituality has its roots in Tradition —always with the capital T— and like to draw a hard line between the teachings they like, which are in accord with Tradition, and those they don't, which are either mere misguided goofiness or the products of the sinister forces of Counter-Tradition, which plays the notional role of Satanism to Traditionalism's One True Church.

So far, so good —but what exactly is this Tradition? Read Evola's *Revolt Against the Modern World* or any of his other major works, and when you get past the dogmatic posturing and the denunciation of rival views, what you'll find is exactly the same sort of freewheeling pastiche of concepts from early twentieth century popular culture that Evola himself condemned so savagely in other occult writers of his day. If you pick up such pop-culture standards of the time as Friedrich Nietzsche, J. J. Bachofen, and especially Otto Weininger's bestselling pop psychology book *Geschlecht und Charakter* (*Sex and Character*), you have the foundations of

24 John Michael Greer, *Green Wizardry*, New Society, 2013, pp. 211–227.

Evola's ideas. While Evola's books are worth reading, his ideas are anything but timeless Tradition. Quite the contrary, they represent a specific, personal, historically conditioned take on things.

That's true, in turn, of all the other contenders for the title of Timeless Wisdom of the Ages. If any one small-t tradition has a claim on that status in the Western world, it's Neoplatonism, and that's just because the Neoplatonists played so large a role in occultism from late Roman times through the end of the Renaissance. Even so, there's nothing timeless about Neoplatonism; it evolved and adapted, flowed and changed, absorbed and was absorbed by other teachings over most of two millennia. Check out the esoteric teachings of China or India, and you'll find exactly the same thing: not a petrified idol but a living, flowing movement of ideas in history.

The irony here, and it's a rich one, is that exactly this point could have been learned from a good many of the small-t traditions of Western esoteric spirituality, Neoplatonism among them. As Plato himself pointed out in no uncertain terms, it's crucial not to mistake eternal realities for experiential phenomena or vice versa; no matter how carefully it's drawn, no circle is *the* Circle, the transcendent principle of which every existing circle is an expression.[25] Nor, it probably needs to be said, does the ability to draw a more or less exact circle depend on being given access to some privileged lineage of circle–drawing. The same points are just as true of spirituality; no tradition that has to put up with the inconveniences of actually existing is or can be identical to the ageless wisdom that stands eternal in the heavens; nor do historical lineages confine that wisdom which, as an expression of the living Spirit, notoriously "bloweth where it listeth."

That's the first point that unfolds from the history surveyed above. The second is, if anything, even more controversial: that this living, flowing movement of ideas in history isn't headed toward some one and only one true occult philosophy of the future.

The notion that human knowledge progresses toward some kind of perfection in the future is hardwired into most contemporary thinking. It's an important expression of the faith in progress that provides the modern world with its established religion.[26] Like every other established religion, it raises a sprawling superstructure of faith on a very modest foundation of

---

25 The classic source here is of course Plato's dialogue *Meno*. See Plato, *Collected Dialogues*, Princeton University Press, 1961, pp. 353–384.
26 See John Michael Greer, *After Progress*, New Society, 2015.

fact: in this case, the broad general tendency for certain kinds of technical knowledge to build up over historical time. Human beings know, for instance, a great deal more about how to grow vegetables than they knew ten thousand years ago, or a thousand years ago, or even a century back; surviving agricultural handbooks from Roman times contain some very useful tips, for example, but a competent organic gardener these days knows quite a lot of things about enriching the soil, countering pests, and the like that Roman gardeners simply didn't know.

That tendency isn't inevitable or invincible. History is full of examples of technical tricks that were lost, for a time or forever. An entire technology of gearing and mechanical computation, best known by way of the famous Antikythera mechanism, vanished at the fall of Rome and hasn't been completely recovered yet; the famous "Baghdad batteries" among other anomalous remains show that electricity was discovered in ancient times, and then lost until the eighteenth century.

For that matter, nobody nowadays has any idea how ancient Hindu blacksmiths made the famous pillar of iron in Delhi that's been soaked by thousands of years of monsoons without ever showing a spot of rust, or how the Inca managed the astonishing stonework of Cuzco and Macchu Picchu. Knowledge can be lost, knowledge has been lost, and there's every reason to expect that, when today's industrial societies are pushing up metaphorical daisies in the graveyard of dead civilizations, a great deal of what passes for common knowledge these days will vanish forever.

The history of magic shows both processes—the tendency to build up an ever-larger accumulation of knowledge, and the temporary or permanent loss of large parts of that accumulation—at least as clearly as any other field of knowledge and practice does. If anything, where magic is concerned, the losses are far more striking than the buildup. Ancient Egypt had, by all contemporary accounts, an immense body of magical ritual and technique, but almost all of it vanished long ago, leaving scholars and occultists alike to puzzle over the fragmentary remains.[27] The ceremonies of the ancient Greek *goetes*, the rites and lore of the old Druids, the rituals of the Eleusinian mysteries, the incantations of the Neoplatonist mages, the practices of folk wizards across early medieval Europe: all of it is gone forever.

---

27 Robert K. Ritner, *The Mechanics of Ancient Egyptian Magical Practice* (University of Chicago, 1993) is a useful summary of what's known on that subject, and an equally useful guide to what has been permanently lost.

What we have, when we look out over the wreckage of the Western world's magical past, is a vast wilderness of ruins, in which the occultists of the last few centuries have traced out a few pathways and raised up a handful of modest shelters out of the fallen fragments of ancient temples. Here and there, inscriptions are still readable, and it sometimes happens that those of us who go digging in the ruins are able to clear the debris from another such inscription and add to the slow recovery of knowledge. Of the overall plan of the site we still have no certain conception, though there's no lack of speculation on the subject, and too many dogmatic claims; whole regions of the ruins remain unexplored, and their relationship to the better-known portions can only be guessed at; as often as not, when new discoveries get made, they don't add to the existing body of knowledge, but rather replace some part of what we thought we knew, which then has to go out with the trash.

Even if magical knowledge were cumulative, in other words, we're nowhere near the point at which some kind of unified field theory of magic could be put together. So much has been lost, so many whole fields of occult philosophy and practice still have to be recovered or reinvented from scratch, that even if such a theory was possible, we've got centuries of hard work ahead before enough of a knowledge base can be amassed to bring such a project within reach. Still, that far from minor difficulty simply sets the stage for a much more serious difficulty, which is that magical knowledge isn't cumulative; it's not the kind of knowledge that moves toward one best answer.

In his brilliant little philosophical handbook *A Guide for the Perplexed*, renegade economist E. F. Schumacher pointed out a crucial distinction between two classes of problems, which he called convergent and divergent problems.[28] Convergent problems are those that have a single right answer, and inquiry into convergent problems naturally converges on that single answer; the longer you pursue the work of inquiry, the more the data constrain the range of answers that will fit, until—in a phrase made famous by Sherlock Holmes—having excluded the impossible, what remains is the truth. Convergent problems are the natural prey of modern science; they're what the scientific method is meant to tease out of the haze of data, and the successes of modern science have encouraged a great many people to think that all problems are convergent in nature.

The difficulty with this confident belief is that it doesn't happen to be

28 E. F. Schumacher, *A Guide for the Perplexed.* Jonathan Cape, 1977, pp. 139–156.

true. There's another class of problems, which Schumacher called divergent problems: problems that have no one right answer. Divergent problems are by and large problems of value, while convergent problems are problems of fact. Put another way, convergent questions ask about the properties of perceiving objects, while divergent questions relate to the properties of perceiving subjects. Thus one common kind of convergent problem asks, "what is in the world?" One common kind of divergent problem asks instead, "what should I do about it?"—and for that latter question there's no one answer that applies in all cases and to all those who ask it.

It's become popular in recent years for rationalists of a certain stripe to insist that convergent problems are more important than divergent ones, or even that those branches of knowledge that are subject to convergent solutions are the only kind of knowledge that matters, while those that present divergent problems are somehow illegitimate or irrelevant. This is nonsense—popular nonsense, at least in an age of fashionable abstractions, but nonsense nonetheless. What you should do for a living and whom, if anyone, you should marry are divergent questions; the answers that emerge from inquiry into them differ necessarily from one person to another; but how you answer these questions has a far greater impact on your chances for a happy and productive life than any merely convergent question.

Philosophy, now that it's succeeded in spinning off the quantitative sciences into orbits of their own, has finally gotten most of the way back to its original purpose as a set of tools for responding to divergent problems. It's a routine gibe of rationalists these days that philosophy isn't "real knowledge," since it doesn't progress. This is precisely the same sort of idiocy as denouncing a hammer because it isn't a very good saw. Philosophy doesn't converge on a single answer, which is what rationalists mean here when they talk about progress; it diverges along with the problems that it studies, so that it can provide the widest possible range of options for individuals who are trying to make sense of their own intuitions of meaning and value, and apply those to the task of living a happy and productive life.

Two completely different philosophies can work equally well, in turn, because there's an inherent feedback loop that comes into play any time you turn sustained attention on your own sense of meaning and value, or any other property you have as a perceiving subject. That feedback loop, interestingly enough, is the same one that Erwin Schrödinger discovered when poking at quantum particles: you can't observe the phenomenon without changing its behavior. Adopt any philosophy that doesn't clash unbearably with your basic intuitions of meaning and value, and that philosophy will reshape those intuitions in its own image. The value of a humanistic education, in turn, is that it provides the individual with the necessary breadth of raw material —philosophical, literary, artistic, cultural—to transform those basic intuitions into foundations for the rare but necessary quality we call 'wisdom.'

Occult philosophy is a branch of philosophy, not a quantitative material science. That may seem too obvious to need stating, but the repeated calls for a definitive theory of magic make it clear that some people in the occult community, at least, don't seem to have gotten the memo. What differentiates the various systems of magic from each other isn't that one is 'more advanced' than the other, or for that matter 'more traditional,' with or without the capital T; it's that they unfold in a divergent manner from different postulates and different cultural frameworks, and thus appeal to different people. What's more, the feedback loop mentioned above slams into high gear once magic enters the picture, because the technical methods of magic reshape the activities and content of the mind far more powerfully than the practices of ordinary philosophy do.

One interesting consequence of this last detail is that every theory of magic provides a precise and accurate description of what magic can do, for those people who adopt that theory of magic. That's just as true of the rationalist theory that magic is superstitious nonsense, by the way, as it is of the most rarefied theurgic Neoplatonism or the most up-to-the-elbows–in–entrails sort of robust folk sorcery. The rationalist believes that all magic is mere superstitious nonsense; his whole philosophy supports that belief, and so if for whatever reason he attempts to perform magic, the results he gets will be precisely those you would expect from superstitious nonsense.

What's more, if someone else casts a hostile spell on him, his perception of the situation will continue to support his belief that magic is mere superstitious nonsense. He'll simply slam face-first into a series of random disasters, in which he'll be able to see no pattern or meaning whatsoever. Now of course this means, among other things, that he's very sharply limited in terms of potential responses. Since magic doesn't exist for him, he can't very well dispel what's been tossed at him, turn it back on its sender, or do any of the other things that less rigidly restrictive theories of magic permit as a matter of course. Of course that's exactly the point; the philosophy you accept determines what you can perceive as well as what you can do, and if the thing you value most is living in a completely material, rational, magic-free cosmos, that price might well be worth paying.

The same principle, in turn, applies to every other theory of magic. If, as Dion Fortune proposed, magic is the art and science of causing change in consciousness in accordance with will,[29] the particular approach to magic that you embrace will have profound effects on what you perceive in the universe around you, and what you can do in response to the things you perceive. If you believe, like most Chaos magicians, that gods and spirits are simply forms established by the human imagination, then it's probably a safe bet that the only gods and spirits you'll meet are those that your imagination has created. (If you insist on imposing that view on them, after all, why would any other kind of god or spirit be interested in talking to you?) If you start instead from the presupposition that gods and spirits are real, independent, conscious beings, your chances of encountering those gods and spirits who do in fact act like real, independent, conscious beings—and who thus know things you don't, for example, and can teach them to you—go up sharply. The same principle applies to every other dimension of magical theory.

Nor is there any Archimedean point from which it's possible to dive into, and back out of, all other magical systems. If your theory of magic defines, say, the existence of deities as a feature of a worldview into which human beings can choose to enter and leave, then you can have that experience, too, but the deities you'll experience will be the kind who can inhabit a worldview created by you, and the realm they inhabit will be a worldview rather than a world. Embrace a more traditional view of deities, and you may just find yourself encountering something a good deal more robust, not because you've created it but because you've opened yourself to interaction with it, and encouraged it to open itself to interaction with you.

The operative mage is thus to some extent—but only to some extent—conjuring in a hall of mirrors. It's crucial to be aware of the ways that magical theory constrains magical perception and action, but it's at least as crucial to recognize that the things we don't perceive can still exist, and that things that we very badly want to exist may pull a no-show on us no matter how much frantic intensity we put into believing in them. The failure of December 21, 2012 to live up to the expectations piled onto it by millions

---

29 This definition doesn't seem to appear in any of Fortune's published works, but is credited to her by a number of her students. See, for example, W.E. Butler, *Magic: Its Ritual, Power, and Purpose*, Aquarian, 1975, p. 12.

of true believers is a recent case in point, and a good object lesson about the pitfalls in believing that reality is whatever you want it to be.

A commonplace of occult theory has it that the magical universe is more complex and multidimensional than any human mind can possibly grasp. Faced with a universe incomprehensible in its fullness, every mage, and every magical theory, must therefore choose a handful of the available options, work with those, and develop as much proficiency as possible with them. That limitation, like most limitations, is a source of strength, not of weakness. Some of the best martial artists you'll ever meet are those who know just a couple of punches, a kick or two, and a few blocks, but can do any one of them extremely well.

Magic is subject to the same principle, and this offers a solution to the implied conundrum explored in this essay. Where does magical power come from? From every one of the places from which the magical systems we surveyed draws it, and infinitely many more beside. Does magical power come from outside the human mind, or from within it? Both, of course. Magic is *everywhere*; magical forces surge and flow through every atom of matter, every cubic Angstrom unit of space, every picosecond of time. It's purely a question of where you, yourself, as an operative mage, want to tap into the flow of power, and what you want to do with it—and that, as already hinted, is a divergent problem rather than a convergent one.

*   *

*

The Pulsation of the Cosmos

The Moon's Thirty Phases

Freedom Cole

OUR DAY IS based on the rotation of the Earth, the week and month on the cycles of the Moon, and the year on the revolution of the Earth around the Sun. Everything is changing within the background of the stars. The dancing luminaries are a clock revealing the nature of Time whose nature drives everything onwards (*kalanātmaka*) and manifests our experience.

Thoughts arise and lead us to actions and life unfolds. Rarely does one look at where these thoughts come from. Time turns, we breathe—thoughts and desires endlessly arise and move us to action. Time (*kāla*), breath (*prāṇa*) and thought (*buddhi*) are intricately tied together as a tri-manifestation of cosmic consciousness (*Mahat*).

It's all consciousness manifesting and we get lost inside of it. Time veils our awareness of where we have been and where we are going. We only see what's happening in the present, unless we look at time—the clock that spins existence. To know the movement of time is to literally understand the functioning of the universe, both externally and internally. The alignment of conscious action or ritual with the correct time is the way of the seer, the wise one who sees.

This chapter will look at the nature of time from the heavenly luminaries and give a good understanding of the thirty phases of the Moon. You will learn how they are calculated, how to know their frequencies, and how to utilize them in life and ritual. The first step is understanding the calculation of the lunar phases. The deeper our understanding of this science, the deeper the possible depths of our ritual. Logical science is the right eye, and intuitive understanding is the left eye. Together they create depth, and the weakness of either distorts one's vision. We have to dig into the science behind the function of time to use it ritually.

Then we dig into the structural keys to intuitively grasp the nature of the Moon's phases. The Moon's constant endless cycle of coming to fullness and then returning to the place where everything is empty. The waxing Moon invokes us to work for some purpose in our days. The waning Moon calls us into the realm of sleep at night. The day-night cycle drives our habitual patterns embedded in our culture. We wake, work, eat and sleep. Sometimes people, step outside their routine and wonder why, others don't even think to question. I look at the knowledge of Time as a way to free ourselves from the unawareness that many don't even know they are bound within. Knowing the Moon phases gives us insight into the mind that leads us around with our overly self-identified emotions. We are full and we are empty, we are full and we are empty; pulsing—an emptiness that is completely full.

MOON PHASES: LIGHT AND SHADOW

The universe is spinning and generating vibration. The Sun and Moon are keeping rhythm. We stand upon the Earth as we observe these luminaries and we interpret how they impact us by how we perceive them, from a geocentric viewpoint. We also understand the dynamic of how they move from a heliocentric view. Half of the Moon is always illuminated by facing the light giver. In Bṛhat Saṁhitā, Varāhamihira says

> *The Moon is always under the Sun therefore one half is bright*
> *And the Moon's own shadow is on the other portion,*
> *just like half a pot is bright in the Sun.* 4.1

From the viewpoint of Earth, we see the one half that is bright from different angles, and it creates different phases. During half moon, we see half the light side and half the shadow. During full moon we see only the light side. As humans we have our light and dark sides and both are always present. The more light that we see, the more dark that is hidden.

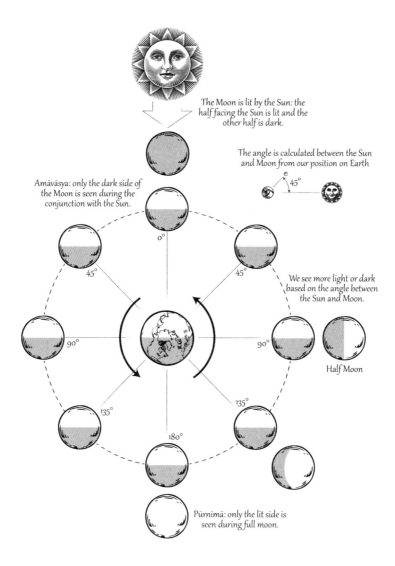

The Moon is lit by the Sun: the half facing the Sun is lit and the other half is dark.

The angle is calculated between the Sun and Moon from our position on Earth

45°

Amāvāsya: only the dark side of the Moon is seen during the conjunction with the Sun.

0°

45°

45°

We see more light or dark based on the angle between the Sun and Moon.

90°

90°

Half Moon

135°

135°

180°

Pūrnimā: only the lit side is seen during full moon.

Every month the Moon goes through all its phases. The time period from new moon to new moon is called a *synodic month*. During each phase the Sun and Moon will have a certain angle of relationship to each other. At the final moment of full moon the Sun and Moon are 180° apart. At half moon, the Sun is 90° from the Sun. At the beginning of new moon, the Sun and the Moon are seen as having the same longitude in the sky (0° of angle between them). As dancers have steps and musicians have key, the Sun and Moon have angles.

MOONRISE

When the Moon is waning it will rise later and later in the night. At the waning half moon it will rise at midnight. Until it reaches the end of the waning cycle, where the Sun and Moon are perceived as being in the same place in the zodiac, and the Moon will rise when the Sun rises and set with the Sun so it will not be visible in the sky.

As the Moon begins to grow fuller it will begin rising almost an hour later each day. First an hour after sunrise, then after a day, it will rise two hours after sunrise. After another day about three hours after sunrise. The waxing half Moon will eventually rise at 12 noon, and be directly overhead when the Sun sets. These phases were on the top of grandfather clocks until a century ago. Modern society, living with artificial light, has become unaware of these phases and their impact on life. But ancient cultures were very aware of these phases and connected to them similar to the modern individual's need to know the date (created by Pope Gregory) in order to plan life and make decisions.

The ancient astronomers noticed that the moon moves about $.5°$ an hour, which is the angular diameter of the Moon as perceived from the Earth. In this way, each hour the Moon moves its own size relative to the background of the stars. This is $1°$ in 2 hours, which is the approximate time it takes for a sign to rise. During a night's observation the Moon can be seen to move about $6°$ against the background stars (as six signs have crossed the ascendant). The next evening after this, the Moon is seen to be approximately $6°$ from where it was the previous sunrise. With this simple observation, the Moon can be seen to move about $12°$ a day. The $360°$ circle of the sky divided into $12°$ portions of motion creates 30 lunar phases.

Egyptians, Babylonians, Indians and the early Greeks are known to have utilized these 30 phases. The Indians called these phases tithi. The Babylonians called them *ūma,* in the Akkadian language, which literally means 'day'. In the ancient world, before the Roman calendar, the exact lunar phase (tithi) indicated the number of the day. These are the days in which rituals and festivals to the gods were celebrated. These are the days in which auspicious and inauspicious actions were chosen.

LUNAR TIME: THE MOON'S 30 PHASES

The synodic month (new moon to new moon) takes approximately 29.530588853 (29 days, 12 hours, 44 minutes, 3 seconds). This time averaged into 30 portions, called tithi, can be seen as a 'lunar phase' or a 'lunar day.'

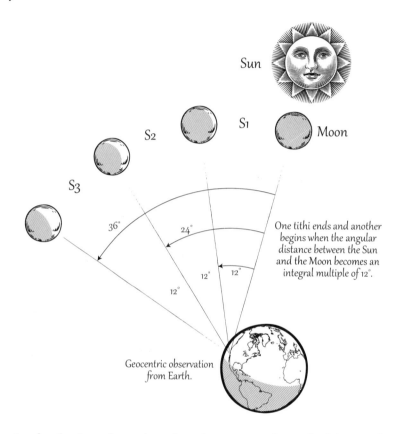

One tithi ends and another begins when the angular distance between the Sun and the Moon becomes an integral multiple of 12°.

Geocentric observation from Earth.

A solar day is 24 hours based on the rotational speed of the Earth, and would be seen as the Sun returning to a point in the sky in which it was previously.[30] The *mean* synodic month divided into 30 portions makes a lunar phase (*tithi*) approximately .9483 that of a solar day. The *mean* tithi is 23 hours 37 minutes and 28 seconds; when the median synodic month is divided by 30. In actuality, each tithi varies in length, just as the synodic

---

30 The Babylonians and the Hebrews use Sunset to mark the day for New Moon calculation purposes. The Hindus use Sunrise, and modern science use midnight to mark the beginning of the day.

cycle can vary by up to thirteen hours. A tithi can vary from 20 hours up to 26 hours, but for ease, we say it lasts 23.5 hours.[31]

The lunar day/phase is calculated by an increase in 12° of arc between the Sun and the Moon. The solar day is a solar-masculine calculation. To number our days based on the Sun alone is to invoke in our culture a consciousness that revolves around the masculine. The tithi calculation balances the male-female dynamic as it takes into account both the Sun and the Moon and therefore was considered by the ancients to carry the energy of the god and the goddess. The angle between them is the mood they create.

In astrology, there is nothing that is empty of meaning—*everything* means something. The 30 lunar phases of 12° are a mirror reflection of the 12 solar signs of 30°. The calculation and mathematics of astronomical data reveals a deeper significance. Everything can be differentiated based upon its archetypal nature and the significance of that nature. Clarity in how something is calculated delineates its use. To gain insight into the synodic month and its divisions we can look deeper at the observable luni-solar variants; the tropical and sidereal calculations of the Sun and Moon.

The twelve sidereal signs of 30° are calculated from the star Spica showing the relationship of the Earth to the starry heavens (*svarga loka*), indicating a perceptual realm of being. The sidereal moon cycle is divided into 13° 20' portions of 27 lunar constellations (*nakṣatra*). These lunar divisions show the perspective or lense the individual sees the world through.

The twelve tropical signs of the zodiac are 30° each calculated from the spring equinox. They reveal the Earth's relationship to the Sun (*bhuvar loka*) which is the realm of the mental-emotional being. The phases of the Moon are a reflection of this division. The synodic moon cycle is divided into 30 portions of 12°, showing us the sentiment or emotional nature of the time. This means that the moon sign is the perspective/lense and the moon phase is the emotion. These interact to create experience. Here we will only focus on the phases.

---

31 According to *Sūrya Siddhanta*, the minima of a tithi is 54 ghatis (21hours and 36 minutes) and the maxima of a tithi is 65 ghatis (26 hours). According to the research of S.D. Sharma (Astro–research Section, in his paper *Maxima and Minima of Tithis*, p.115) the minima can be 50 ghatis (20 hours) and maxima can be up to 67 ghatis (26 hours and 48 minutes).

Tithi	Tithi Name	Tithi	Tithi Name
1	PRATIPAD	9	NAVAMĪ
2	DVĪTIYĀ	10	DAŚAMĪ
3	TRTĪYĀ	11	EKĀDAŚĪ
4	CHATURTHĪ	12	DVADAŚĪ
5	PAÑCHAMĪ	13	TRAYODAŚĪ
6	ṢAṢṬĪ	14	CHATURDAŚĪ
7	SAPTAMĪ	S15	PŪRṆIMĀ
8	AṢṬAMĪ	K15	AMĀVASYĀ

WAXING AND WANING

The thirty phases are divided into 15 portions in the waxing phase called the white half (*śukla pakṣa*), and 15 portions in the waning phase called the black half (*kṛṣṇa pakṣa*). Modern nomenclature shortens this to 'S' for waxing and 'K' for waning. The second day of the waxing moon would be called S2, the third day S3. And K5 would be the fifth day of the waning moon.

The fifteenth waxing tithi, which is 12° before the direct opposition of the Moon and Sun, is called the full moon (*pūrṇimā*). *Pūrṇa* means full, complete, filled. The moment after opposition, the waning phase begins and the energy is immediately shifted. Full moon ceremonies should take place within the phase (approximately 23.5 hours) previous to the Sun–Moon opposition moment. In many Gregorian calendars they may list a day as full moon even if the moment of fullness happens at 2am that morning. A ceremony celebrated on that day will be in the waning energy of the goddess who is no longer in fullness—similar to sex with a woman after she has completed ovulation. A ceremony celebrated the previous day while the Moon is still in the mode of increasing will harness completeness and fulfilment—it is the fertile time.

The fifteenth waning tithi is called *Amāvāsya*; *ama* means together, and *vāsya* means to dwell. Amāvāsya is when the Sun and the Moon are coming to dwell together. This is the dark moon, which is the menstruation of the Mother Goddess. The Moon gets darker and darker, creating tension, until at the end of this tithi there is a conjunction of the Sun and Moon called a syzygy. Then they separate and the Moon begins to grow in light. The 12° after syzygy is called *Pratipad* (or *Prathama*) which means the initial, first or new. This is the first tithi, which is correctly called the new moon[32], and it was this tiny crescent that was sighted at sunset to begin a new synodic month in the ancient world. It is because it is first sighted at sunset that many cultures began their day from sunset, as the new month began then. In the ancient world, this meant the rent and other bills were due, as it is on the first of the Gregorian month in our culture. New moon rituals are to be performed the day *after* the time of conjunction (the time listed in many calendars), while full moon rituals are done *before* the listed time.

LUNAR DAYS: TIMING WITH THE MOON

Before the man-made numbering of the Roman calendar, the tithi indicated the number of the day. The sixth day of the month was the sixth tithi after syzygy. A tithi can change at any time of the day or night. For civil purposes, the day was named after the active tithi at sunrise. A financial transaction or a day at work would be recorded based on the nomenclature of the tithi at sunrise and the planetary day of the week.

Religious festivals had more specific rules for timing. Some holy-days are calculated by the tithi at sunrise, others have more detailed requirements. Gaṇeśa worship is performed on the day that the tithi at the third quarter of the day (noontime–3PM) is the waxing fourth (S4). Ancestor worship is done where the tithi is Amāvāsya on the fourth part of the day (3PM–sunset).

For astrologers who advise people on beneficial times to begin activities, the exact tithi at the moment of the activity is utilized. The waxing fifth (S5) is an auspicious time to begin one's studies. If the fourth waxing tithi becomes the fifth waxing tithi at nine in the morning, then the first class could be set for that day, after the tithi changes to the fifth.

The ancients were very aware of the phase of the Moon and its anomaly. They kept exact measure of the tithi by noting the position of the Moon during sunrise or sunset and the position of the Sun during moonrise or moonset. These measurements allowed them to be aware of the speed and exact angle of the luminaries.

---

32 The Sanskrit dictionaries have translated Amāvāsya as New Moon which has created a serious misnomer in many translated works since. It does not differentiate pre–syzygy to post syzygy. The Greeks called the 30th lunar day *Héné*, meaning Old Moon and the first day after the syzygy as *Noumênía, meaning new-moon*.

A tithi is independent of the zodiac and so is not tropical or sidereal, therefore the lunar phase is the same for all systems of astrology. The moment a tithi ends and another begins is the same on all parts of the earth's surface. The angle between the Sun and the Moon is not dependent on the longitude (or latitude) of the region. But sunrise varies according to the longitude of the location, and the local time of the tithi beginning will differ accordingly. If a tithi changes at midnight (0:00) Universal Time (UT). It will change at 5 PM (18:00) in California (PST) and 5:30 am in India (IST). This is the same moment on the Earth, but different time zones.

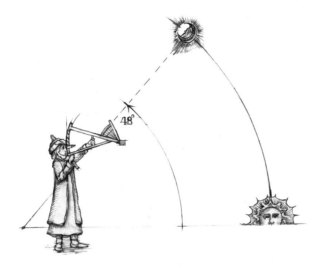

This means that the tithi at sunrise is different in different places on the planet. In the above example, if the tithi became S7 at midnight Universal Time, sunrise in California that day would have been S6, while in India it will be S7. In this way, the new moon happens everywhere on the Earth at the same planetary moment, but at different local times which gives it a personal predictive flavor at each location.

Lunar holidays are calculated based on the solar month and lunar phase. Your own luni-solar birthday is calculated by the Sun returning to its sign at birth and then the Moon returning to its phase at birth. This date will vary earlier or later than the Gregorian birth date. This birthday is the time the god and goddess created you.

COSMIC PULSATION: SPANDANA

You can see the pulsation of the universe if you know how to look. The Moon is moving approximately .5 degree an hour. Each hour is changing between the energy of male (solar) or female (lunar), indicating how we expend ourselves. A solar and lunar hour together create a sign of the zodiac which takes two hours to rise on the horizon. These signs are divided into masculine (odd) and feminine (even) and indicate the nature how we are interacting. The day itself is solar and the night is lunar which directs our daily activities. The waxing half of the lunar month is solar and more energetic and outgoing, while the waning half is lunar, introverted and contemplative. The half year where the days grow longer is solar and each lengthening day empowers the devas—good thoughts. While the other half of the year, where the nights grow longer, is lunar and the inner mental realms with all our inner demons grow stronger.

The play of opposites and the energetic currents that are created by this opposition keep life in motion and unfolding. The Sun and Moon are pulsing (*spandana*); a cosmic heartbeat. The solar-lunar pulsation is the pulsation of *time*, the pulsation of collective *thought*, and the pulsation of the solar system's life *breath*. The two parts of the year from solstice to solstice are the exhale and inhale of the spiritual realms. The waxing and waning Moon is the exhale and inhale of the mental realms. The day and night are the exhale and inhale of the physical realm. We are not controlled by time, we are time. The pulsation (*spandana*) within us, that causes our heart to beat and breath to move, is a reflection of this life force; the essence of the core pulsation of the universe. In that pulsation, we have access to all realms.

SYNODIC MOTION

The Synodic month is the period in which the Moon gains one complete revolution over the apparent or visible motion of the Sun. The quickly moving Moon is leaving and then chasing the slow and steady moving Sun. We see this on the face of the clock, as the minute hand moves quickly like the Moon, the hour hand moves slowly forward like the Sun. At noon, both hands are in union on the twelve. Then the minute hand has to go through all twelve numbers plus one more to find union with the hour hand again, since it has moved forward. The minute hand moving from the twelve back to twelve is like the sidereal lunar month (27.3217 days). The minute hand moving from the twelve and needing to go one more number to meet the hour hand is like the synodic lunar month (29.5306 days). This movement happens twelve times a year, making twelve synodic lunar months just like the twelve hours of the day.

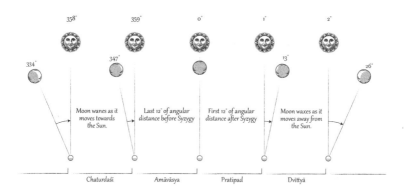

The tithi calculation is not a static angle but one in which both luminaries are moving, similar to how both hands on a clock are moving and the angle between them is not based on the movement of the minute (moon) hand alone, but has to be a constant awareness of the hour (sun) hand motion as well. The Sun (from a geocentric perspective) is moving approximately 1° for every 13° of lunar motion, resulting in 12° of angle.

TWELVE KĀLĪS

The Sun moves approximately 30° in a synodic lunar month which creates twelve solar months in the 360° orbit of the Sun. These twelve divisions are called the twelve spokes on the Sun's wheel in the Vedic hymns. The number of sun signs is not based on space, but based on Time.

The dark moon phase is the 12° before the syzygy and the new moon phase is the 12° after syzygy. The western astronomical definition of 'new moon' is the moment when the Sun and Moon have the same longitude (syzygy), which means they are in a conjunction (0°). After syzygy with the Sun, the Moon moves approximately 390° through the sky to return to another syzygy. That is 30° past the last place where the Sun and Moon were conjoined. In this way, there is a new moon that happens in each of the 12 solar divisions, and there are twelve Amāvāsya tithis in a year.[33]

In the Tantras, these are correlated to twelve aspect of non-dual consciousness. The dark moon, Amāvāsya, is the phase of the non-dual awareness personified as the dark goddess Kālī. The Greeks associated the dark goddess Hekate with the last tithi. The name Kālī is the feminine of kāla which means dark, black, or time as well as death (your time has come): she is therefore the Dark Mother, or Mother of Time or Mother of Death and Destruction. Kālī is also called Jyeṣṭhā which means the pre-eminent, more excellent than, or the eldest. As the eldest she is seen as the goddess that came before the others, creating the womb of Time in which all things were born into. As the eldest, she is properly portrayed as old and emaciated with sagging breasts. She is the last tithi, the emaciated moon, the old moon, the dark moon—and she has twelve forms in the heavens above.

MYTHOLOGY OF THE THIRTY TITHI

The thirty lunar phases, or the waxing/waning fifteen, show up in various mythologies of the ancient world. In Egyptian mythology, Osiris was associated with the Moon. He was the first ruler of Egypt along with his sister/consort Isis. Everyone loved Osiris and this brought about the jealousy of his brother Set (shadow/Rāhu). Set dismembered Osiris into fourteen parts. The dismemberment is the waning moon, and the dark moon (Amāvāsya) was a mourning for his loss where no beneficial activity was recommended.

When Osiris was murdered, he became a lord of the ancestral realm. The Moon in the Vaidik paradigm is also the lord of the ancestor realm (pitṛ loka), and also indicates the blood—meaning the family line. Ancestor worship (śraddha) is done during the lunar phase of Amāvāsya. It is said to be the time when the veils between the living and the dead are thinnest. A day in the ancestral realm is equal to a month in the earth realm (bhū

---

33 To be exact, there are 12.36827268 lunations per year. Every three years the one third extra part of lunation creates the space for an additional month. The intercalary month (adhika māsa) is added to keep the solar and lunar cycles in harmony and thereby allowing a functional luni–solar calendar. Therefore a normal year has twelve Amāvāsya while every three years there is an additional thirteenth, known as the supreme form of Kālī.

loka). So to feed the ancestors each Amāvāsya, is to feed them in their every morning.

With the seed of Osiris, Isis created a son, Horus, the Sun god. He is born on the winter solstice (original Christmas), which is the morning of the spiritual realm. He was crowned on the Spring Equinox (Easter), which is the noon time in the realm of the gods. Isis collects the portions of Osiris and Horus (Sun) defeats Set (darkness/shadow) and restores life/light into his father Osiris. The new moon now visible with light (*Pratipad*) was be a celebration of the return of Osiris and the full moon was a celebration of his complete restoration. Osiris, the renewal deity of grains and wine (his body and blood), then becomes a savior deity.

The Akkadian Moon-god, Sin, (called Nanna in Sumerian) can be represented by the number 30, representing 'she who is made of 30 portions.' The union of the Sun and Moon was seen as a sexual act from which the crescent moon was born. Similar to Vaidik astronomical terminology, the Moon before syzygy was the invisible moon (*naṣṭa-indu-kalā*) while the new moon was called the visible moon (*dṛṣṭendu*).

The Vedas call Amāvāsya as the portion 'dwelling together' (*saṁvasati*).[34] It calls this dwelling together as union (*saṁgamanī*).[35] It was not considered a very auspicious time as we see a prayer in the Atharvaveda praying for protection from thieves, flesh-eaters, spirits (*piśācas*) and those who hunt on the dark night of Amāvāsya.[36]

The darśa-yāga is the 'new moon' sacrifice performed on the first lunar day of the month. The Sun-Moon hymn is to be read on the first crescent which is called the 'appearance' (*darśa*). The name comes from looking at, viewing, or appearing which refers to the first appearance of the waxing crescent. The Sun-Moon hymn starts with the childlike dance of the Sun and the Moon which allows the Moon to be born new again.

The new crescent is seen as a new leaf on the stem of the soma vine.[37] As the soma vine is described as having fifteen leaves which increases (*vardha*) and decreases (*hīya*) like the Moon waxes and wanes.[38] The Sun–Moon

---

34 Atharvaveda 7.84.1 (Amāvāsya Sūkta)
35 Atharvaveda 7.84.3 (Amāvāsya Sūkta)
36 Atharvaveda 4.36.3
37 Atharvaveda 4.86.3 Sūrya-Chandra Sūkta
38 Charaka Saṁhitā, Cikitsāsthānam, Chapter I.4 Rasāyanādhyāya v.7

hymn prays to let us grow/thrive (*pyāyana*) like the new moon which is growing from a single leaf to a full plant.[39]

In the Hindu Pantheon, there is the goddess Satī. Sat means being, existence, truth, and satī translates as a virtuous wife. The goddess Satī was shamed at the sacrifice her father hosted so she burnt herself alive. The shame is symbolic of the last phase of the dark moon and the burning herself is the conjunction with the Sun. Her husband, Śiva, mourns her loss and carries her dead body around. Slowly, Viṣṇu removes the body parts, as Śiva wanders and these parts fall into different places making them sacred.

When the goddess is reborn as Parvati, she must do intense penance (*tapasya*) to purify herself. This is the burning of syzygy, and the purification associated with the new moon day. Śiva and Parvati then return to their dance of love.

In the Tantras, there is a concept that each portion (*kalā*)[40] of the moon phase is a goddess. They are the sliver of light that the Moon gains or loses as it waxes and wanes, and that light is personified as a goddess and worshipped. They are called either the fifteen Nityās or the sixteen Kalā depending on the tradition. The first crescent and the last crescent are the same goddess and the second to last crescent and the second from new crescent are the same goddess as they are that same portion (kalā) of light. In this way, there are fifteen Nityās (or sixteen Kalā). In Tāntric ritual, these goddesses are invoked and worshiped in a diagram of sixteen lotus petals.

The Moon is also seen as feeding the gods as it gets closer and closer to the Sun. As she loses each sliver of light, the gods are fed. Abhinavagupta says the waning Moon nourishes (*āpyāyana*) the gods, losing one tithi at a time until the Moon reaches the fifteenth portion where she is the goddess Amā, offering libations to the whole universe. By giving up her light, all the stars/gods shine brighter. The goddess of this final tithi has been called the Emaciated One (*śuṣkā*) as well as the 'Lioness of the Nectar of Union' (*utsaṅgāmṛtakesarī*).[41]

---

39 Atharvaveda 4.86.5 Sūrya–Chandra Sūkta
40 Kāla (pronounced kaaa–la) means time, kalā (pronounced ka–laaa) means a portion.
41 Manthānabhairavatantram, Kumārikākhaṇḍa 3.116, 3.132

RITUAL

To one unconscious of time, desires arise from natural inclinations and a person believes that to be themselves. Our wrong views and negative emotions get manifested as events in our life, which we ourselves created. Unconscious of time, points of power pass randomly and life is left unfold by fate. To the knower of Time, the mind has power to redefine itself. Not a new year's resolution that forgets itself in a few weeks or months but change that manifests itself more deeply over time. Reality is generated by the nature of the mind's deep contents and tendencies. A mind that we have little control of unless we get doorways to its functioning. That functioning is hidden in the movement of the Moon and its dance with the solar system's Sun. Within us is our own moon (mind) dancing with our sun (soul). It is the root male-female/god-goddess opposites that turn the mechanism of what we experience as consciousness. Their time is not a factor in reality, it is the actual reality we 'experience.'

When a car mechanic looks at the engine of a car, he knows how it works and if he wants to change something, he will either know or figure out how to do it. A ritualist looks at the cycle of time and uses its parts to alter manifestation. The Vaidik and Tāntric ritualist uses five aspects of time (*pañchāṅga*). The qualitative nature of time is seen through five elements of the luminaries' motion. The seven days of the week (fire) shows what activities have strength. The sidereal lunar position within the twenty-seven nakṣatra (air) shows the perspectives and mental direction of time. The lunar phases of thirty tithi (water) show the emotions and desires that are present within the collective field. Lakṣmī is the goddess of the water element and so the tithi are also a crucial indicator for prosperity. Each tithi is divided in half to create another variation called a causal portion or karaṇa (earth) that relates to productivity. And there is another calculation of the Sun and Moon combination (ākāśa) which shows how well people get along.

Tithis, indicating the qualitative water element of time, show the emotional state. Ritual requires a state of mind—the power of emotion to empower intention—to give it body and flavor; the right 'taste'. Cake is sweet, if not, its bread. Sweetness gives cake its nature. The taste gives us the emotional experience of a food. If I tell my wife that I am completely in love with her in a flat tone—it means very little, while if I hold her tight and stare in her eyes romantically and tell her deeply 'yes', she is overcome and her heart melts.

Emotion is power and one's ability to call forth the appropriate emotion is not acting, it is ritual skill. A ritual will lack impact without emotion. The use of tithi is a way to harness that emotional capacity in its most natural alignment. Ritual aims to align with the appropriate mental state that is required for the particular ritual success.

Some people feel controlled by consciously using the tithis to plan life events, but they are already controlled by them. Being aware allows for more conscious use of our life force. Using tithi for electional astrology, one will see the desires of the mind at the initiating time of an event. What people will want, what will make them happy and how easily they will be gratified or not satisfied. This relates to the quality of the desire that is experienced, while the nakṣatra will show how the emotion arising with it is integrated into the person and utilized by the psyche.

Modern psychology has stopped electrocuting people but they are still creating iatrogenic diseases with psycho–pharmaceutical tranquilizers that are falsely advertised as balancing brain chemistry. Some alternative therapists have people beating a stuffed bag to get their anger and aggression out. Vaidik and Tāntric thought utilizes ritual on the lunar phases where particular psychological energies are active. Fasting on Ekadaśī (11) is used to remove anger. The root cause for anger/aggression is purified, and its opposite, which is the perception of divinity in all things, replaces anger: boundaries merge, and needs become shared. The churning of anger is hidden in the symbolism of the mythology of the lion–headed god.

Fasting on a day where one's personal psychological issues are activated is difficult, generally more difficult than other days. The first few times there may even be mental suffering because a churning is taking place. It is more than a fast, it is a consciousness shift which requires the deeper aspects of the being to alter. Alternative health supports fasting for cleaning out physical toxins from the body, but fasting also helps us digest emotional and psychic toxins. Tithi fasting as a remedial measure can be difficult for a westerner who doesn't have a daily calendar based on tithi. But I give these remedies and make my clients get in touch with this calendar because it is so effective.

Emotions over rule our rationality and control us all in some area of our life. Without knowledge we are at the hands of these emotions—and pushed forward into a fate that was pre-written. Either by long periods of proper mediation, or through access to the causal structures by astral techniques, we gain control of emotions that have dominated us. Then we have a place to make a choice and then we own our life.

FREQUENCIES OF THE PHASES

Anything we divide up has *meaning* based upon the numerology of the divisor and how the archetypes act through the quotient. Meaning is deeper than rationality. The rational mind filters through the I-sense (*ahaṅkāra*) of the psyche. Image works at a deeper level of the extra-rational psyche where archetypes can weave open ended conceptual realities and holistic understandings.

Believers of scientism consider themselves advanced because of their rationalism but they are just the rebellious children of Christianity's illogicalness, and have the same short sighted vision. Rationality is only one faculty of mind. Archetypal language has the capacity to transmit an extra-rational understanding that opens the mind to infinite ways of perceiving. To define a nakṣatra or tithi with a sentence of words is a limited rational understanding of it. To define it in the archetypal energy of a deity is to give it unlimited possibilities within the field of a frequency delineated in the image and myth of an archetypal being.

Tithi	Ruler
PRATIPAD (1), NAVAMĪ (9)	SUN
DVĪTIYĀ (2), DAŚAMĪ (10)	MOON
TṚTĪYĀ (3), EKĀDAŚĪ (11)	MARS
CHATURTHĪ (4), DVADAŚĪ (12)	MERCURY
PAÑCHAMĪ (5), TRAYODAŚĪ (13)	JUPITER
ṢAṢṬĪ (6), CHATURDAŚĪ (14)	VENUS
SAPTAMĪ (7), PŪRṆIMĀ (S15)	SATURN
AṢṬAMĪ (8), AMĀVĀSYA (K15)	RĀHU

Here we will look at the factors that flavor the nature of a tithi. Planetary lords and elemental rulership are the core essence of a tithi's nature. The ruling deity is the special nature (*prabhava*) of the lunar phase. Then there are the deities that are worshiped on the phase which give further insight into how we can utilize this portion of time.

The tithis are ruled by the planets in the order of the days of the week plus Rāhu (*vārachakra-krama*). The first tithi is ruled by the Sun, the second by the Moon, the third by Mars, and onwards. After Saturn comes the north node (*Rāhu*) to rule the eighth tithi. This repeats twice through each half lunar month (creating four quarters like a week).

Element	Tithi	Name
FIRE (AGNI)	1, 6, 11	HAPPY (NANDA)
EARTH (PṚTHVĪ)	2, 7, 12	FORTUNATE (BHADRA)
SPACE (ĀKĀŚA)	3, 8, 13	TRIUMPH (JAYA)
WATER (JALA)	4, 9, 14	EMPTY (RIKTA)
AIR (VĀYU)	5, 10, 15	FULL (PŪRṆA)

The fifteen tithis of the waxing and waning halves are also broken down into five groups according to the five elemental aspects of desire. The elements are seen to create cycles of a six pointed star when mapped into the degrees of the zodiac. The planetary and elemental natures are integrated. The planet which rules the tithi is used to determine the nature of desire and its strength on that particular lunar day. The element is used to see the expression of the desire.

Tṛtīyā tithi (3rd) is ruled by Mars but as it is Jaya (ruled by ākāśa) so it gives a lot of energy to work together, as ākāśa is the binding force that holds things together. Ekādaśī tithi (11th) is ruled by Mars and it is Nanda (ruled by fire) so the fighting desire is very strong. Mars is passionate, energetic, and creates conflict, it is not good for marriage, though good for war and leadership. Fasting on Ekādaśī removes anger issues, because this is the energy arising on this day. Vaiṣṇavas religiously fast on this eleventh tithi to perfect their peaceful nature. No one will fight with the one who has done this fast for some time. Fasting is the root remedy, ritual can be done in addition to clear that energy from ourselves. This tithi can also be utilized to harness these intense energies for activities that need fierceness.

Pratipada, the first tithi, is ruled by the Sun and it is a Nanda/fire tithi. It is associated with purification, internal cleansing from the past so a new month can begin. The sixth tithi is ruled by Venus but a Nanda/fire tithi; fire and water are inimical elements and battle each other. This is the tithi of the war god Skanda or the Greek huntress goddess Artemis. The fourteenth tithi is ruled by Venus and it is a Rikta/water tithi, so this is the phase where infidelity is strongest. Those that have had problems being faithful or have suffered infidelity from their partners can fast on this tithi to protect themselves from those desires (in themselves or their partner). The waning fourteenth is the most unfaithful, and old lovers or those that have intimate desires will often be in touch during this time. In this way, the various phases take on a certain nature.

The full moon (S15) is ruled by Saturn and is a Pūrṇa/air tithi. Satya Nārāyaṇa (the god of truth) is worshipped on this day, to remove the negativities of Saturn. For those who want to overcome issues with dishonesty or being lied to, this phase is the time to fast and do ritual for the god of truth.

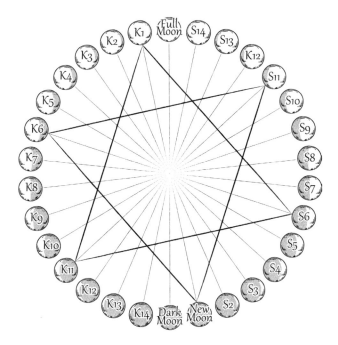

The eighth phase of the Moon is ruled by the north node, Rāhu, and has a deceptive energy. Fasting on this phase removes the energy of deception from yourself. If someone deceives us, it is because we have karma with deception, so by fasting on this day, it prevents those actions. It removes deceptive ideas from our consciousness and thereby removes the energy that attracts deception to us. All these tithi remedies work on the understanding that the outside is reflective of some aspect of our own self; the gullible invite a deceiver since they are deceiving themselves by not being aware of the light and the shadow. The tithi fasts and rituals work with the deep seated desires that live in our unconscious mind where thoughts, both light and shadow, arise from. Fasting on the dark moon is the greatest cleansing of the shadow self. For someone with a shadow that controls them, or someone who often loses their mind to other's control, the dark moon fast with the worship of the goddess Kālī brings inner strength and clarity.

Intense emotions are triggered in our life, and we believe that we are angry or anxious or some other type of intense emotion. Relationships are destroyed because of emotional upsets and how they are handled. Understanding the cycles and seeing what astrological movements brings up issues in our personal life allows us to be able to be unattached to intense waves of negative emotions. If you begin fighting with your partner as the dark moon energy grows strong, you can just let go of the issue and choose to resolve things in a few days. In allowing the friction to pass, what was considered an issue can be cleared up quickly and easily. As a general thumb rule, one can do fasting and ritual on Ekadaśī (11th) for Mars related issues, full moon for Saturn related issues, and dark moon for Rāhu related issues.

The rikta (empty) tithis are not considered for beneficial actions, but it is recommended to pay debts on those days, so they go away faster. Particularly, rikta tithis falling on a Tuesday or a Saturday make the debt go away quickly (just don't buy something you want to have for a long time on those kind of days).

There are certain combinations that are more beneficial or more dangerous when certain tithis line up with certain days of the week. For example, when the ninth tithi (navamī) falls on a Saturday, the actions that day are said to get burnt up (dagdha). When a bhadra tithi takes place on a Wednesday, then the endeavor is likely to be successful (siddhi-yoga). There are also specific ritual days that are created by the tithi-weekday alignment. For example, when the waxing tenth tithi (daśamī) falls on a Thursday, it is a special time to worship Lakṣmī, the goddess of prosperity. The day-tithi combinations are a chapter in themselves.

✶   ✶   ✶

[See Table, facing page] *Varāhamihira, Bṛhat Saṁhitā, XCIX, v. 1–3. I have replaced Brahmā for lotus-born (Kamalaja), Nirṛti for dark mother (Kālī), Bhaga for Manmatha, and Aryamā for Dharma to fit the most prevalent nakṣatra terminology. For 'six-faced,' I have used the name Skanda, though pure Vedic is Agni-devatā.

Tithi	Deity*	Energy
1	BRAHMĀ (CREATOR)	CREATING, CULTURE, ARTS
2	VIDHĀTṚ-HARI (SUPPORTER)	BUILDING, PLANNING
3	VIṢṆU (SUSTAINER)	EXPANDING, PROTECTING
4	YAMA (DEATH)	TRANSFORMATION
5	CHANDRA (MOON)	GROWTH, NOURISHMENT
6	SKANDA (WAR-GOD)	BURNING, CLARIFYING
7	INDRA (KING OF HEAVEN)	CONTROL, POWER
8	VASUS (THE SHINING ONES)	FAME, BEING SEEN
9	NAGA (SERPENT GOD)	DECEPTION, PRESUMPTION
10	ARYAMĀ (COMPANION)	LOVE, MARRIAGE, FAMILY
11	RUDRA (LORD OF ANGER/ RAGE)	POWER OF DESTRUCTION
12	SAVITṚ (SUN'S CREATIVITY)	WAKING UP, REALIZING
13	BHAGA (SOURCE OF LUCK)	RELATIONSHIP, SEXUALITY
14	NIRṚTI (DISORDER GODDESS)	BREAKING, INTENSITY
FULL	VIŚVADEVAS (UNIVERSAL PRINCIPLES)	NOBILITY, GOOD CHARACTER
DARK	PITṚS (ANCESTORS)	AUTHORITY, KARMA

DEITY

There are two systems of deities for the tithi. One is an older Vaidik system that we can use to understand the natural frequency of the tithi. These are the same as the rulers of the lunar constellations (*nakṣatras*), which can be found in many popular books. Varāhamihira says "Since Rohiṇī star and Pratipad (new moon) is presided over by Brahmā, all works that are allowed under the star can be performed under the tithi too. Similarly in regard to the star Abhijit and Dvītiyā; Śravaṇa and the third tithi, Bharaṇī and the fourth," etc. The electional prescriptions of the nakṣatras lines up with fifteen of the lunar waxing and waning phases.

   Traditionally, the nakṣatra are to be understood through their deity. They are even sometimes called by the deity's name. I have given a simple translation of their names and listed a key funtion, to get the reader started, but to understand them more requires studying the myths associated with them.[42] Then, after having a structure, the best way to get to know the energy of the tithi are to have them marked on a calendar. You can be aware of what is happening each day and see the correlation in your own life. The tithi do have a slightly different impact on different people based upon areas of one's own strengths and weaknesses that get activated. Being aware of the cycles and watching their impact on you is very important.

   Before looking at the next tithi and deity relationship, it is important to understand the Moon from another perspective—the mooning cycle. A woman's menstruation cycle is called her Moon cycle. This internal cycle is regulated by the external Moon as it relates to the woman's natal Moon. The external cycle shares many of the same features as the internal. As the Moon waxes towards fullness it becomes more and more fertile. The full moon is correlated to ovulation, and the dark moon is correlated to menstruation. When ovulation happens, there is heightened energy, and when menstruation comes, there is stress. The closer to the dark moon, the more stress becomes palpable in the air and things that would normally not be a big deal, can become explosions. The dark moon is the first day of menstruation, when the flow of blood is heaviest. The energy is drained and people are easily tired and irritated. Events near this time often suffer a low turnout—unless the Moon is aspected by benefic planets, meaning there are lots of good friends and support around.

[See Table, facing page]
* I add Demeter based upon Hesiod's mention to spread her grain on the middle seventh (K2).
† I move Aphrodite from the correlation to the fourth to match her Hindu counterpart Lakṣmī.

42 I give key myths succinctly in *Science of Light*, v.1, pp.235–271.

	Hindu	Greek
1	AGNI	APOLLO
2	BRAHMĀ	DEMETER*
3	GAURI	ATHENA
4	GAṆEŚA	HERMES
5	SARASVATĪ	HORKOS
6	SKANDA	ARTEMIS
7	SŪRYA	APOLLO
8	KṚṢṆA	POSEIDON, ASKLEPIOS
9	DURGA	
10	RĀMA	
11	LAKṢMĪ	APHRODITE†
12	VIṢṆU	
13	BṚHASPATI	ATHENA
14	ŚIVA	
FULL	SATYA	
DARK	KĀLĪ	HEKATE

Menstruation normally lasts about four days. So the first few days after the dark moon are still not completely beneficial energy and they lack their full capacity and focus. The fourth lunar day is when the Moon is seen to have regained its balance of light. This is why Gaṇeśa, the lord of beginnings is connected to the fourth tithi. Being aware of this cosmic moon cycle, major events in life are not started close to either side of the dark moon.

The Hindu system of tithi deities is based on the days that they are often celebrated. This system can show how to work with the energy of the tithi. I have similarly added the Greek deities in the same way.[43] When doing a fast or other remedy, ritual to the deity celebrated on that phase will give the energy to overcome its weakness.

Tāntric rituals with particular deities are done regularly on the corresponding tithi. Gaṇeśa unlocks the doorway to our goals, he is the first tithi after the Moon's cleansing. Tāntric worshippers of the goddess, can spend years worshipping Gaṇeśa to get the needed access to the domain of the goddess. Afterwards, they do ritual once a month on the fourth tithi to

43 Source information from Hesiod's *Works and Days* (v.765–282). I rely here heavily on the interpretation of Apollonius Sophistes at Biblioteca Arcana.

ensure the acquired powers remain with them.

The Moon phases are often grouped into sets of ten to make a trinity. The Moon in the first period of ten days of the lunar month is considered to be of moderate strength, the second period of ten days is very auspicious.[44] In the third ten days, the Moon has little strength unless aspected by benefic planets. As a trinity, the first ten days are related to the goddess Sarasvatī, the middle ten phases relate to the goddess Lakṣmī, and the last ten phases relate to the goddess Kālī.

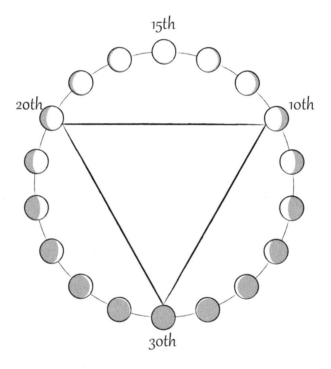

The Ancient Greek use of the 30 phases utilizes the division into three groups of ten (decad). They were called the waxing ten, middle ten and waning ten. Hesiod says things like the first ninth (S9) is harmless for men, but the mid ninth (K4) improves towards evening, meaning it's not good in the morning. He indicates that the fifth lunar day in each phase (S5, S15, K10) were considered dangerous, particularly to break an oath. "Beware the terrible fifth day, when the Furies helped Strife to bear the maligned

44 Jātaka Prāijāta II.10, and Sārāvalī V.16

Horkos, who punishes those who break their word."[45] In the Hindu view, the fifth tithi is auspicious as it's ruled by Sarasvatī, mother of the Word and goddess of art and learning. This tithi is the best day for academic works. Athena was worshipped on the third phase (S3, S13, K8) in each trinity as well, as Artemis on the sixth (S6, S12, K11).

Hesiod says this lunar calendar of thirty phases was designed by Zeus, the all-wise, to help men discern properly. He says to mark the (lunar) days and to make sure to tell your [illiterate] slaves of their personalities.[46] He lists certain days to perform certain works, like the twelfth phase to dust the loom and start weaving, or the twenty-seventh (K12) to yoke a horse. These were not meant to be the only good days to do these activities, these were meant to be the first days to do these activities. Working with the magic of the Moon, one ensures the first time you yoke a new horse is an auspicious day for the well-being of that horse, or in our case, the day we buy a new car.

Before the Greeks had rigorous methods to keep track of the exact phase, they averaged the lunar days. On shorter months, they removed the 29th lunar day, which in a natural calendar falls on any tithi in which the Moon is in perigee. In the ancient Greek lunar calendar, Hekate's thirtieth day was always present as a day to connect to the ancestors.

COSMOS

We can say that the entire universe is within us; that the planets and stars and cycles of time exist within us. Or we can say that we are within the universe and just a fractal portion of its manifestation. There is a pulsation that moves us, that is moving the universe. To be aware of this pulsation merges us with the cosmos.

We can conceive of the universal reflection in many different ways, and there are various Tāntric systems of chakras, breath and energy. This system I am about to discuss is rooted in Kashmiri Śaiva Trika Tantra as taught in the Tantrāloka by Abhinavagupta.

Kasmiri Tāntra focuses heavily on the pulsation (spanda) of existence. Abhinavagupta explains that the active-resting nature of the Sun and

---

45 Robert Saxton, *Hesiod's Calendar*, p.78
46 Hesiod's *Works and Days*, v.765–828

Moon is the pulsation of life revealing itself through the breath.[47] We can see the solar day and lunar night mapped into the inhale and exhale. The repose of the night is an inhale of rejuvenation while the exhale is the exertion of the day.

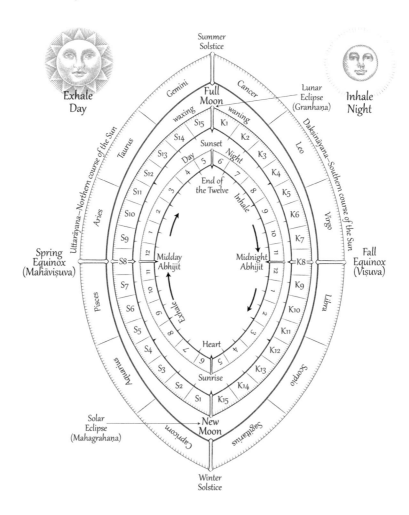

Just before the end of the exhale the breath slows down to nothing, then there is a transition (*sandhi*), and the inhale begins. Again at the end of the inhale, the breath slows down to nothing, there is a gap—prāṇa resides in the heart, and then the exhale begins. The normal breath is calculated to be four seconds: two seconds in and two seconds out when not

47 Tantrāloka 6.8–14

watched and elongated.[48] The gap in between these two is an eighth of a second. The transition from the lunar inhale to the solar exhale is an eighth of a second, where consciousness resides in the gap without thought.

The gap at the end of an exhausting exhale is the sunset of the day. This place was called the End-of-the-twelve, because the breath was said to go down the nasal passage which was four fingers width and then eight finger width more into the space in front of the breather. The inhale therefore starts from the air eight fingers width in front of the nasal passage and the prāṇa flows in and then down to the space of the heart. The gap at the end of a night of inhale correlates to sunrise within the heart. The breath's eighth of a second gap proportionately becomes 24 minutes before and after the exact moment of sunrise. The sacred time to do sunrise or sunset ritual is the twenty–four minutes before and after the exact moment of the day's transition. That transition time is a space of in between; solar and lunar unity. The breath is normally residing more to the solar or lunar aspects of consciousness, but at this time, the center is activated.

This same pulsation of life is seen in the breath of the lunar month and solar year. The new moon resides in the heart while the full moon is at the end of the twelve. The winter solstice is in the heart, where the Sun is reborn and then the days of exertion increase with exhale. On the lunar inhale, the days grow shorter and the nights grows longer, similarly on the inhale, the Moon loses its portions of light (kalā), and its dark/night energy increases. When the Moon is bright, having more sun energy, the stars are dimmer in the night sky. As the lunar/night of the Moon grows, the sky becomes darker and the stars shine more brightly. This loss of light from the Moon that brightens the stars is seen as feeding the gods, which brings many aspects of our inner selves into greater visibility.

> *By the Moon's nature of nourishing [the gods] it one by one gives up a part for each tithi,*
> *The fifteenth part (dark moon) comes near to the heart,* 6.93
> *There, Amāvāsya, who is the emaciated Moon, enters into the Sun...*

---

48 A breath (prāṇa) of four seconds is equal to 0°01' of arc, therefore it takes 60 breaths for 1° of arc, 900 breaths an hour, 21,600 breaths a day. The breath is an astronomical unit as well as a function of life. The breath directly measures/moves with the spin of the Earth and movement of the stars.

The dark moon enters the heart and the new moon leaves. Just as the breath and day have their transition, the proportional gap for the lunar month is half a tithi (almost twelve hours) on both sides of the conjunction (or opposition) of the new and full moon. Above we have discussed the fifteen phases (tithi) of the waxing and waning Moon. However in the Tantras a sixteenth portion (kalā) is discussed, one that very few knew how to calculate—or indeed the origin of—before this was written. The Kalā are similar in most respects to the tithi, except for the transcendental sixteenth portion which is always there, hidden.

Nectar, in the form of the Moon, is in two [divisions, each of] sixteen parts.
6.95
All the gods drink the fifteen [tithi], but the final portion [known as] Amā (togetherness),
is the secret remainder in the final place offering libations to everything as Dark Moon (Amāvāsya). 6.96
In this way, the fifteen portions of the Moon progressively wane,
But the sixteenth is that immortal (amṛta) form of the Moon's course. 6.97
The fifteenth [tithi] is the portion where the Moon is vanished,
There, is the transcendental half portion that is known as the junction of the phases. 6.98

The last half of the waning phase, where the Moon is losing all of its light, is the fifteenth tithi. This is clarified to differentiate it from the ascended or transcendental (ūrdhvaga) portion of the sixteenth which is the junction zone between the waxing and waning phases of the Moon. One half of the sixteenth tithi resides above the last half of the (lunar) fifteenth tithi. The other half is above the first half of the (solar) new moon tithi. It has both aspects of the duality of consciousness. She is the power located in the gap (sandhi) personified—she is timelessness beyond time.

In the waxing exhale, the pure perceiver in the heart illumines the senses and their objects. Similar to the Moon growing brighter, objectivity increases. The greatest duality exists in the full moon, and therefore also the greatest prosperity. On the waning moon, the objectivity decreases and the mind is drawn inward. In the core of the new moon, within the heart, is the pure perceiver unattached to all objectivity. It is not just a time of reflection, but a time to see the self. The sixteenth portion is the transcendent perceiver consciousness, where we are fully non-dual.

The sixteenth portion is always present, but our conscious awareness is limited. It is this gap in the lunar cycle where we aim to tap into the timeless realm. This gap is also the place that twice a year when the synodic cycle crosses the draconic cycle the lunar node (Rāhu) moves within the gap conjunct the Sun and Moon, and an eclipse is created. Normally, the I-sense blocks us from seeing the non-dual source within the sacred transition zone. The conjunction of the Moon with the Sun and Rāhu in the gap, heats up and melts the Moon, who flows forth like nectar/honey. This represents the opening of deeper levels in the sea of consciousness, and the ability to attain (drink) the highest states.

Then the solar disc is concealed/dissolved by the Moon who is flowing nectar,
In its melting state, during this union, Rāhu seizes and drinks. 6.101
The Sun is the means to acquire knowledge, the Moon is the object of knowledge...
Rāhu is the delusioned subject, who is skilled in obscuring them. 6.102
But, he is really just a form of ignorance (tamas), and unable to sustain the dissolution,
That non-dual union shining forth is the principle dissolver of the measurer (the individual). 6.103

The Sun (the nature of knowing) is the means of measuring (*pramāṇa*) knowledge, and the Moon (the nature of action) is what is measured (*meya*). Rāhu (the nature of will) is the measurer (the individual) of this world (*māyā*), and he is confusing subject and object. Rāhu represents the limited perceiver who creates the illusion of all levels of separate existence. Modern developmental psychologist, Robert Kegan, has done extensive research with the mundane levels of the stages of subject-object relationship in a maturing individual. The gateway to the transition in the levels of consciousness live in the space of the gaps—the in between transitions. In the eclipse, the cognitive functions are transcended to a spiritual consciousness giving access to the pure perceiver, free of all objective identification, which leads to mystic union with the entire Cosmos.

The solar eclipse is considered auspicious (*puṇya*) for spiritual work because 'the three aspects which create the perception of the world merge in union to create non-duality between the subject, object and the means to perceive them'.[49] In this way, the eclipse empowers the limited perceiver

---

49 Tantrāloka 6.104

(*māyā-pramātā*) seeking spiritual insight to recognize the supreme perceiver, from which everything else is an extension. The solar eclipse can have a negative impact for the material aspects in the external world, but is sacred for spiritual practice because of the perceptibility of the non-dual source which can truly dissolve the individual (the measurer).

Abhinavagupta recommends bathing, meditation, oblations, mantra recitation to be performed between the devouring of the Sun and its liberation.[50] Spiritual knowledge and all types of supernatural powers are available during this time. Similar practices are recommended for a lunar eclipse, but with the intention of manifesting worldly gains. The full moon is dual consciousness and its power can be harnessed to achieve worldly success. We are often limited by our karma, but during the eclipse, the ritualist is only limited by their own ritual skill.

Both lunar and solar eclipses are powerful for spiritual or worldly ritual, but one is clearly more supported in the correlating gap. The spiritual power of the full moon in general takes more conscious work to attain, but it is overflowing and abundant when reached with the proper consciousness, breath and time.

This leads to our final important gap in time. Half way into the inhale and half way on the exhale is the solar noon and exact midnight. The points are called Abhijit, or the 'victorious' time. In my Utkal astrological tradition, we teach that the noon time Abhijit (which is twenty four minutes before and after solar noon), is the most powerful time for work events, while the midnight Abhijit is the most powerful time for spiritual practice. In the day, objectivity is increasing but this halfway point is the midpoint between the inner core essence and the outer self. Actions at this time can be in alignment with both the material world and our inner essence, which leads to success. The midnight Abhijit is also a midpoint but in the direction of decreasing objectivity. Here we can balance the material needs to support our inner growth.

In the lunar cycle, the midpoint falls in the eighth tithi (Aṣṭamī), the half moon. Kṛṣṇa is associated with the waning eighth tithi, while Radha is associated with the waxing eighth tithi. In the breath, this gap is located at the level of the hard palate, and this is where the internal alchemy happens.

The breath goes in through the nostrils and down into the heart and then back out the nostrils. The Abhijit position is where the prāṇic move-

50 Ibid., 6.107

ment can alter from the common consciousness to the seer. On the exhale, the prāṇa passes through the midpoint and reaches upwards to above the crown of the head (the upper end-of-the-twelve). On the inhale, the prāṇa is pulled through the crown and passes through the midpoint, down to the heart. Air may still move through the nostril, but by moving the consciousness in this crown to heart cycle, the prāṇa follows it. By practicing this breath within the gaps of time, consciousness is cleansed and the higher capacities are within reach. This technique practiced with deep concentration during an eclipse will reveal the prāṇic movement and consciousness shift that happens only subtly at other times.

In the year, we can see that this mid-point falls on the equinoxes. They are the time that the day and night, Sun and Moon energies are at their greatest balance. Horus was crowned on the spring equinox. This time gives us access to our higher potentialities. I am not sure ancient cultures would have needed to build big stone monuments to mark the time just for agricultural purposes. They built them because they knew the power of time. Abhinavagupta gives greater importance to what was the beginning gap for him in each realm. In the material realm, he calls the sunset great. In the mental realm, he calls the new moon (and its eclipse) great. On the daivik realm, he calls the spring equinox great. These are power times to access our inner potentialities.

CONCLUSION

This has been a journey worshiping time through the game played by the Sun and the Moon. We have understood the intricate nature of stellar calculations and how they relate to our conscious reality. I hope we all have greater awareness of the thirty lunar phases and can utilize them to lead a more successful lives and more powerful rituals with their magic.

* *
*

When the Stars Aren't Right

Sorcery For When You Can't Wait

Jason Miller

I AM A Sorcerer. I do it and teach it professionally. There is no day-job. It is my career, and I make a pretty decent living at it, so I guess I am pretty good at it. I have made my name in this business by being strategic and practical and as focused on non-magical actions and events as I am on magical ones. I don't really care which of the two has the greater impact, so long as the goal is reached. Clients want results, that's what matters in the end. I mention all this not to boast, but to explain why I might have a different take on planetary powers than some of the other contributors to this book.

Astrologers and Sorcerers are both concerned with the planets and their influences but often in ways that seemingly contradict each other. Pure astrological magic is based on timing operations to coincide with optimal moments when the planets and stars best reflect the goal of the operation. You form a company, propose marriage, or create your talisman at the precise moment that the stars are aligned best for what you want to do. In the case of the Astrological Talisman, you are taking a sort of snap-shot of the Stellar moment and infusing that energy into the talisman so that it broadcasts that power whenever it is worn or worked.

The Sorcerer, however, has to compensate for problems as they arise and cannot always wait for a perfect moment. This is especially true when the problems are not yours, but your clients. If you are a Sorcerer worth your salt, your regular practices have your day-to-day life running fairly smoothly, so you might be able to wait for the optimum moment to implement a strategy. The client, however, is by definition a person with a problem that needs to be solved.

This is the dilemma we face: necessity vs the ideal. How do we stop the perfect from becoming the enemy of the good? As I write this essay its 97 degrees outside, but I am nice and cool in my air-conditioned office. In a similar vein, a Sorcerer faced with less-than-helpful astrological weather has to take on responsibility for changing the temperature.

ASTROLOGY VERSUS MUNDANE FACTORS

The first thing to consider is exactly how important astrological conditions are in comparison to other non-magical conditions. Ignoring mundane considerations is, in my experience, the leading cause of failure in magic. Jupiter, Venus, and the Sun might be in a perfect position to lend their abundance, enchantment, and glory to your job interview two weeks from now, but if you put it off till then, you might do much more damage to your chances than any magic can compensate for. Mercury retrogrades, and Saturn direct be damned, if the company needs you now, the best magic is to get your ass in there ASAP. This seems almost too obvious to mention, but let me tell you, it's not. The list of people I have consulted with who are willing to do completely daft things like delay interviews because of astrology, pour powder on resumes, or douse themselves in foul smelling oils in the name of getting the magic right is long indeed. When we spend all of our time on magic and the occult, sometimes we can lose sight of expectations that fall outside of our specialty. Some of us set aside our own career advancement and romantic interests because our love of the mysteries is so strong. We are what we think about all day long. It is only natural, that when we need to change careers, start a business, find a lover, or care for our health, we think primarily in terms of magic, astrology, and other spiritual influences.

It is not that the magic isn't helpful, of course it is, or why would I even be writing this? But we need to remember magic is an influence on events that gets weighed against other influence. It is not the single determining factor. This is as true for stellar magic as it is for any other kind of Sorcery. The influence of the planets and stars needs to be weighed against all the other considerations. Unfortunately, because it is easier, more interesting, and more entertaining for us to think about magic than it is to start digging through business books, researching medical procedures, or learning to be more charming, it is magic that winds up being the primary focus in our quest for change and success.

Knowing my reputation for grilling people on doing the non-magical work in a clever and effective manner, clients often assure me that they are 'doing all the mundane stuff', and so could I just give them the magic spell to make everything work out please. Yet, time and time again, I see people that have clearly taken less time to actually write their resume than they did in charting the perfect moment to send it out.

DIVERSIFY YOUR DAEMONS

The Sorcerer stands in the path of power, not only the power of the stars and planets above but the planet that he stands upon. The classical elements, the spirits of nature, the genii of plants, the sorcerers own mind—these are just some of the 'universal points of transmutation' that Andrew Chumbley spoke about when defining Sorcery. Now, I am not denying that the movements of the stars and planets have an impact on your work, no matter what you are doing, but clearly the influence of astrology is far more important if you are making a Talisman of the Pleiades to support your occult studies than if you are calling upon the spirit of the wormwood plant.

If we think of the planetary powers as currents, we can see that while they have some influence upon just about everything, certain types of magic beckon us to wade deeper into that wave than others. If you are calling upon Hekate to bind someone with a definiens tablet, you might want to check the astro-weather to make sure it is conducive to that kind of work, but if not. you may decide to proceed anyway since in this case it is Hekate as a Chthonic Deity that we are concerned with. If, however, it is Saturnus himself you are petitioning to wrap someone up in lead, the position of the planet can make or break the operation because that power is more intimately tied to the planet.

While I do not subscribe to the "it's all in your head and whatever you believe is true" camp, I do think that certain influences hold greater sway if you are standing deep in that current. Some may not feel the influence of the planetary hours keenly but if you are invoking Tapthartharath, the spirit of Mercury, or doing a Talisman from the *Picatrix*, doing it at the wrong hour it can really screw up your results, because the operation is so closely tied to that system of hours. I have seen cases where this holds true even though the operator was unaware of the error at the time.

Because of this, the practical Sorcerer is keenly aware of how much the planets are going to affect any given operation. He can utilize the timing to his benefit or minimize its impact by relying upon other points of transmutation.

The planets are only one level that magic happens on. You can appeal to higher or lower powers to achieve similar goals. Agrippa taught that Natural Magic, Celestial Magic, and Divine Magic are the three main categories of the Occult Sciences. If the needs of the Sorcerer do not lend themselves to the movements of the Celestial bodies, it is quite easy to go over their heads to the divine powers or slip in under the radar by using the natural world for powers that fit your needs. You can even go underground if you don't mind working with the demons and denizens of Hades. Make no mistake: your overall operation will still be affected by Astrological powers, but not as deeply as it would if you called upon those powers directly for aid.

As an example, a student of mine recently told me that he was getting nowhere with using Jupiter, Sol, or Mercury to build wealth. I suggested he start working with Yakshas and other types of earth elementals. A few weeks of offering later and that wealth he was looking for started to flow. Eventually he decided to work with Pluto and really made a huge leap forward. The uber-rich are called Plutocrats for a reason, after all.

FIGHT THE POWERS THAT BE

At times, the Sorcerer may decide to attempt to counteract current astrological conditions through the agency of magic. This is not un-traditional. A common feature of Gnostic Christianity was the Hebdomad: the seven planets as Archons that were hostile to the humanity and seek to keep us shrouded in ignorance. Gnostics taught techniques for by-passing these Archons and mitigating their influence. In the modern era practices like the Banishing Ritual of the Hexagram ritual have been said to banish planetary influences and yield a sort of 'clean room where the magician can do his magic.

A method of by-passing the influence of planets that has gained much popularity recently is a method drawn from PGM XIII 824 where six of the

Greek vowels connected with the planets are chanted in the six directions (N, S, E, W, Above, and Below) and the seventh chanted at the center of your being. Modernized versions of this have appeared in Stephen Flowers' book *Hermetic Magic*, *The Book of Abrasax* by Michael Cecchetelli, and my own *Advanced Planetary Magic* chapbook. The idea is a simple one, by arranging the powers of the spheres around you in an orderly fashion, you create a buffer between yourself and the actual position of the planets. Think of it as astrological climate control.

It is also possible to contact the gods and spirits connected with the planets and ask them to provide different methods for working with the powers of the planets in different conditions. In the summer of 2007 I embarked on a project with my friend and long-time friend, illustrator, and partner in crime Matthew Brownlee to generate a new group of planetary seals that would be able to access the powers of the planets in a very direct manner. We wanted these seals not only to channel the forces of the powers invoked, but we wanted them to be able to overcome retrogrades, eclipses, and other unfortunate planetary alignments. I conjured the intelligences and spirits of each planet and asked for a vision to be shown to Matt that he could work into a sigil. Below are the seals in descending Chaldean order.

Obviously within each seal is the basic outline of the ordinary astrological symbol for the planet. Beyond that are elaborations that hint at the movement and actions of each planet in a very direct way. Rather than relate to a kamea or analytical method for deriving the deal, the artistic appearance is the action.

Saturn's ribbons bind and constrain the sickle and cross. Jupiter's flowing lines seem to reach up and pull unseen riches back into it. The wheel of mars spins its spokes like a chariot wheel and launches a loop pulling a target right into the tip of the arrow. In sun we see hints of the swastika, flares of unstable fire, and just the hint of the number 6 in the central spiral. Venus appears as a woman posing with one hand on her hip and another against her head, a classic pose. Here again is also the lasso of enchantment. Mercury is wispier than the others and has lines that hint at the serpents of the caduceus as well as the lightning flash. Nothing about the image is straight on. Luna of course has the classic crescent as well as the waves that she controls through gravity and a spiral effect that is indicative, perhaps, of lunacy.

I have written extensively on these seals in my books and course, but they are simple enough to be employed in just about any ritual that involves planetary powers. I encourage you to use them when you think that perhaps the time is less than ideal to work with a particular planet.

HACK THE PLANETS

If you have ever seen those life-hacking articles about using toilet paper rolls to boost the bass on your phone, or using ketchup bottles for pancake batter, you know that with a little ingenuity you can sometimes expand your use of things well beyond their intended use. The planets can also be hacked and applied in ways that Lilly or Agrippa might not have thought of.

Most occultists have an appallingly simple idea of the powers of the planets that goes something like this:

Moon: sex and dreams and astral
Mercury: intelligence and movement
Venus: love and sex
Sun: inspiration and health
Mars: war and killing
Jupiter: wealth and expansion
Saturn: death and restriction

This leads to very limited thinking. Everyone that needs money goes to Jupiter like he is their dad giving them money to go out on a Saturday night. People want love magic: they go to Venus, as if there are no reasons for their lack of companionship beyond not having enough Venus mojo. People feel threatened: they go to Mars to kick butt, as if this is the only tool that a soldier has. Many Sorcerers I meet won't touch Saturn with a 10-foot wand, as they are more afraid of its malefic influence than any demon they might summon.

The best tool a Sorcerer faced with inopportune timing for one planet is to learn how to be flexible with the others. The variety and fullness of each planet is unfortunately lost on most magicians, and this is an area where a little study of traditional astrology would pay off. Most people might not think of Mars as the patron planet of Bakers, but William Lilly did.

I find that all seven planets can be called upon to affect just about any situation, you just have to know how to apply them. I have laid down a Two Week Challenge to my students that encourages them to start a working on a Monday and invoke a planet to impact their situation every other day for two weeks. This lets you hit all seven planets on their appropriate day in the Chaldean order.

Let's take a look at some different scenarios and see how each planet can impact a situation.

When it comes to business or money, you can invoke Luna to help make sure that you are working in alignment with the tides of commerce, affecting the deep minds of customers with a new marketing campaign, or revealing deception from backstabbing partners, bosses and co-workers.

Then call upon Mercury to make sure that motion is on your side. There is nothing more key when it comes to Financial magic. People treat money magic as a static goal or set number, but there is never stasis in business or personal finance: if you are not moving forward, you are moving backward. If your money is not moving around and making more money, then you are probably losing money. Mercury, and the motion he governs, is key.

Venus is all about relationships. Have you ever been involved in a business venture that did not require you to influence other people, sell things, or otherwise have people in your corner? Me neither.

The Sun. Gold right? Also inspiration, illuminating new ideas. No idea, no product. Let's not forget leadership, fame and glory. It is worth noting that while Jupiter is the king of the Gods, the planets all revolve around the Sun. There are times when you simply need to plant yourself firmly, radiate your light, and let everyone else start to revolve around you. In the new economy where businesses need to not only serve customers, but develop communities, this is incredibly important.

Of course you can call upon Mars to overcome competition, but I have had a lot of success drawing upon Mars for discipline and drive as well. Never underestimate the power of drive and discipline for finance. There is a reason that so many businessmen love *The Art of War*.

Jupiter is a no-brainer: expansion, governance, accretion, benevolence etc. This is the one everyone calls on, so let's leave it at that.

That just leaves spooky Saturn. Everybody is scared of Saturn, but limits are important. Jupiterian expansion needs the limits and strictness of Saturn to keep it focused, and make sure that systems do not expand unchecked. Think about all that Solar flare and Jupiterian expansion as an explosion. Saturn is like the barrel of a gun that can restrict it and make sure it hits a target. Also, very simply, if you want something to happen, you can use Saturn to restrict the opposite from happening.

If you are in a situation where Jupiter is negatively afflicted in your chart, or if you are working during a time when Jupiter is retrograde or otherwise not aligned well, you have a lot of other options as a Sorcerer.

Let's take a look at love work: Luna is all about the loving. Deep mind, sexual drives. Not exactly stretching our minds with this one.

Call on Mercury to make yourself witty, confident, and funny. Looks may be the thing that gets initial attention, but wit, confidence, and humor will beat looks for sealing the deal and establishing a real connection every time. Not to mention that Mercury can grease the wheels of fate to get you in the right place at the right time.

Venus is the love goddess, and thus the obvious choice—we need not go on.

Sol will illuminate you and let you shine bright amongst dimmer lights. Honestly, I wonder why more Solar Love talismans are not in production. There is no better glamour than the warmth of the Sun.

Martial power might seem like a stretch for love work, until you realize just how much there is to be conquered in the pursuit of love. Love poems that draw upon the language of the hunter and prey or frame love as a conquest are so common that it is cliché.

There is also an enormous amount of fear for people to overcome in the quest for love. Fear of rejection, fear of failure, fear of ridicule—the drives of love and sex are so primal that they turn the volume up on everything and make it impossible for us to keep our cool. One of the most successful love spells I ever did for a client was a Mars spell to overcome fear of rejection and build confidence. All the Venus work in the world did him no good until he got that under control. It was Ares after all that Aphrodite had the passionate affair with.

Has anyone had more sex than Zeus? Jupiter is really good for love magic. It's power, and confidence and all things benefic, what can be more attractive than that. Having money doesn't hurt either when it comes to finding lovers, so even the common application of Jupiterian magic is useful here.

Saturn is tricky for love, even when thinking outside the box. It can be used to end bad relationships, deal with pain. You can also petition the planet to remove its influence and free you from its grip. People rarely think about that, but it works. More nefarious sorcerers might invoke Saturn in love spells that strongly bind someone or curse them until they love you. Such work is certainly traditional, but that still doesn't make it a good, or ethical, idea.

You can also combine Saturn to constrain the power of another planet. One student adapted an invocation I wrote calling upon both Saturn and Venus to strengthen their marriage. On the day of Venus at the Hour of Saturn they chanted Eta and Omega over and over, building up to the charm used to bind hairs from her and her husband together,

> *As Aphrodite arose from Cronus's phallus*
> *May this hour give rise to love*
> *May Saturn's bindings hold love firm*
> *May Saturn's firmness make love strong*
> *May Saturn's strength make love deep*
> *And may love last till death do us part.*

Healing is often done with the Sun, but it's easy to see how Luna might work on the mental anguish, Mercury can move you toward good health, Venus can heal the emotions, Mars can do battle with disease directly, Jupiter encourage sovereignty over your own body, and Saturn might be petitioned to bind and control symptoms, or even give more time.

Anything used for healing can be used to harm, and so while Mars and Saturn are obvious planets to run to, as a sort of sword and shackles for your enemy, the other planets are easy to play with as well. The Moon literally is the planet for causing lunacy. The Sun's light can burn and cause cancer. No one started more wars than Aphrodite, and the powers of Venus can turn people against each other as sure as it can turn bring them together. Mercury is a god of thieves. Jupiter of course, while usually thought of as the greater benefic, is a powerful force in battle, both in terms of governing the forces you call upon, and granting you luck, and potency in the presence of your enemies.

ARCANE ADAPTATION

Following a tradition strictly can be a wonderful and rewarding thing: whether it is finding virgin-spun thread for grimoire work, long sadhanas in Tantra, or perfect timing in Astrology. The rules and protocols of a tradition give a goal to aim for and an example to measure our work against. The particular needs and time constraints of any given person in their particular situation at their particular time often come up against the protocols of tradition and demand some flexibility.

Through knowing how to use the planets and stars in flexible ways we find creative avenues to achieving our ends. When we need to we can use the planets and stars themselves to overcome problems that they would otherwise create. Even when no answer can be found in the sky above, we can look beyond the visible heavens to the realm of the Gods, or below them, to roots beneath our feet. Sorcerers are always pragmatists. They adopt and adapt. They assess the situation, check the weather, and make a plan based on what can be accomplished in the time needed with the tools available. We need to be aware of what would be perfect, but we should never let what's perfect become the enemy of the good.

*   *
*

On Identifying Presiding Daemons and Geniuses from an Astrological Chart

According to Three Books of Occult Philosophy

Eric Purdue

IN BOOK 3, chapter 26 in the influential book *Three Books of Occult Philosophy*, Agrippa wrote a somewhat detailed series of instructions on how to find the names of spirits, or more specifically daemons and geniuses, from an astrological chart. This chapter has caused some confusion over the years, particularly with some of Agrippa's terms such as 'almutez' and 'hylegical places', common terms in medieval astrology, but almost unknown to modern astrology. In the Llewellyn 1993 annotated edition,[1] Tyson misinterpreted some of these terms, so that replicating Agrippa's system as intended was nearly impossible from Tyson's notes. Additionally, as Agrippa promised in the last chapter of *Occult Philosophy*, some material is organized, some disorganized, and some is veiled. Thus important information to put this technique into perspective and practice is found not only elsewhere in the book, but in other sources.

The art of identifying the planetary significators for daemons and geniuses is not practiced widely in either modern astrological or occult circles. The modern astrological world tends to shy away from occult prac-

---

1 Henry Cornelius Agrippa, *Three Books of Philosophy* 3:26 ed. Tyson, Donald, Llewellyn 1993 notes 2 and 5.

tices, instead largely favoring psychological models and prediction. The occult world tends to avoid deep study of astrology, perhaps because of perceived 'new age' trappings and the lack of more complex techniques in many popular grimoires. However in the pre-Enlightenment age, magic and astrology were inextricably mixed.

The three Hermetic sciences are alchemy, astrology, and magic. The medieval Arabic astrological magic text *Picatrix*[2] further describes these as: ...[magic] operat[ing] on spirit by spirit, ...images[3] with spirits on bodes, ...alchemy with bodies on bodies. The link between all three of these is astrology. Agrippa wrote: "all secrets, and all kinds of divination have their roots and foundations in astrology, since without it, little or nothing will seem to be accomplished"[4]. Thus, astrology is the foundational language and framework for magic and alchemy according to this system. While famous grimoires such as the *Keys of Solomon* have less complex astrological rules than *Picatrix*, its importance is plain.

Modern astrology has largely divorced itself from spirituality, which may sound strange considering there is an entire branch of astrology called 'spiritual astrology', but as spirituality as a whole has become a more distant concept in the 21st west, and definitions of 'spirit' are often murky, it begs the question, what is spirit? And, while modern occultists have written volumes on working with demons, what exactly *are* daemons?

DAEMONS AND GENIUSES

Agrippa tends to use genius and daemon interchangeably. Daemon is the Latinized form of the Greek *daimon*, and genius is essentially the Roman equivalent. There are three basic 'beings' that Agrippa delineates: spirits, intelligences, and daemons. Agrippa seems to use 'spirit' as an almost generic term for all incorporeal beings outside of God. However intelligences and daemons are always mentioned explicitly, and there is a hierarchy.

The first and highest are the supercelestial intelligences, which Agrippa says some call gods. These are closest to God and partake the most from divine nature.

2 *The Picatrix*, tr. Greer and Warnock, Adocentyn Press 2010, book 1: ch. 2.
3 I.e. talismans
4 Henry Cornelius Agrippa, *Three Books of Philosophy*, tr. Purdue, Eric, Three Hands Press 2018, book 2: ch. 53

The second are the celestial intelligences. These are the same intelligences mentioned in Agrippa's famous planetary tables in book 2. In addition, there are intelligences over the fixed stars and twelve zodiacal signs.

The third are worldly daemons who rule over various places, things, people, and activities on Earth. This includes terrestrial spirits such as nymphs and satyrs.

One way to think about this hierarchy, and this is a general rule in Hermetics, is that the higher in chain of being, the closer one is to God (or the First Cause). Thus the higher orders of spirits tend to be more like what we would think of as Classical gods. This was an attractive model to monotheist Christians and Muslims. These spirits dispose the will of God to the lower orders, which are heavier and more flawed, but still often useful. Because these lower orders of spirits are less corporeal than humans, they could still provide a valuable link to the divine.

Generally speaking, anything with a soul has three parts:[5] mind, reason, and the idolum. Ficino[6] compares these to the parts of the body-mind being the head, reason the body, and the idolum the feet. The intelligences are like the mind of a spirit, and the idolum are the daemon. To take this analogy in a more literal way, the intelligences are the higher, more pure 'thought form' of a soul, and the daemon is the mover. In Agrippa's chapter on the planetary tables,[7] the sigils of the planetary intelligences as for 'good' and the sigils for the planetary daemons as 'evil' are obviously meant to be used to benefic and malefic magic, I suspect, considering daemons are not equated as inherently evil in any other portion of the book, he also means that the intelligences as more pure and less corporeal, and the daemons as denser and more corporeal.

This is not to say there aren't evil daemons. Agrippa is quite clear that some spirits and daemons are good and some are evil. Good daemons tend to be helpful and are conducive to happiness and have life-giving properties. Evil daemons cause unhappiness, illness, strife, and death. In addition, as a whole Agrippa does not equate daemons with fallen angels.

Quoting Iamblichus, Agrippa describes[8] the threefold daemon (or

---

5 Agrippa, *Three Books of Philosophy* 3: 36.

6 Marsilio Ficino, *Platonic Theology*, tr. J. B. Allen, Michael. Tatti Renaissance Library, 2004 book 13: ch. 2.

7 Agrippa, *Three Books of Philosophy* 3:22

8 Agrippa, *Three Books of Philosophy*, Iamblichus *On the Mysteries*, tr. Taylor, Thomas London 1818 book 9:ch. 1.

genius) of man. The first is the sacred, the second is of the nativity, and the third is of the profession. When the genius or daemon of the profession or place agrees with the daemon or genius of the individual, success and happiness come easily. When these do not agree, success and happiness is difficult.

From this I believe it is heavily implied, and sometimes explicitly stated, that the dispositions of the planets in astrology show daemonic influences and can determined through astrological methods.

Thus in order to answer this question, we need to be able to identify the planet(s) ruling the nativity, and name the daemons themselves. Now we will discuss these various methods according to Agrippa and other sources.

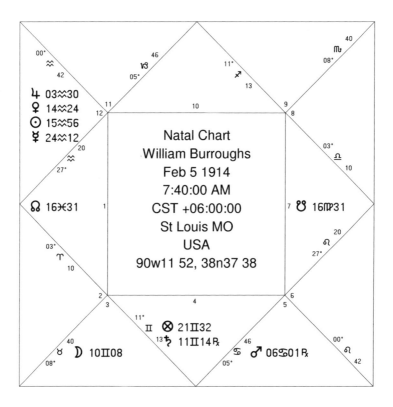

TECHNIQUES

The Ruler of the Chart

In book 3 chapter 21 of *The Occult Philosophy*, Agrippa[9] says that one can find the nature of their genius from the dispositions of the planets in the natal chart. Agrippa gives several methods, sometimes with no citations or little details, but we can read between the lines using medieval and classical astrological techniques. To understand these techniques, we must discuss some core concepts.

Because it is easier to understand these concepts with practical examples, we will use the natal chart of William Burroughs for illustration. I chose Burroughs because 1. his life is well documented and eventful, and 2. because we have a birth certificate, and thus an accurate chart. I am using the Alchabitius house system, because this was a popular house system from Agrippa's time and throughout medieval astrology—though we have no documentation of which system he actually used. What is certain, is that by the 16th century, most European astrologers used some quadrant house system.

Agrippa lists six methods:

> · The planet that is the lady of the nativity
> · The planet with the most dignities
> · The house that the Moon enters after the sign it is in at birth
> · The Sun or Moon
> · A certain angle of heaven or from all of them
> · The good genius from the eleventh house and the evil genius from the sixth

These techniques range from the Hellenistic period to the late medieval period. We will discuss each in turn.

Before we go further, we must discuss the concept of essential dignity more fully.

---

9 For this entire section, Agrippa quoted directly from Georgius' *Harmonia Mundi* Parisii 1545 cantici 3, tonus 1, chapter 9. As such, it is difficult to tell exactly what methods Agrippa may or may not have used if any.

Essential Dignities

In astrology, especially pre 19th century astrology, we must determine how a planet will exhibit its nature and its overall strength. The method we use for this is called essential dignity. There are five levels of "strength" in descending order: rulership, exaltation, triplicity, term, and face.

Each planet in each degree is in one or more dignities. In some cases an entire sign is dignified, sometimes part of a sign will be dignified, and it matters whether astrological chart is for a day or night birth or event. It might be easier to visualize with a table.

Sign	Ruler	Exalt.	Trip. D.	Trip. N.	Terms (Egyptian)					Face			Fall	Det.
♈	♂	☉	☉	♃	♃6	♀12	☿20	♂25	♄30	♂	☉	♀	♄	♀
♉	♀	☽	♀	☽	♀8	☿14	♃22	♄27	♂30	☿	☽	♄	✕	♂
♊	☿	✕	♄	☿	☿6	♃12	♀18	♂24	♄30	♃	♂	☉	✕	♃
♋	☽	♃	♀	♂	♂7	♀13	☿20	♃27	♄30	♀	☿	☽	♂	♄
♌	☉	✕	☉	♃	♃6	♀11	♄18	☿24	♂30	♄	♃	♂	✕	♄
♍	☿	☿	♀	☽	☿7	♀17	♃21	♂24	♄30	☉	♀	☿	♀	♃
♎	♀	♄	♄	☿	♄6	☿14	♃21	♀28	♂30	☽	♄	♃	☉	♂
♏	♂	✕	♀	♂	♂7	♀11	☿19	♃24	♄30	♂	☉	♀	☽	♀
♐	♃	✕	☉	♃	♃12	♀17	☿23	♄27	♂30	☿	☽	♄	✕	☿
♑	♄	♂	♀	☽	☿7	♃14	♀22	♄26	♂30	♃	♂	☉	♃	☽
♒	♄	✕	♄	☿	☿7	♀13	♃20	♂25	♄30	♀	☿	☽	✕	☉
♓	♃	♀	♀	♂	♀12	♃16	☿19	♂28	♄30	♄	♃	♂	☿	☿

How to read the table

Each sign has planets that rule it in five ways: ruler, exaltation, triplicity, term, and face.

One planet rules the entirety of each sign.

One planet may or may not be the exalted ruler of each sign. For instance, Aries' exalted ruler is the Sun, but Gemini has no exalted ruler.

There is a day triplicity ruler, and a night triplicity ruler. The one you use depends on if the chart is a day or night chart.

There are five term rulers for each sign. Each planet rules a portion of the sign. In this table, the number under the planet is the **last** degree that planet rules. Using Aries as an example, Jupiter is the term ruler from 0 degrees Aries to 6. Venus rules 6°01' to 12°, and so on.

Each sign has three face rulers, each ruling 10 degrees. In this table, the 1st planet rules the first 10 degrees, the 2nd rules the 2nd 10 degrees, and so on. For example, in Aries, Mars is the face ruler for 0° Aries to 10°. The Sun rules from 10°1' to 20°, and so on.

This table lists the rulers in descending levels of "strength": rulership is the most powerful, and face is the weakest.

It is possible for a planet to have no dignity. This is called peregrine, and while this can be an important consideration for delineation, this doesn't have much bearing for this article.

Detriment and fall in the last two columns are debilities, which are weaknesses, and for the purposes of this article will only be used for one technique later.

Example with William Burroughs' chart:

The Sun is at 15°56' Aquarius.

In the table, you will see that Aquarius' ruler is Saturn.

There is no exalted ruler for Aquarius.

Burroughs' chart is a day chart, and the day triplicity ruler is also Saturn.

At 15 degrees, the term ruler is Jupiter.

The face ruler is Mercury.

Thus at 15 degrees Aquarius, the Sun can be said to have three planets ruling it: Saturn, Jupiter, and Mercury. Notice the Sun doesn't rule any of the dignities, and is in detriment. This is a debility or weakness, but this is outside the scope of this article.

Now to return to the techniques.

The Planet that is the Lady of the Nativity

This is quoted from a short mention by Porphyry in his 39th epistle. Unfortunately Porphyry didn't explain how to determine this, but most likely Agrippa interpreted this as the planet that rules the rising sign. In the medieval and renaissance periods, the other method to determine the ruler of the nativity (the planet with most dignities) is the Agrippa's second choice, so the sign ruler is more likely here.

The ruler of the ascendant was traditionally the most often used as the significator for the chart or the person for whom the chart was made. The ascendant signifies the body and being of the individual.

Sun signs as a distinct identifier and technique is almost unheard of in Renaissance (and prior) astrology unless the Leo happened to be the rising sign. Sun signs were more common in the 19th century and beyond. Agrippa and Porphyry would never have used the Sun sign to identify the personal daemon.

In Burroughs' chart, the rising sign is Aquarius, so Saturn would also signify his personal daemon.

The Planet with the Most Dignities

There are two probably methods to find the planet with the most dignities. Agrippa lists Firmicus Maternus[10] as the source for this technique, but the technique changed dramatically by Agrippa's time, so it isn't clear which Agrippa preferred or even understood. There are two ways to do this. The first is closer to Maternus' method, and the second is the later medieval version. We will begin with the simplest.

Version 1

Since we know that there are several levels of rulerships and dignities, it might be tempting to automatically look at planets in sign rulership. However, as one can see in the essential dignities table, such as the Sun in Aries, one planet can hold several different dignities. While Mars is the sign ruler, the Sun is the exalted ruler, the day triplicity ruler, *and* the ruler of the second face of Aries. Mars also has three rulerships in Aries—sign ruler, one of the terms, and one of the face, the latter two dignities are weaker than two of the Sun's.

To make this easier to grasp, medieval Arabs developed a point system for the different dignities. Firmicus Maternus would not have used a point system, but the overall method is similar. The points given to the dignities are:

SIGN RULER =5 POINTS
EXALTED RULER = 4 POINTS

---

10 Firmicus Maternus, *Matheseos Libri VIII*, tr. Rhys-Bram, Jean, Astrology Classics, 2005, book 4. Ch. 19.

TRIPLICITY RULER = 3 POINTS

TERM RULER = 2 POINTS

FACE RULER = 1 POINT

We take a planet and determine which dignities that planet has and add the points together. The planet with the most points is the most dignified planet.

To make this easier, we will make a table of all 7 planets in the chart. Here is the list of planets in Burroughs' chart with all of their dignities. Remember, this is a day chart:

	SATURN	JUPITER	MARS	SUN	VENUS	MERC.	MOON
Sign R.							
Exalt.							
Trip.	3						
Term			2				
Face							
Total	3						

Saturn is again the significator. Burroughs' chart has several planets with no dignities. There are only two planets—Saturn and Mars with dignities. Saturn is in its triplicity, and Mars in term. Since triplicity is stronger than term, Saturn is more dignified.

Version 2

There is a more complex method, which was first described in the 12th century astrologer Abraham Ibn Ezra's *Book of Nativities*.[11] Instead of considering how dignified each planet is, we look at how many dignities a particular degree has regardless of which planet is actually there.

The planet which has the most dignities in any particular degree is called an *al-Mubtazz*[12] in medieval Arabic astrology, and later Latinized to *almuten* or *almutazz*. To illustrate this, imagine the Sun is at 16° Aries in a day chart. In the essential dignities table, we will consider every possible rulership for that degree in a day chart and add the points together:

---

11 Ibn Ezra, *The Book of Nativities* tr. Epstein, Meira, Arhat 2008 p. 13.
12 Al-Mubtazz means victor or ruler in Arabic.

SIGN RULER = MARS—5 POINTS

EXALTED RULER = THE SUN—4 POINTS

TRIPLICITY RULER = THE SUN—3 POINTS

TERM RULER = MERCURY—2 POINTS

FACE RULER = THE SUN—1 POINT

MARS = 5 POINTS

THE SUN = 8 POINTS

MERCURY = 2 POINTS

This is called a simple almuten—a ruler for one particular degree. At 16°
Aries, the Sun has the most dignities, even more than Aries' sign ruler
Mars, so the Sun can be said to rule that degree. To find the most dignified planet in a chart according to this almuten system, we use a *compound*
almuten.

Ibn Ezra explains that we find the ruler of the chart from finding the
most dignified planet amongst the degrees of the Sun, Moon, ascendant,
Part of Fortune, pre natal lunation,[13] plus 7 points for the planetary ruler
of the day, 6 points for the planetary ruler of the hour, and a list of points
for each house.

This might require some more explanation:

   · The degree of the pre-natal lunation can be found through al-
     most any astrological software or an ephemeris. Ephemerides
     might be confusing for novices, but there are many resources
     online that can help.
   · The planetary ruler of the day and hour can also be found in
     almost any astrological software. Some online tools might
     assist.
   · The point value of the houses is based on their relative
     "strength". In traditional astrology, some houses are seen as
     more powerful than others. The 1st house is the strongest, fol-
     lowed by the 10th, and the 6th house is the weakest. Here is a
     table showing these point values.

---

13 I.e. the degree of the new or full Moon just prior to birth. This is also called a *syzygy*
or a *syzygy ante nativitatem* (SAN in some astrological software).

House	1	10	7	4	11	5	2	9	8	3	12	6
Points	12	11	10	9	8	7	6	5	4	3	2	1

Finding the Almuten

We first make a table. An example for Burroughs' chart is below.

Make a column for each planet.
There is a row for each item listed above in Ibn Ezra's list.
Next we enter the point value for **every** dignity for that degree. Note that if a planet has more than one rulership for that degree, then we enter more than one point value. For example, for Burroughs' Sun, Saturn is the sign ruler (5 points) and the triplicity ruler (3 points), Jupiter is the term ruler (2 points), and Mercury is the Face ruler (1 point).

Then we give 7 points for the planetary day ruler and 6 points, both Jupiter, for the hour ruler.

Enter the appropriate points for the house each planet is in. For example, Saturn is in the 4th house, so we enter 9 points in the Saturn column. Note that traditional astrology has something called the "5 degree" rule, where if a planet is 5 degrees or less from the next house cusp, we consider that planet in the next house. In Burroughs' chart, Mercury is in the 12th house at 24° 12' Aquarius, and the 1st house is at 27° 20 Aquarius. Mercury is just over 3 degrees from the 1st house. We can thus consider Mercury as being in the 1st house even though he is physically placed in the 12th.

Finally add these points together, and the planet with the most points is the almuten of the chart.

Note: the pre-natal lunation is at 5° 29' Aquarius, and the day and hour ruler is Jupiter.

	SAT	JUP	MARS	SUN	VEN	MERC	MOON
Sun 15 Aqu 56	5, 3	2				1	
Moon 10 Gem 08	3	2	1			5	

	SAT	JUP	MARS	SUN	VEN	MERC	MOON
ASC 27 Aqu 20	5, 3, 2						1
POF 21 Gem 32	3		2	1		5	
Lunation 5 Aqu 29	5, 3				1	2	
House Dig.	9	8	7	8	8	12	9
Day Ruler		7					
Hour Ruler		6					
Totals	33	23	10	9	9	24	10

Saturn is the almuten of the chart. What is interesting about this technique, is that it is possible for the almuten to be an entirely unexpected planet—one that does not rule the ascendant, or even one that is essentially dignified. An almuten can be a planet that is weak and afflicted, and in natal astrology, this can be a valuable insight. For magical purposes, this can uncover the true power behind the horoscope in surprising ways.

I suspect Agrippa favored this method because it was a common technique in medieval astrology, and he was certainly familiar with Ibn Ezra, as *Book of Nativities* was quoted several times throughout *Occult Philosophy*.

The House that the Moon Enters after the Sign it is in at Birth

Agrippa again sourced Firmicus Maternus for this method. This is a relatively simple technique, though not worded in a very clear way.

In the astrology of Greece and Rome, houses and signs were essentially overlapped in an astrological chart. If your ascendant was in Aries, then the entire 1st house was Aries, the 2nd house was Taurus, and so on. In later Hellenistic and then medieval astrology, astrologers developed different house systems, and ways of dividing the chart and Sun's ecliptic, so that houses were independent from the signs. However, medieval astrological literature continued to call signs houses and both were used interchangeably. Consequently, one has to read between the lines to discern whether a house or a sign is intended.

In this case, a sign is almost certainly intended, mostly from the wording of using both sign and house in the same sentence, but also because astrological literature, especially medieval, commonly considers sign placement rather than house placement for several other considerations.

The other area of confusion is that a sign wouldn't be a significator for a daemon. Signs in traditional astrology were used differently than modern, in that signs are rarely significators, though there are some exceptions. Planets are generally the first choice. What seems to be intended here is the planet that is the sign ruler for the Moon's next sign.

In Burroughs' chart, the Moon is at 10° 8' Gemini. The next sign the Moon enters is Cancer, which is ruled by the Moon.

The Moon is the significator of the daemon.

The Sun or Moon

The source for this is unclear as this is credited to the Chaldeans.

Since this can be either the Sun *or* Moon, then there must be some way to decide which planet is the best significator. Typically this would be either by essential dignity, house placement, or both if there is a conflict. We have previously discussed both of these concepts above.

In Burroughs' chart, the Sun is afflicted by detriment, and the Moon is peregrine (no dignity). Peregrine, while weak, is still better than detriment, so the Moon is preferred here.

If the two planets happened to have the same dignity, we would then consider house placement. The Moon is in the 3rd house, and the Sun in the 12th. The 3rd house is a stronger house than the 12th, so the Moon would again win out.

The Moon is the significator.

A Certain Angle of Heaven or From All of Them

This is attributed to the Hebrews with no other citation, so the source is unknown.

The angles in astrology are the four cardinal direction houses—i.e. the 1st, 10th, 7th, and 4th houses. Since Agrippa says "a certain angle or all of them", he implies two techniques.

TECHNIQUE 1

By "certain" angle, I suspect he means the angular house with the most dignities. Since signs themselves cannot be dignified or likely significators, then we must identify a planet. This is accomplished with a simple almuten table for each house, again using Burroughs' chart:

1ST HOUSE	SAT	JUP	MARS	SUN	VENUS	MERC.	MOON
27 Aqu 20	5, 3, 2						1
Total	10						1

10th house	SAT	JUP	MARS	SUN	VENUS	MERC.	MOON
11 Sag 13		5, 2		3			1
Total		7		3			1

7th house	Sat	Jup	Mars	Sun	Venus	Merc.	Moon
27 Leo 20	1		2	5, 3			
Total	1		2	8			

4th house	SAT	JUP	MARS	SUN	VENUS	MERC.	MOON
11 Gem 13	3	2	1			5	
Total	3	2	1			5	

Taking the planets with the most point in each angle separately, the 1st house has Saturn at 10 points, the 10th has Jupiter with 7, the 7th house has the Sun with 8, and the 4th has Mercury with 5.

Saturn is the significator.

TECHNIQUE 2

To find the most dignified planet over *all* of the angles, we must create a complex almuten table similar to what we did above for the chart almuten, except by using four the angles only:

	SAT	JUP	MARS	SUN	VENUS	MERC	MOON
1st house 27 Aqu 20	5, 3, 2						1
10th house 11 Sag 13		5, 2		3			1

	SAT	JUP	MARS	SUN	VENUS	MERC	MOON
7th house 27 Leo 20	1		2	5, 3			
10th house 11 Gem 13	3	2	1			5	
Total	14	9	3	11		5	2

Saturn is the significator.

The Good Genius from the Eleventh House and the Evil Genius from the Sixth

There is no cited source for this, however the Roman astrologer Firmicus Maternus called these the houses of the good and evil spirits respectively. More generally, the 11th house is the house of friends, groups, and hope, and the 6th is the house of illness.

Quite simply, the planet that rules the sign on the 11th house, signifies the good daemon, and the planet that rules the sign on the 6th house signifies the evil.

In Burroughs' chart, the 11th house is in Capricorn, and the 6th house is in Leo. Thus the good daemon is signified by Saturn, and the evil daemon is signified by the Sun.

This concludes the explanation of the six techniques for finding the planetary significator for the personal daemon as given by Agrippa. While William Burroughs' chart overwhelmingly prefers Saturn as the significator in most of these methods, do not let this example make you think the significator will be so consistent in every chart. Often there can be multiple possible significators among the different techniques, so it is up to the practitioner to make their own conclusions of what is the best.

Planetary Natures

This will be a brief discussion on planetary natures, but this subject can be very complex and large. Astrology books customarily contain long lists of planetary rulerships, correspondences, and natures. This section will briefly summarize common descriptions of the natures.

What is the purpose of this? Quite simply, when you identify the planetary significator of your daemon, the nature of the planet gives you a clue of the nature of the daemon. Note, this list is very basic, but once one is familiar with the essential dignities, they can fine-tune these characters even more.

Saturn is cold and dry and rules old age, wisdom, death, is solitary and slow, and is a co-ruler of astrology and magic. He is the greater malefic and his day is Saturday.

Jupiter is warm and moist, pleasant, moderate, generous, rules justice, law, and reason. He is the greater benefic and his day is Thursday.

Mars is hot and dry, wrathful, rules soldiers and weapons, blood, cutting, and fire. He is the lesser malefic and his day is Tuesday.

The Sun is hot and dry, honorable, rules kings and leaders, good judgment, and is sumptuous. He is both benefic and malefic and his day is Sunday.

Venus is cool and moist, rules love, younger women, jewels, music and musical instruments, art, games. She is the lesser benefic and her day is Friday.

Mercury has a variable nature and has a quick wit, loves learning, business, and is the co-ruler of astrology and magic. He is malefic when with malefics, and benefic when with benefics and his day is Wednesday.

The **Moon** is cool and moist and rules messengers and older women, sailors and the sea, hunters, a wavering and eclectic disposition, peaceful. She is both malefic and benefic and her day is Monday.

Picatrix gives some additional natures,[14] dividing the planets into three categories. the animal, natural, and rational spirit.

- · The natural spirit is signified by the Moon and Venus, and is a lover of food and drink, and physical delights.
- · The animal spirit is signified by the Sun and Mars and is a lover of conquering others and aggression.
- · The rational spirit is signified by Jupiter and Mercury and is a lover of knowledge, intellect, and goodness.

Saturn is missing from this list, perhaps because he rules the occult and is the most superior of the traditional planets.

While these lists are not exhaustive, my hope is that this will start an investigation into the natures of the planets, and in turn the personal daemons. Agrippa scatters this information throughout the *Occult Philosophy*,

14 *Picatrix* book 4: ch. 5

but some other good sources are *Picatrix*, William Lilly *Christian Astrology*,[15] al-Biruni *The Book of Instruction in the Elements of the Art of Astrology*,[16] and Guido Bonatti *The Book of Astronomy*.[17] There is no one book that explains everything. Instead, astrologers tended to give long lists of attributes and correspondences from which one must read between the lines to gather a full picture.

Finding the name of the good and evil daemons

Once the significator is identified, the name of the good and evil daemons must be found. Agrippa detailed a series of techniques in *Occult Philosophy* book 3 chapter 26. As with finding the significators, there are several methods to finding the names. Before explaining these further, all of these techniques have one thing in common: overlaying an alphabet on the zodiac.

Agrippa clearly preferred the Hebrew alphabet, as this is the only alphabet he mentions in this section. He also says to end the name with a Hebrew suffix of *iah* or *el* to the end of the name, as these suffixes refer to divinity. However one can use any alphabet they wish. Agrippa writes about the Latin and Greek alphabets in book 2 chapters 18–20, but what seems to matter is that there are also numerical correspondences to each of the letters, because once numbers are identified, then sigils can be made.

Casting the alphabet

Agrippa gives slightly different ways of doing this depending on the method used. Most of this listed techniques require the alphabet to be cast from the degree of the ascendant. He says to cast it from the horoscope, which is another name for the ascending degree. From this point, place one letter of the alphabet, Hebrew in this case, on each degree around the zodiac in the order of the signs (clockwise), repeating all the way around until you return back to the ascendant.

For example in Burroughs' chart, his ascendant is at 27° Aquarius. The first letter in the Hebrew alphabet is א. The next degree is 28° Aquarius

15 William Lilly, *Christian Astrology*, London 1647.

16 al-Biruni, *The Book of Instruction in the Elements of the Art of Astrology*, tr. Wright, Ramsay, British Museum 1933.

17 Guido Bonatti *The Book of Astronomy*, tr. Dykes, Benjamin. Cazimi Press, 2007.

which would have the letter ב, the next is 28° Aquarius ג, and so on. Each of the 22 letters cycle through the chart until you reach the last degree before the ascendant. This is the order for the good daemon.

The evil daemon uses the opposite order starting with the cusp of the 7th house which is opposite the ascendant, and move *against* the order of the zodiac or counterclockwise. For example, Burroughs' 7th house is at 27° Leo. Place א there. The previous degree is 26° Leo with ב, then 25° Leo with ג, and so on.

There is one exception to this system, which we will point out at that time.

Agrippa gives four ways to find the names, which we will discuss in turn:

- The almuten of the angels of heaven.
- The good daemon from the almuten of the 11th house, and the evil daemon from the almuten of the 12th.
- From the five hylegical places.
- From the almuten of the five hylegical places.

The almuten of the angels of heaven

This is the same almuten found above in technique 2 of "a certain angle of heaven...". Here is the almuten table for Burroughs' chart:

	SAT	JUP	MARS	SUN	VENUS	MERC	MOON
1st house 27Aqu20	5, 3, 2						1
10th house 11Sag13		5, 2		3			1
7th house 27Leo20	1		2	5, 3			
10th house 11Gem13	3	2	1			5	
Total	14	9	3	11		5	2

The almuten here is Saturn. Saturn is at 11° Gemini. The Hebrew letter on that degree for the good daemon is פ. Agrippa instructs us to add a monosyllabic name of divine omnipotence at the end such as "el" or "iah". Thus the good daemon for Burroughs, if we use el, would be פאל. The evil daemon for that degree is כ, or כאל. Pronunciations are approximate due to the sometimes "irrational" nature of these names.

The good daemon from the almuten of the 11th house, and the evil daemon from the almuten of the 12th

We must find the almuten for the degree of the 11th and 12th house cusps. As these are simple almutens, tables are not needed.

Dignities for the 11th house at 5° Capricorn:

```
SATURN—5
JUPITER—1
MARS—4
SUN
VENUS—3
MERCURY—2
MOON
```

Saturn is the almuten of the 11th house. This is the same as good daemon above, thus Burroughs' good daemon is פאל.

The dignities for the 12th house at 0° Aquarius:

```
SATURN—5, 3
JUPITER—
MARS—
SUN
VENUS—1
MERCURY—2
MOON
```

Saturn is the almuten of the 12th house. Again this is the same as the evil daemon above, thus Burroughs' evil daemon is כאל.

From the five hylegical places

These next two techniques are quite different than the others. First let's discuss the hylegical places.

In pre-modern astrology, it was customary to identify a planet (usually the Sun or Moon, but it could be other planets or points) as the *hyleg*. The hyleg can be seen as planet that signifies the life of the person, and is an important planet that is used in death calculations and finding sensitive times for illness.

The hylegical places are five points on the chart that signify life as well. These five points vary among astrological writers, but most agree that they are the degrees of:

- The ascendant
- The Sun
- The Moon
- Part of Fortune
- Pre-natal lunation

Note the similarity with the complex chart almuten above. It is also notable that these five points (with the addition of the 10th house or midheaven) are also used in the traditional timing system used in most pre-modern astrology called primary directions.

Instead of finding a single-letter name, minus the divine suffix mentioned by Agrippa, this will result in a five-letter name.

What also makes this different is alphabet scheme. For this method, rather than casting the alphabet from the ascendant, we cast it from the beginning of Aries. Thus in every astrological chart we use this technique with, 0° Aries will always be א, א Aries will always be ב, and so on for the good daemon.

For the evil daemon cast from 29° Pisces, and work backwards against the order of the signs, so 29° Pisces is א and 28° Pisces is ב. Instead of using the letters of the five hylegical points themselves, we use the points *opposite* the five hylegicals. For instance, if a planet is at 0° Aries, we use the letter on the degree of 0° Libra.

For Burroughs' chart, the five hylegicals with their corresponding letters are:
- The ascendant—27° Aquarius ר
- The Sun—15° Aquarius ח
- The Moon—10° Gemini ר
- Part of Fortune—21° Gemini ע
- Pre-natal lunation—5° Aquarius ר

Assembled with "el", Burroughs' good daemon's name is רחרערא‎ל.

For the evil daemon, we first find the degrees opposite the five hylegical places mentioned above:

· Opposite the ascendant—27° Leo ס
· Opposite the Sun—15° Leo ה
· Opposite the Moon—10° Sagittarius ג
· Opposite the Part of Fortune—21° Sagittarius ג
· Opposite the pre-natal lunation—5° Leo ס

Assembled with "el", Burroughs' evil daemon is ל׳אסהנגס.

From the almuten of the five hylegical places

Once again we must make an almuten table. This will be a single-letter name, and we will cast the alphabet from 0° Aries for the good daemon and 29° Pisces for the evil.

The basis of this almuten table is the five hylegical points. However, for the evil daemon, we do not use the points opposite the hylegicals.

	SATURN	JUPITER	MARS	SUN	VENUS	MERCURY	MOON
27° Aqu	5, 3, 2						1
15° Aqu	5, 3	2				1	
10° Gem	3	2	1			5	
21° Gem	3		2	1		5	
5° Aqu	5, 3				1	2	
Totals	32	4	3	1	1	13	1

The almuten is Saturn which is at 11° Gemini

Burroughs' good daemon with "el" is ויאל, and his evil daemon is גאל.

Conclusion

As with many traditional magical systems, there are multiple variations of individual techniques. *The Occult Philosophy* shows different methods, sometimes with similar results, sometimes with variable results. It is up to the practitioner to work with the system that makes sense to them.

Agrippa does not give instruction of what one does with these daemons. I suspect that once the significators are chosen, and their names discovered, they can act as a focus for ritual and meditation. Another possibility is to use the daemon as a significator for spiritual considerations in natal delineations, and as showing the true nature of a person as *Picatrix* implies, especially with the chart almuten.

In addition, the planetary sigils in book 2 ch. 22 in *Occult Philosophy* can be used to ensoul an image or talisman with the personal daemon. Using the same logic as shown in that chapter, unique sigils can be made by using the good and evil names of the personal daemon.

Another application is as part of the delineation of a natal chart. The combination of the chart almuten, with other considerations not mentioned in this article, such as the ruler of the 9th house (spirituality and religion and God), the ruler of the 3rd house (the Goddess), the ruler of the 11th (the Good Daemon), and the ruler of the 12th (the Evil Daemon), often inform other areas of life, linking spiritual and mundane matters.

An important key to understanding and research into the techniques of pre–modern astrology and magic is to take them on their own terms, rather than imprinting our modern worldviews on them. While initially difficult, this will lead to more practical and concrete predictions and results.

Agrippa is a representative of the nexus between astrology and magic. Today these are often seen as separate disciplines, this wasn't always the case. Astrology is the 'language' of medieval and renaissance European textual magic, and to many astrologers of that period, magic was the application of astrology. Breaking up the divisions that seem to lie between astrology and magic today will open new ways of understanding them. While the practical application of using the daemon is somewhat open, now with recent translations of traditional material available to us, we can now investigate these with new and informed eyes.

*   *

*

The Azured Vault

Astrological Magic in Seventeenth-century England

Al Cummins, PhD

ALTHOUGH DEBATES ABOUT the precise influence and nature of the stars arguably became increasingly heated in the early modern period,[1] it can nevertheless still be said "belief in natural astrology was almost universal in Tudor England."[2] The seventeenth century arguably marked a zenith in its popularity and utility.[3] Lifted restrictions on printing presses in the middle part of the century led to "several years of virtually complete freedom

---

1 See D.C. Allen, *The Star-Crossed Renaissance: The Quarrel about Astrology and its Influence in England.* London, 1966; Richard Dunn, 'The Status of Astrology in Elizabethan England 1558–1603', (Ph.D. thesis, University of Cambridge, 1992); Brian Copenhaver, 'Natural Magic, Hermetism, and Occultism in Early Modern Science', in David Linberg & Robert Westman (eds.), *Reappraisals of the Scientific Revolution.* Cambridge, 1990, pp. 261–301. For specific debate around sigils and astrological images, see Anna Marie Roos, 'Israel Hiebner's Astrological Amulets and the English Sigil War', *Culture and Cosmos*, 6, 2: pp. 17–43.

2 Bernard Capp, *Astrology and the Popular Press: English Almanacs 1500–1800.* London, 1979, 31.

3 For more on seventeenth-century English astrology and its environmental, political, and social functions—as well as its ties with occult philosophy and magical practice—see Alexander Cummins, *The Starry Rubric: Astrology and Magic in Seventeenth–Century England.* Milton Keynes, 2012.

of the press",[4] and the resultant print 'explosion' made almanacs, translations, and typeset versions of occult manuscripts (which had already been
circulating privately around Europe) more available than ever before.[5]
Seventeenth-century English folk learned their astrological magic from
handbooks,[6] almanacs,[7] herbals and kitchen physic manuals,[8] as well as
treatises on natural magic and occult philosophy and grimoires of ritual
magic.[9] Such learning and experimentation is evidenced not least in the
manuscripts and workbooks of various kinds of early modern magicians.[10]

Seventeenth-century England is also an important period to examine
in the history of astrological magic, as these records—from both personal and professional correspondence, as well as private diary and journal
notes, and even patient case-files—of particular sets of affiliations of magical and astrological practitioners sharing information, teaching their trade,

4 Christopher Hill, *Some Intellectual Consequences of the English Revolution.* London,
1980, p. 7
5 For solid foundations in print and social history of astrology, the exemplars are
still Capp's *Astrology and the Popular Press* and Keith Thomas, *Religion and the Decline of
Magic.* London, 1971.
6 See, for example, William Lilly, *Christian Astrology.* London, 1647 and Henry Coley,
Clavis Astrologiae Elimata: or a Key to the Whole Art of Astrology New Filed and Polished.
London, 1676.
7 These ranged from mainly calendrical pamphlets of 'common notes and moouable
Feasts', such as Daniel Browne, *A New Almanacke.* London, 1620, to polemical political
and theological tracts, like John Booker, *The Bloody Almanack.* London, 1642.
8 See Nicholas Culpeper, *The English Physitian.* London, 1652 and Joseph Blagrave,
Astrological Practice of Physick. London, 1671.
9 See Jean Baptiste Porta, *Natural Magick.* London, 1658 and, most importantly, Heinrich Cornelius Agrippa, *Three Books of Occult Philosophy*, trans. 'J.F.' London, 1651, which
since its initial complete publication in Cologne in 1533 had also been 'accessible and
widely considered by English intellectuals during the sixteenth and early seventeenth
centuries.' Owen Davies, *Popular Magic: Cunning-folk in English History.* New York, 2007,
122. The 'pseudo–Agrippan' *Fourth Book of Occult Philosophy*, trans. Robert Turner (London, 1665) included the *Heptameron*, a popular system of planetary angel conjuration.
10 See the decrypted diary entries in C. H. Josten (ed), *Elias Ashmole (1617–1692):
his autobiographical and historical notes, his correspondence, and other contemporary sources
relating to his life and work.* Oxford, 1966 and Michael Hunter & Annabel Gregory (eds),
An astrological diary of the seventeenth century: Samuel Jeake of Rye, 1652–1699, ed. Oxford, 1988. For a transcription of a seventeenth-century magical practitioner's working
notebook of charms, conjurations and prayers, along with tables of correspondences,
recipes, and copied sections from grimoires and books of occult philosophy, see David
Rankine (ed.), *The Grimoire of Arthur Gauntlet.* London, 2011, which presents and an-
notates MS Sloane 3851.

and passing on their papers and their magical objects.[11] The most central figures in these cross–generational seventeenth-century "networks" of astrologer magicians are Simon Forman (1552–1611), Richard Napier (1559–1634), William Lilly (1602–1681), and Elias Ashmole (1617–1692), but the wider lines of transmission and influence clearly extended out further to many other practitioners. As but two pertinent examples of this such networking, we know the highly regarded Arabic manual of astrological magic, the *Picatrix*, was shared, copied, studied and passed on between practitioners;[12] and that in 1611 Forman sent Napier some of his brass moulds with which to cast astrological sigils, along with instructions for use and reflections on practice.[13]

Astrological knowledge and practice could be found in many—indeed, I would argue *any*—areas of seventeenth–century English life. Almanacs contained agricultural information on best times to 'plough, sow, geld animals or fell timber',[14] and it was quipped that an almanac without weather predictions was 'like a Pudding without Sewet, or a Christmas-pye without Plums.'[15] During the Civil Wars, both sides had paid astrologers as both intelligencers—deriving private political and military advice from the overhanging promontory—and public propagandists.[16] Astrologer

11 See Lauren Kassell, *Medicine and Magic in Elizabethan London: Simon Forman—Astrologer, Alchemist, and Physician* (Oxford, 2005), 215, 229; Michael MacDonald, *Mystical Bedlam: Madness, Anxiety and Healing in Seventeenth Century England* (Cambridge, 1981), 213; also Josten, *Ashmole*, 1208, 1454–5, 1663–4.

12 In 1592, for instance, Forman made his own copy of the *Picatrix* (MS Ashm 244, f. 97), and on 5 January 1648, Ashmole records (in cipher) delivering a copy of the *Picatrix* to William Lilly. (MS Ashm 1136, f. 184). We also have records of Forman's notes from *Picatrix* in his writings and calculations (MS Ashm 244, ff. 45, 97; Ashm 431, ff. 146–146v; Ashm 1491, p. 1128), including quoting it in his biblical commentary on Genesis, alongside Augustine and others (MS Ashm 802, ff. 3–12, 1–2; for further on the unusual foliation of this rebound document, see Kassell, *Medicine and Magic*, 194 n 21), and drawing on this text in his own expositions of natural magic, alongside Hermes, Paracelsus and others (MS Sloane 3822, ff. 68–75; MS Ashm 244, ff. 35–60). For more on this reception and circulation of *Picatrix*, see David Pingree (ed.), *Picatrix: The Latin Version of the Ghayat al-hakim*, Studies for the Warburg Institute, 39 (1986), xix, liii–lv.

13 MS Ashm 240, f. 106.

14 Capp, *Almanacs*, 63.

15 Adam Martindale, *Country Almanack For the Year 1676* (London, 1676), sig. B 2.

16 See Harry Rusche, 'Merlini Anglici: Astrology and Propaganda from 1644 to 1651', *English Historical Review*, 80 (1965): 322–333; Patrick Curry, *Power and Prophecy* (Cambridge, 1989); W.E. Burns, 'A Whig Apocalypse: Astrology, Millenarianism, and Politics in England During the Restoration Crisis, 1678–1683', in J.E Force & R. H. Popkin (eds.),

physicians were not only the cheapest medical practitioners available but, considering they were the first doctors to keep patient case–files and that the most popular alternative diagnostic technique was uroscopy, the most empirical and nuanced in their healing practices.[17] Finally, magical practitioners from all walks of life and social classes—including the folk magicians called 'cunning-men' or 'wise-women'—engaged with astrology and astrological magic in their popular divination practices (chiefly it seems to find lost items and offer advice for the lovelorn), to construct magic items and to conjure spirits.[18]

It is these last two features that I wish to concentrate upon in this chapter: the variety and vivification of astrological magical items. We will examine how the immaterial was approached through the material to consider some of the astrological dimensions of adjuration, 'Invocation', and theurgic angel summoning through the tools of conjuration and sigil–craft. These are the two reflections of Prospero's *Azured Vault* offered here: Below, the Keys wrought from the worldly; Above, the Leap 'twixt Heavens and Earth.

Millenarianism and Messianism in Early Modern European Culture: The Millenarian Turn (London, 2001).

17 See Kassell, *Medicine and Magic* and MacDonald, *Mystical Bedlam*. See also Michael MacDonald, 'The Career of Astrological Medicine in England', in *Religio Medici: Medicine and Religion in Seventeenth-century England*, ed. O. P. Grell & A. Cunningham (Aldershot, 1996), 62.

18 See Charles Burnett, 'Talismans: Magic as Science? Necromancy among the Seven Liberal Arts' in Charles Burnett (ed.), *Magic and Divination in the Middle Ages: Texts and Technicians in the Islamic and Christian Worlds* (Aldershot, 1996), 1–15; Richard Kieckhefer, *Forbidden Rites: A Necromancer's Manual of the Fifteenth Century* (Pennsylvania State University, 1998); Stephen Wilson, *The Magical Universe: Everyday Ritual and Magic in Pre–Modern Europe* (London, 2004); Don C. Skemer, *Binding Words: Textual Amulets in the Middle Ages* (Pennsylvania, 2006); Owen Davies, *Grimoires: A History of Magic Books* (Oxford, 2009), as well as Davies' previously mentioned *Popular Magic*. For the role of astrology in early modern manuscript copies of older grimoires, see MS Sloane 3826 collected in Don Karr & Stephen Skinner (eds.) *Sepher Raziel: Liber Salomonis, A Sixteenth-Century English Grimoire* (London, 2010) and Stephen Skinner & David Rankine (eds.), *The Goetia of Dr Rudd* (London, 2007*)*, which collects 'Liber Malorum Spirituum seu Goetia' from MS Harley 6483 with MS Harley MS 6482, MS Sloane 3824 and MS Wellcome 3203.

KEYS OF THE AZURED VAULT: TOOLS OF
ASTROLOGICAL *MATERIA*

HERBS

The most obvious *materia* of astrological magic are plants. Early modern herbals understood and utilised the potencies of natural materials in terms of their inhering occult virtues; that is, imbued by an expressly astrological cosmogony, and thereby arranged into astrological taxonomies. It was outlined that God, as "beginning of all Vertues...gives the seal of the Idea's to his servants the Intelligencies", who themselves empower 'the Heavens, and Stars, as instruments' whereby the potencies and affective properties of nature are 'conveyed' to instil "all Vertue of Stones, Hearbs, Metals, and all other things."[19] Thus, "from the tempers of the Elements disposed, answering the influencies of the Heavens, by which the Elements themselves are ordered, or disposed",[20] all things received their virtues from astral sources. Astrological understanding and engagement with the world itself underlay early modern ecology. The power of the stars burned in every blossoming of Nature.

Such virtues might not even appear expressly astrological. The 'astro-magus' and geomancer John Heydon (1629–1667) claimed "the signatures of plants, which indeed respects us more properly and adequately then the other, and is a Key (as Rosie Crucians say) to enter man into the knowledge and use of the Treasures of nature": for example, the kernel of walnuts "is good for the Brains, which it resembles."[21] We should however bear in mind this operational magical principle underlay zodiacal magic itself, as the Signs are thusly considered 'either for their properties [i.e. virtues] they hold with living Creatures, or by reason of the situation of the Starres in those places which somewhat resemble that effigies and *similitude* of living creatures."[22] Awareness of the principle and particularities of signature was to be literate in the language of nature's affectivities; to write in such a language was to perform magic, to utilise the hidden properties and effects of nature.

---

19 Agrippa, *Three Books*, 30.
20 Ibid., 30–31.
21 John Heydon, *A New Method of Rosie Crucian Physick*. London, 1658, 24
22 Lilly, *Christian Astrology*, 87.

However, the astrological magical utilities of herbs are perhaps best exemplified—and certainly most crucial to seventeenth-century medicine—in *sympathia* and *antipathia*: arguably the crux about which magical remediations were affected. Thus the famed herbalist and astrologer Nicholas Culpeper (1616–1654) details the applications of "Carduus Benedictus, or blessed Thistle...a herb of Mars, and under the sign Aries:"[23] not only could this plant be useful against "infirmities of the Gall, because Mars governs Choller", but it also 'strengthens memory, and cures deafness [a Saturnine condition] by Antipathy to Saturn, who hath his fall in Aries, which rules the head.'[24] The web of interrelations constructed by astrological rulerships, correspondences and symbolic comprehensions meant sympathy and antipathy were profoundly useful and eminently practical magical principles.

Sympathy and antipathy are, of course, central to the very operation of magic. Magic itself is defined as, *inter alia*, 'the differing, and agreement of things with themselves.'[25] Given proper deployment and utilisation of virtues, such differing and agreement generate essential forces of push and pull that a canny astrological magician could use to achieve miraculous things. Sympathy was a means of integrating strategies for engagement and interrelation into a cosmological and thoroughly magical worldview.

Charm–Packets

Not only were plants bearing particular remediating virtues used to compose medicaments to be taken as pills or even poultices, herbs could also be used as talismans, and astrologer physician Joseph Blagrave (1610–1682) even recommended 'in the curing of all kinds of evils, I do usually cause the patients to wear a select number of Solary herbs gathered at the hour of the Sun'.[26] Transfer of properly cultivated and innervated astral virtues was still the key affective utility, whether by ingestion or more subtle contagion.

The yellow–flowered St Johns Wort (*Hypericum perforatum*) was a particularly popular solar herb. Simon Forman recommended hypericon 'against haunting and frenzy if worn around the neck.'[27] Culpeper seems to even find its Solar and Leonine qualities in its typical habitat ("in Woods and

---

23 Culpeper, *English Physitian*, * a 3.
24 Ibid., * a 3.
25 Agrippa, *Three Books*, p. 5.
26 Blagrave, *Astrological Physic*, p. 156.
27 Kassell, *Medicine and Magic*, 188; MS Ashm 1494, p. 568

Copses...open to the Sun") and the very elections for its cultivation: 'their seed is ripe in the latter end of July or August.'[28] It was also explicated, "it resists all Putrefaction by its Solar Virtue."[29] Many magical practitioners would employ 'paper charms to protect against evil spirits, frustrate the malevolence of witches, and soothe troubled minds': such charms have been characterised as generally including "pseudo-scriptural prayer and the names of God and the archangels...'in a little paper close written and tied with taffeta with a leaf of mugwort or St John's wort' and worn around the patient's neck."[30]

Early modern English astrological magic utilised and combined with Christian cosmological frameworks—especially angelology—and natural-magical herbalism in its techniques for gaining knowledge and affecting the world. Indeed, the Scriptural passages formed crucial components of magicians' "astral talismans and parchment charms to protect their clients from witchcraft", "based ultimately on religious beliefs and practices"; indeed, "to many villagers they seemed consistent with popular piety."[31] After all, every 'wonderfull vertue, and operation in every Hearb, and Stone' came from "a Star, beyond which, even from the governing Intelligencies every thing receiveth, and obtains many things for itself, especially from the Supream Cause' Almighty God."[32]

SEALS

While powerful magics could be worked with "the Influence of Herbs and Roots, they are not esteem'd so strong as the Metals",[33] for "Metals do best of all help; being prepared and used in due time and means."[34] Astrological *sigils*—from which Austin Osman Spare must have derived his (typically idiosyncratic) terminology and influence upon later chaos magic—were specific markings cast in metal, and generally the size of coins.[35] The fa-

---

28 Culpeper, *English Physition*, p. 119.

29 Israel Hiebner, *Mysterium Sigillorum, Herbarum & Lapidum*. London, 1698, p. 89.

30 MacDonald, *Mystical Bedlam*, 214; MS Ashm. 1473, f. 619, 659; see also Thomas, *Religion*, pp. 186–7.

31 Ibid., p. 176.

32 Agrippa, *Three Books*, 31.

33 Hiebner, *Mysterium Sigillorum*, 100.

34 *Paracelsus of the Supreme Mysteries of Nature*, trans. Robert Turner. London, 1655, 99.

35 Lilly described a sigil owned by his mistress as "of the bigness of a thirty-three shilling piece of King James' coin." William Lilly, *History of His Life and Times* (London,

miliar planetary metals were utilised: lead for Saturn; tin for Jupiter; Sun, gold; Venus, copper; Mercury, quicksilver (or, occasionally, alloys); and the Moon, silver.[36] Magical utility of particular metals was explicated more specifically:

> *Quicksilver hath power of and over enchanting and enchanted. Led hath power over witchcraft. Copper hath power of binding. Tyne against thunder lightining and diseases. Silver dothe preserve and hath power in magik and enchantment. Yron doth bind and command and threaton.*[37]

So a copper sigil of Venusian Libra could be given as "an admirable Remedy against all Bewitchings of Women, which hinder the act of generation, and especially in those whom they hate."[38] Moreover, the instructions for this sigil's framing demonstrate a particularly astrological (especially electional) metallurgy:

> *This Sigil is to be made of pure {Venus} [i.e. copper], and to be melted, poured out and made when the Sun enters Libra, which somtimes happens on Sunday the 13 or 14 of September, according to the progress of the yeer: And this is to be noted, That when Venus is the ruling Planet, or Reservator of the yeer, the Sigil will be of much more virtue, especially if those wear it, who were born under the same Planet; and if it be made and prepared for them. When {Venus} is in the sign Libra, the Signes, Characters, and Words which you see in the following Figure, are to be engraven in the Seal; afterwards in the day and hour of Venus, in the first or eighth hour, which Venus governs, let it be applied.*[39]

Finally, metals and herbs could be combined, as with the *zenexton*—a paste combining animal, mineral, and botanical ingredients sealed in a stamped metal case worn as a medallion against the plague—which seems to been especially popular throughout the seventeenth century.[40] In returning to

---

1715), 32.

36 Agrippa, *Three Books*, 75, 80, 83, 86, 89, 94, 258. These were also found in standard astrological handbooks and books of medical sigils alike. Lilly, *Christian Astrology*, 60, 64, 68, 72, 75, 79, 82; *Supreme Mysteries*, 3.

37 MS Ashm 1494, pp. 483–44.

38 *Supreme Mysteries*, 146–47.

39 Ibid., 146.

40 Martha R. Baldwin 'Toads and Plague: The Amulet Controversy in Seventeenth-

the interrelation of herbal medicaments and cast metal amulets, the term *seal* was indeed appropriate, given that 'some astrological physicians, including Napier, supplied their patients with astral sigils bearing the symbol of an appropriate astrological entity with which they were to stamp their medicines before taking them.'[41] Marking in such a manner both demonstrates the general array of occult preparations and consecrations of magical medicines—which might also include incantations or written charms—as well as further highlighting the importance of *impressionability* as an affective principle in occult philosophical conceptions of the imagination.[42]

SIGIL-BAGS AND KAMEA

Astrological charm-bags were detailed by astrologer mathematician Israel Hiebner (1619–1668): a planetary sigil was cast in its metal which had been mixed with suitable ingredients while molten (such as protective rue for Jupiter, sharp urine and vinegar for Mars, soft 'Fat, Wax or Honey' for Venus), stamped or engraved, and then put in a colour-coded silk bag—black for Saturn, blue for Jupiter, red for Mars, "golden colour'd, or yellow" for Sol, 'Grassgreen' for Venus, purple for Mercury, and white for Luna—and hung to protect by sympathetic governance from maladies associated with their planet.[43]

These sigil-bags were, however, of a far different order to Blagrave's herb talismans. While Blagrave argued "an *exact time* must be obtained whereby to erect your [decumbiture] Figure aright, whereby to give judgment upon the disease, its cause and termination",[44] Hiebner insisted sigil casting itself must be framed at precise elections. It has been argued an emphasis on exactitude is the key to understanding how the publication—a work dedicated to the production and utility of magical objects—was regarded

---

Century Medicine', *Bulletin of the History of Medicine*, 67 (1993): 230–37.

41 MacDonald, *Mystical Bedlam*, 194; MS Ashm. 421, f. 171–171v, 144–5.

42 For more on this, see Agrippa, *Three Books*, 141–51; Pico della Mirandola, *On the Imagination*, ed. Harry Caplan (New Haven: Yale University Press, 1930). See also Katherine Park, 'The Imagination in Renaissance Psychology', M.Phil. thesis. University of London, 1974; Stuart Clark, *Vanities of the Eye: Vision in Early Modern European Culture*. Oxford: Oxford University Press, 2007; Yasmin Haskell (ed.), *Diseases of the Imagination and Imaginary Disease in the Early Modern Period*. Turnhout: Brepols, 2011.

43 Hiebner, *Mysterium Sigillorum*, 162–77.

44 Blagrave, *Astrological Physick*, sig. Bv. Emphasis added.

as such a "landmark event among reforming and scientific astrologers."[45]
Hiebner insisted: "you must have an exact Watch made, that shows the
Hours, Quarters, and Minutes," for the Sigil "must be stamp'd in a Minute,
because this Impression occasions the Power of the heavenly Influence; for
the Heavenly Influences of the Stars are as quick and nimble, as an Arrow
out of a Bow, or a Bullet out of Gun, so quick must this Impression be."[46]

This precision also extended to Hiebner's use of cutting–edge astronomical observations of the physical planets in his astrological magical
sigils, and the figures of Saturn, Venus and the Moon bear particularly
close resemblance to the engravings of Johannes Hevelius' *Selenograph-
ia* (1647)[47]—'the acknowledged authority on telescopic astronomy.'[48]
Hiebner's sigils also included planetary number squares (*kamea*): 'tables
of the planets, endowed with many, and very *great virtues* of the heavens,
in as much as they *represent that divine order* of celestial numbers, impressed
upon celestials by the Ideas of the Divine Mind, by means of the Soul of the
World, and the *sweet harmony* of those *celestial rays*, signifying according to
the proportion of *effigies*, supercelestial intelligencies'.[49] These arrangements of numbers both abstractly signified and offered a portal for immanent celestial forces; forces which could be contained in these objects and
deployed to affect change in the sublunary world. As exact figures of the
cosmos—both astrological and mathematical—they were, naturally, to be
found on all Hiebner's sigils.[50]

Kamea were also deployed in their own right, to both beneficial and
deleterious effect. Offering a unique access to the 'Intelligencies' mentioned in many Platonically-inclined occult philosophical explications of
astral virtue, the tables (if properly prepared with appropriate material
and timing) could produce tangible effects as magical items in themselves.
The kamea of Luna, if made when the Moon occupied favourable astrological aspects and 'engraven on silver...causeth security in a journey, increase
of riches, and health of body, drives away enemies and other evil things

---

45 Roos, 'The English Sigil War', p. 17

46 Hiebner, *Mysterium Sigillorum*, 178.

47 Ibid., 162, 172, 176.

48 Mary Winkler and Albert Van Helden, 'Johannes Hevelius and the visual language
of astronomy', in J.V. Field & Frank A. J. L. James (eds.), *Renaissance and Revolution: Hu-
manists, Scholars, Craftsmen, and Natural Philosophers in Early Modern Europe*. Cambridge,
1993, pp. 97–116, 98.

49 Agrippa, *Three Books*, 318. Emphasis added.

50 Hiebner, *Mysterium Sigillorum*, pp. 162–177.

from what place thou pleaseth'.[51] This sense of locative specificity—of the *placement* of the talismanic engraving—is crucial, as such tables also included a detrimental averse form; so, 'an unfortunate Moon engraven in a plate of Lead, where ever it shall be buried, it makes that place unfortunate'. We find exactly such an early modern lead cursing object in Lincoln's Inn in London, bearing a lunar kamea, along with the names and seals of lunar spirits, and the imprecation: "That Nothinge maye prosper Nor goe forwarde that Raufe Scrope [the apparent landlord of the pub where the kamea was placed] take the in hande."[52] Given this number square actually replicates an error traced back to the 1651 'J. F.' translation of Agrippa's *Three Books*, this object is also a testament to the use of a copy of this supposedly theoretical tome of occult philosophy for operative—indeed, malevolent—sorcery.[53]

CONSTELLATED RINGS

Hiebner also offered brisk instructions for framing planetary magic rings by engraving a suitable planetary gem during an election and setting it in its metal—all with the particular proviso to ensure the stone is "put into the inside of the Ring, so as to touch the Skin."[54] Such instructions were also be utilised to make talismans to be hung around the neck, and the necessity of direct bodily contact also accords with specifications made of Paracelsian medical sigils, such as a seal of Taurus which "if it be so hanged that it may touch the Navel, the Sign Taurus being turned next the flesh and the body, it giveth the best help to men or women."[55] The notion of a stone close to the skin also recalls, more mythically, the ring of Gyges who found "when he turned the collet inward he became invisible, and when

51 Agrippa, *Three Books*, p. 319.
52 W. Paley Baildon, 'Sixteenth Century Leaden Charm (obverse and reverse) found at Lincoln's Inn', *Proceedings of the Society of Antiquarians of* London, Second Series, 18 (1901): 146, passim.
53 See Jim Baker, *The Cunning-man's Handbook: The Practice of English Folk Magic 1550–1900*, (London, 2014), 272–3. This error trail also extends to later manuscript works such as MS Harley 6482, further emphasising the *Three Books*' influence. See McLean, *A Treatise of Angel Magic*, p. 121.
54 Hiebner, *Mysterium Sigillorum*, pp. 162–77.
55 Specifically, 'the Nature and Property of this Sigil, giveth a most excellent Remedy to them who have lost their Generative Virtue'. *Supreme Mysteries*, 140.

outward visible."[56] The contagion of the magical item's virtues is most effective and affective when brought into contact the user. This myth was, of course, related in Agrippa's treatment in the apt–titled chapter 'Of rings and their compositions'.[57]

Napier "out-went Forman in physick and holiness of life; cured the falling-sickness perfectly by constellated rings, some diseases by amulets, &c."[58] Lilly also relates that one such ring was made to cure a young woman of epilepsy, which it did successfully until her family (convinced by Puritans of the ungodliness of such an artefact) threw it away, whereupon the fits returned.[59] Asked to replace it, Napier refused, primly stating "those who despised God's mercies, were not capable or worthy of enjoying them."[60]

Forman recommended a ring made of electrum 'against Enchantments and witchcraft and against sprites', and 'worne of the harte finger [perhaps the "ring finger"], helpeth the cramps, launces and falling evil'; further noting it "changeth collour yf any sicknes or evill be towards the man."[61] So the protective uses of rings might extend to early warning systems of potential curses or other magically adverse conditions.

Like using sigils to stamp medicaments, rings could also be used to prepare other magical remedies: Kassell informs us that, in 1597, Forman "prescribed Jackemyne Vampena, a Dutch woman married to an English merchant, a series of potions, including one in which a ring engraved with the symbol of Jupiter had been immersed."[62] Thus contact exposure and contagion, the transfer and enervation of virtue, galvanised the innate capacities of materials—'as in a grain of mustard-seed, bruised, the sharpness which lay hid is stirred up'[63]—to actually cause a desired magically effectual substance.

Forman later designed and constructed himself a personalised astrological ring—"a golden setting holding a large coral stone engraved with the sign of Jupiter, under which was wedged a piece of parchment bear-

---

56 Plato, *Republic*, ed. Edith Hamilton & Huntington Cairns. Princeton, 1961, 2.359d–360b, 607.

57 Agrippa, *Three Books*, 94–5.

58 Lilly, *History*, 123–4.

59 Ibid., 124–5.

60 Ibid., *History*, 125.

61 MS Ashm 1494, p. 483–4.

62 Kassell, *Medicine and Magic*, 222; MS Ashm 411, f. 95, 99v, 115, 118v.

63 Agrippa, *Three Books*, 105.

ing Forman's name and an inscription of the words and symbols for Virgo and Mercury, the astrological [sign] and its ruling planet at the time of his birth."[64] Worn on the little finger of his left hand, it operated both as anti–witchcraft protection and would grant him "favour & credit & to mak on[e] famouse in his profession & to overcome enimies."[65] More generally, Forman's notes for astrological magical rings demonstrate identical methods as those espoused by Agrippa:

the manner of making these kinds of Rings, is this, viz. when any Star ascends fortunately, with the fortunate aspect, or conjunction of the Moon, we must take a stone, and Hearb that is under that Star, and make a Ring of the Metall that is sutable to this Star, and in it fasten the stone, putting the Hearb, or root under it; not omitting the inscriptions of images, names, and Characters, as also the proper suffumigations.[66]

Forman notes the combination of botanical materials (such as 'peony, bay, vervain'), parchment images ('lion, ram, and goat and their associated astrological symbols'), and—with such *materia* usually mounted under— precious stones ('ruby, diamond and heliotrope'), consecrated with prayer and incense.[67] The detail that images and glyphs (that is, pictograms and ideograms) were to be not only engraved on the stone but also marked on parchment is a useful clarification.

PARCHMENT LAMEN

The *Heptameron* is only one of many systems of magic that require a pentacle to be 'made in the day and hour of Mercury, the Moon increasing, written in parchment made of kids skin'[68] and displayed in order to summon its angels and 'Aeriall' spirits effectively.[69] Such lamens, to ensure a spirit pays 'homage' to the conjuror, are found in both contemporary demonological grimoires such as the *Clavicula Salomonis* manuscripts[70] and like-

---

64 Kassell, *Medicine and Magic*, 222.
65 Sloane 3822, f. 11.
66 Agrippa, *Three Books*, p. 94.
67 Kassell, 222 n. 42; Sloane 3822, f. 77v.
68 *Fourth Book*, p. 79.
69 Ibid., p. 84.
70 The Goetia of the *Lemegeton* (or the *Lesser Key of Solomon*) often required that a spirit's 'Character or Seal...must be worn as a Lamin by the Magician who calls him, on his breast else he will not do you homage.' Skinner & Rankine, *Goetia of Dr Rudd*, f. 103; MS Sloane 3825, f. 100v.

wise in charm–based 'folk magic' treatises.[71] Should such a connection seem tenuous—'Goetia' (publically vilified by early modern occult philosophers and later adopted by nineteenth–century lodge–based ceremonial magicians) and 'folk magic' still not necessarily being considered obvious bedfellows—please note both of these sets of instructions are found in the expanded 1665 edition of Reginald Scot's *Discoverie of Witchcraft*,[72] now acknowledged to be 'what amounted to the first grimoire printed in the English language', which while published with the intention 'to prove the worthlessness of its contents... unwittingly ended up democratizing ritual magic rather than undermining it.'[73] Indeed, Peterson suggests Sloane 3825 (Ashmole's own handwritten copy of the *Ars Goetia*) 'seems dependent on Scot, faithfully copying his frequent mistranslations, elaborations and omissions.'[74] It seems 'unclean spirits' have a habit of smuggling themselves and their chimerical heraldry via parchment.[75]

SIGILS

Perhaps the most detailed records of the construction of seventeenth–century sigils can be found in the diaries of Elias Ashmole, for which we have the decryption and annotation efforts of C. H. Josten to thank for their availability, unlocked from the magician's private coding and scribbled notation. Most broadly, these journals demonstrate the term 'sigil' appears to have had a rather wide variety of specific terms of art and meanings, from 'amulet' to 'seal', 'pentacle', 'lamen', and, even, 'ymage'. Early modern

---

71 See MS Cod. Gaster 1562, in which is contained illustration of a sigil for protection from and conjuration of 'all spirits', such as those found in a manuscript 'written mostly by a certain Thomas Parker in the years 1693–5', which promised 'whoso hath this about him all spirits shall do him homage.' M. Gaster, 'English Charms of the Seventeenth Century', *Folklore*, 21, 3 (1910), 375, 378. Gaster also notes the charms were passed between those 'addicted to astrology'.

72 Reginald Scot, *Discoverie of Witchcraft*. (London, 1584: 1665), pp. 229–38, 243.

73 Owen Davies, *Grimoires: A History of Magic Books*. Oxford, 2009, p. 70. See also S. F. Davies, 'The Reception of Reginald Scot's *Discovery of Witchcraft*: Witchcraft, Magic, and Radical Religion', *Journal of the History of Ideas* 74, 3 (2013): pp. 381–401, 393.

74 Joseph H. Peterson (ed.), *The Lesser Key of Solomon* (York Beach, 2001), xiv.

75 For more on parchment and goetia—especially historically and mythically following the pact from archaic Greece through early modern conjuration to modern praxis—see the *Encyclopaedia Goetica* series: Jake Stratton-Kent, *True Grimoire*. Dover, 2009; Jake Stratton-Kent, *Geosophia: The Argo of Magic*, 2 vols. Dover, 2010; Jake Stratton-Kent, *The Testament of Cyprian the Mage*, 2 vols. Dover, 2014.

magical practitioners distinguished various 'Sigills, Lamels, Talesmes', yet Ashmole himself noted that 'all depend upon one Radix...the Secret power of Figures.'[76] By this he combined principles of reflection and similitude, sympathy and antipathy, contagion and conjuration.

Along with a series of representational objects to ward off domestic vermin—specifically, a batch of "Figure[s] of a Ratt... cast in Lead, and made in full proportion, but had noe Characters upon it"[77]—Ashmole's diaries reveal that his sigils also employed the agency of planetary spirits and of more pictorial image magic. His 'little sigils' of Jupiter and either Mercury, Venus or both stamped in 'Tynn' on 2nd December 1651 apparently included a short Latin excerpt of Scripture, and the seal and name of the archangel of Jupiter, Iophiel.[78] Nor was this quite an isolated case: notary marginalia suggest he made these kinds of sigils—involving spirit names and seals, as well as pictorial images—on 12th and 17th July, 13th September, 29th November, and 3rd and 11th December.[79] He also called upon 'Graphiell' and 'Hagiel' in his castings of 26th February 1652.[80]

The sigil of 3rd December depicted "[Jupiter] in a Chariot drawne by Eagles & Ganymede knelling holding a Cup before him", and was inscribed with further Latin excerpts and the name and seal of Iophiel.[81] Significantly, we also have a specific Jupiterian purpose for both this and other sigils made on the same day: 'for honour and reputation.'[82] This sigil is an interesting combination of the Jupiterian images found in Agrippa: eliding the enthroned king in a 'four–footed chair, which is carried by four winged boys' with the crowned man 'riding upon an Eagle': it also mirrors the spirit rather than the letter of the former's purpose—to "encreaseth felicity, riches, honor, and conferreth Benevolence."[83] Images, it seems, were not regarded as strict, unalterable, indivisible prescriptions, but heraldic formulae of iconographic features to be arranged and combined.

Nor was Ashmole anomalous as an alchemist and astrologer who cast sigils. Lilly recounts he 'had much familiarity with John Hegenius, Doctor of Physick, a Dutchman, an excellent scholar and an able physician,

76 Elias Ashmole, *Theatrum Chemicum Britannicum*. London, 1651, p. 463.
77 MS Ashm 431, f. 137.
78 Ibid., f. 142v.
79 Josten, *Ashmole*, 594 n. 3.
80 MS Ashm 431, f. 133.
81 Ibid., f. 143.
82 Ibid., ff. 143, 127v.
83 Agrippa, *Three Books*, p. 299.

not meanly versed in astrology', to whom Lilly "communicated the art of framing Sigils, Lamens, &c. and the use of the Mosaical Rods; and we did create several Sigils to very good purpose", giving "the true key thereof, viz. instructed him of their forms, characters, words, and last of all, how to give them vivification, and what number or numbers were appropriated to every planet: *Cum multis aliis in libris veterum latentibus; aut perspicuè non intellectis.*"[84] This 'vivification' would chiefly have involved consecratory 'suffumigation' and prayer. And so we come to our second part.

VAULTING THE AZURE: TECHNIQUES OF ASTROLOGICAL *IMMATERIA*

VIVIFICATION

Ingredients and correspondences for astrological magic incenses are detailed in manuscript grimoires,[85] magicians' workbooks,[86] and even—as 'savours'—in more commonplace astrological handbooks.[87] Ashmole's diaries reveal his own planetary incense correspondences.[88] They also offer us records of their employment. At '0.40 p.m.' on 2 January 1678, "at this time exactly I cast my sigil of [Saturn] and [Mercury] for increase of honour and estimation with great men / and presently took them out of moulds and fumed them, with [alchemical glyph for sulphur] and mastic."[89] It is worth remarking that these are not two distinct planetary sigils, but a bi–planetary sigil combining the 'retentive' virtues of Saturn with the 'intellective' virtues of Mercury.[90]

---

84 Lilly, *History*, p. 221.
85 MS Sloane 3826 f. 33v. See also Karr & Skinner, *Sepher Raziel*, 193.
86 *Gauntlet*, 257 n. 334–340.
87 Lilly, *Christian Astrology*, 59, 63, 67, 71, 75, 79, 82. 'Savours', significantly, demonstrate a utility of the sensory and affective attributes of natural materials in operational magic. So herbs with a 'burning' taste, for instance, were employed—via astral virtue, planetary governance, and the doctrine of signatures (which covered not only morphology but *gustative* impression)—to produce literal or other forms of magical heat for Martial sorcerous purposes. Lilly, *Christian Astrology*, 75.
88 [Saturn]—Sulphur, [Jupiter]—Crocus, [Mars]—'Piper', [Sol]—Red Sanders, Crocus; [Venus]—Costus, [Mercury]—Mastick'. MS Ashm 431, f. 154v.
89 MS Ashm 431, f. 113.
90 *The Picatrix: Liber Atratus Edition*, trans. John Michael Greer & Christopher Warnock. Phoenix, 2010, III.1, 32, 35.

Much is made of the use of pleasant and unpleasant smells, especially in the conjuration of spirits. So antiquary and natural philosopher John Aubrey (1626–1697) remarks: "Good Spirits are delighted and allured by sweet Perfumes, as rich Gums, Frankincense, &c. Salt, &c. which was the reason that the Priests of the Gentiles, and also the Christians used them in their Temples, and Sacrifices: And on the contrary, Evil Spirits are pleased and allured and called up by Suffumigations of Henbane, &c. stinking Smells, &c. which the Witches do use in their Conjuration." [91] Lilly also notes that bad odours could be utilised in techniques of spirit–torture common to the antagonist approaches of early modern Solomonic conjuration, although he admonishes reliance on such methods as often connoting a failure on the part of the summoner to observe proper conduct:

> *I was well acquainted with the Speculator of John a Windor, a scrivener, sometimes living in Newbury. This Windor was club-fisted, wrote with a pen betwixt both his hands. I have seen many bonds and bills wrote by him. He was much given to debauchery, so that at some times the Daemons would not appear to the Speculator; he would then suffumigate: sometimes, to vex the spirits, he would curse them, fumigate with contraries.*[92]

Along with suffumigations came prayerful incantation. Ashmole's astrological charts for 6th January 1678 elected a time for a sigil of Saturn and Mercury, and noted 'The *invocation* was for honour and learning viz: things relating to the 10th and 9th houses.'[93] Josten offers some further examples of invocations from Ashmole's manuscripts 'as may have been used for magic sigils'.[94] The apparent conflation of 'invocation' and 'incantation' here must be understood as reflecting pre-modern theological comprehensions rather than magical ignorance. These comprehensions can in part be illuminated by considering the *Ars Notoria*, a late medieval 'Solomonic' ritual text, 'whose goal is to strengthen operator's memory, eloquence, understanding and perseverance, and to obtain knowledge of the seven liberal arts, all of which are sought in various sequences of *prayers* and rituals, and directly infused into the operator via *angels and the*

---

91 John Aubrey, *Miscellanies*. London, 1696, pp. 136–7.
92 Lilly, *History*, pp. 221–2.
93 Ms Ashm 431, f. 113v. Emphasis added. Four days previously, Ashmole had cast another Saturn and Mercury sigil for these same purposes.
94 Josten, *Ashmole*, 1533 n. 3; MS Ashm 421, f. 149.

holy spirit.[95] Simply intoning the Notary Art's prayer-charms and divine names was said to grant knowledge and bring favour. Such combination of religious and magical attitudes, of piety and conjuration, begins to be apparent.

Forman was incredibly interested in *Notoria*, 'which he copied at least three times and illuminated at least twice'; furthermore, Kassell's consideration that this interest 'marks a shift from his attempts to summon visible spirits to efforts to commune with angels' further highlights the theological and affective intricacies of prayerful conjuration.[96] Lilly used the 'magic circle and invocatory methods detailed in a Latin manuscript copy of the *Ars Notoria*' to search for treasure in Westminster Abbey in 1634.[97] Furthermore, the text reached its zenith of public availability mid-seventeenth century when occultist, botanist and medical researcher Robert Turner (1619–1664) published an 'English'd' version in 1656.[98]

As with almost every over type of early modern European magical operation, the works of *Notoria* were to be timed astrologically, specifically 'when [the Sun] Rules in [Gemini] and [Virgo], [Aries], [Leo], [Libra], [Taurus] in these moneths you may begin'.[99] As Agrippa judged, 'verses being aptly, and duly made *according to the rule of the stars*, and being full of signification, and meaning, and opportunely pronounced with vehement affection... and by the violence of the imagination, do confer a great power in the enchanter, and sometimes *transfer* it upon the thing enchanted'.[100] The

---

95 Claire Fanger, 'Plundering the Egyptian Treasure: John the Monk's *Book of Visions* and its relation to the *Ars Notoria*', in Claire Fanger (ed.), *Conjuring Spirits: Texts and Traditions of Medieval Ritual Magic* (University Park, 1998), p. 216. Emphasis added.

96 Kassell, *Medicine and Magic*, 218; Bodleian, Jones MS 1. Kassell also points to Ashm 820, iii, which she suspects Forman owned but did not draw, and Bodley SM 951, an elaborate fifteenth–century version upon which Forman based his copies.

97 Robin E. Cousins, 'Robert Turner of 'Holshott'', in Robert Turner, Patricia Shore Turner & Robin E. Cousins (eds.), *Elizabethan Magic*. Shaftesbury, 1989, p. 142. He had bought the text that same year. Lauren Kassell, 'The Economy of Magic in Early Modern England', in Margaret Pelling & Scott Mandelbrote (eds.), *The Practice of Reform in Health, Medicine, and Science, 1500–2000: Essays for Charles Webster* (Aldershot, 2005), p. 44.

98 For more on Turner's Notary Art, see Cousins 'Robert Turner', 139–41. For an excellent bibliographic and historiographic account of the *Ars Notoria*, see Benedek Láng, *Unlocked Books: Manuscripts of Learned Magic in Medieval Libraries of Central Europe*. Pennsylvannia, 2008, pp. 287–92.

99 *Ars Notoria: The Notory Art of Solomon* trans. Robert Turner. London, 1656), p. 111.

100 Agrippa, *Three Books*, 216–7. Emphasis added.

operating subject was as changed and essential to the operational action as the operated object.

To consider vivification specifically, of enlivening the magical object, consider first that the plant materia of incense was already thought to 'have such an affinity with the Air'.[101] Fumigation was further means to catalyse a quickening. But the truly vivifying link between incense and incantation is, of course, the breath: "suffumigations also, or perfumings, that are proper to the stars, are of great force for the opportune receiving of celestial gifts under the rays of the stars, in as much as they do strongly work upon the Air, and breath", meaning the operator is "affected with the qualities of inferiors, or celestials...quickly penetrating our breast, and vitals, doth wonderfully reduce us to the like qualities."[102]

Consecrations operationalised an enlivening affectivity that encompassed both the material and the operator framing and casting the sigil. Such envirtued expiration enervated the potency of consecratory incantations,[103] as 'magicians enchanting things, are wont to blow, and breathe upon them the words of the verse, or to breathe in the virtue with the spirit, that so the whole virtue of the soul be directed to the thing enchanted, being disposed for the receiving the said virtue.'[104] The consecratory matter and gesture, the action of speaking, indeed the magician's very breathing—from 'spire', after all, and covering both *inspiration* and *spirit*, in all their polyvalent theological and cosmological magical significances—empowered the operator, who in turn empowered the object. Astrological magic is, in many many ways, an intensely *spiritual* affair.

THE SPIRIT AND THE LETTER

Another source of both incense correspondences and magical words was the grimoire *Sepher Raziel*, which attributed its suffumigation instructions to Hermes Trismegistus and listed them by both zodiacal attribution and humoural–elemental 'savours.'[105] This text was certainly owned and worked by Simon Forman, and Lauren Kassell connects the conju-

---

101 Ibid., 23.
102 Ibid., 129.
103 Ibid., 211. For records of such practices, see MS Ashm 431, f. 113v. See also Josten, *Ashmole*, 1533 n. 3; citing MS Ashm 421, f. 149.
104 Agrippa, *Three Books*, 217.
105 Sloane 3826, f. 33v; translated in Karr & Skinner, *Sepher Raziel*, 193.

ration practices of Napier and his mentor Forman, showing the two demonstrably interested in *Sepher Raziel* for both theoretical occult matters
and operative magical activity.[106] One such example is Forman's interest in
the use of specially-prepared inks[107] for the writing of one's own grimoire
or *Liber Spirituum*,[108] Instructions about ink are also found—in this case,
planetary colour-coded inks—in *The Excellent Booke of the Arte of Magick*, a
sixteenth–century manuscript grimoire apparently (at least partially) received through spirit conjuration and scrying techniques.[109] Significantly,
one of the chief spirit tutors delivering this text was the ghost of King Solomon himself, patron of the very Solomonic traditions of magic.[110]

    Solomon also had a connection to *Sepher Raziel* (which was even called
Liber Salmononis): Forman noted the angel Raziel had delivered that book
of astronomy and magic to Adam, which was later found and used by Solomon.[111] In another fascinating interrelation of letter and spirit, Forman
even summoned and conversed with this book's patron, the angel Raziel.[112]
The magician's conversations with the angel are not well documented—
whether by intentional secrecy, loss of papers from then to now, or some
other reason—but we do have records of practical medical advice impart-
ed by the angel on the use of mistletoe which grew on oak trees, which:

> *belongeth to {Jupiter} especially, and {Venus} hath a part therein, and yt*
> *oughte to be gathered and administered in hora {Jupiter}, betwen ye firste*
> *quarter and the full {Moon} and beste in Maye. Yt is good againste the drop-*
> *sie being rubbed theron, and after rub the place with a red cloth.*[113]

Once more, planetary identity, electional timing, moon phase, and co-

---

106 Kassell, *Medicine and Magic*, 221; MS Ashm. 1491, p. 1303–9; Ashm. 1790, f. 116; Sloane
3822, f. 24.
107 MS Ashm 1491, p. 1303–9.
108 See *Fourth Book*, 54–56.
109 British Library Additional MS 36674, f. 47r. For more on the 'Excellent Booke' and
its 'Visions', see Frank Klaassen, 'Ritual Invocation and Early Modern Science: The Skrying Experiments of Humphrey Gilbert', in Clare Fanger (ed.), *Invoking Angels: Invoking
Angels: Theurgic Ideas and Practices, Thirteenth to Sixteenth Centuries*. University Park,
2012, 341–342.
110 See Add MS 36674, ff. 47r, 59r, 61r, 61v, 62r, 62v.
111 MS Ashm 802, ii, ff. 3v, 14r–v.
112 MS Ashm 1491, pp. 1303–9; Ashm 802, ii, ff. 3v, 14r–v; Ashm 1790, f. 116.
113 Ibid., p. 1278.

lour were key features of astrological magic and medicine—even from the mouths of the heavenly choir. However, to better understand this angelic conversation, we must contextualise the early modern summoning of angels.

THE CONJURATIONS OF ASTROLOGERS

Conjuration was not an unusual practice for seventeenth-century astrologers.[114] Many seem to have given it the old college try, and some were even rather good at it. Forman appears to have struggled, as the Elizabethan magus, mathematician and cryptographer John Dee (1527–1608) had, to see many spirits. Napier, as we shall see, had consistent successes in his consultations with Raphael. Some of the best records we have of such contemporary experiments in summoning angels come from John Dee and the soldier and mariner Humphrey Gilbert (1539–1583), who recorded their visionary experiences drawing spirits into stones or crystals.[115] One of the enduring influences on depictions of Dee's conversations with angels was the negative depiction by classical scholar and critic Meric Casaubon (1599–1671).[116] Yet by the latter part of the century, Ashmole planned to write a biography of Dee on the grounds that "I am fully satisfied he was not only a very Learned & pious man, but deserves much better esteeme of our Nation than yet he hath obtain'd."[117] Ashmole certainly poured over Dee's work, and made notes on formulating angelic names from his magical systems, including "the Names of the 16 good Angells for Phisick" taken from Dee's occult tables of letters.[118] He also began his own 'Actions

114 For early foundations, see David Keck, *Angels and Angelology in the Middle Ages*. Oxford, 1998; for links between medieval and early modern angel magic, see Claire Fanger (ed.), *Invoking Angels*. For translations and re-prints of early modern angel magic grimoires from Sloane, Harley and other collections, see Stephen Skinner & David Rankine (ed.), *Practical Angel Magic of Dr John Dee's Enochian Tables* (London, 2004), *The Keys to the Gateway of Magic: Summoning the Solomonic Archangels and Demon Princes* (London, 2005) as well as *The Goetia of Dr Rudd*, and Karr & Skinner, *Sepher Raziel*.

115 Klaassen, 'The Skrying Experiments of Humphrey Gilbert', 346.

116 Meric Casaubon (ed.), *A True and Faithful Relation of What passed for many Yeers Between Dr John Dee... and some Spirits*. London, 1659. See also Stephen Clucas, 'Enthusiasm and damnable curiosity: Meric Casaubon and John Dee' in R. J. W. Evans & Alexander Marr (eds.), *Curiosity and Wonder from the Renaissance to the Enlightenment*. Aldershot, 2006.

117 Josten, *Ashmole*, 187

118 MS Ashm. 1790, f. 47; the manuscript containing these angels is bound in Sloane

with Spirits' journal documenting his experiments.[119]

Angel magic was, of course, ineluctably interwoven with practices of Christian religiosity. Lilly accounts that, visiting Napier in the early 1630s, 'he had me up into his library, being excellently furnished with very choice books: there he prayed almost one hour; he invocated several angels in his prayer, viz. Michael, Gabriel, Raphael, Uriel, &c.'[120] Prayer and piety played a major part in much angel magic. Despite the apparent solemnity of Napier's rituals, Lilly and Aubrey both described an "easy familiarity between the magus and Raphael and assert that Napier asked the Angel's opinion about each of the medical cases he treated."[121] As many magicians knew, Raphael was 'the Medicine of God, & was sent to Toby, and did lay medicines to Tobies eye[s], & healed him of his blindnesse"; indeed "the office of these Angelles is to teache good men, and help them of those things that concerne theyr faith, as of the comming of Gods sonne, and of his déedes and lawes."[122] No wonder this angel should be found ruling the *Heptameron*'s Mercurial spirits of Wednesday who could be summoned "to change bodies mixt of Elements conditionally out of one into another; to give infirmities or health."[123] An excellent choice to call in for medical consults, Napier's 'easy familiarity' is also reflected in the fact that he occasionally disagreed with the archangel's diagnoses.

Specifics on the practices of angel magicians are occasionally obscured, often by the magicians themselves. As MacDonald notes, "aware of Dee's misfortunes, Napier was careful to leave few traces of his secret arts in his main body of papers and did not imitate him by broadcasting his success."[124]

3191. The manuscripts containing these tables were lost between 1608 and 1662, when they were discovered in a secret drawer of a chest and found their way into the hands of Ashmole on 20 August 1672. For more on this remarkable chapter in early modern angel magic history, see Josten, *Ashmole*, 184–8.

119 Skinner & Rankine, *Practical Angel Magic*, 44.

120 Lilly, *History*, 125.

121 MacDonald, *Mystical Bedlam*, 18.

122 Bartholomew Anglicus, *Batman vppon Bartholome, his Booke, De Propietatibus Rerum* (London, 1582), f. 25.

123 *Fourth Book*, 99. Other powers of the Mercurial 'Spirits of the Air of Wednesday' were 'to give all Metals; to reveal all earthly things past, present and to come; to pacifie Judges, to give victories in war, to re–edifie, and teach experiments and all decayed Sciences, and... to raise the poor, and cast down the high ones; to binde or loose Spirits; to open locks or bolts: such-kinde of Spirits have the operation of others, but not in their perfect power, but in virtue or knowledge.'

124 MacDonald, *Mystical Bedlam*, 18.

Dee did indeed suffer accusations of sorcery, diabolism, and necromancy throughout his career for his conjuring activities.[125] Indeed, not all medical resorts to angels were regarded as evidence of piety. At the end of the seventeenth–century, astrologer and almanac publisher John Partridge (1644–1714) attempted to besmirch his rival, astrologer mathematician Henry Coley (1633–1695), with accusations selling amulets,[126] publishing a design for Coley's anti-plague sigil bearing the name and seal of Raphael and glyph of Mercury.[127] This angelic seal and planetary attribution are consistent with those of the most popular system of planetary angel conjuration, the *Heptameron*, printed in the pseudo-Agrippan *Fourth Book* and copied into magicians' work-books.[128]

Although exact details about Napier's angelic consultations are unclear—such as when "conferences with spirits began, how often they occurred, and whether he ceased to practice angelic magic"—MacDonald considers that 'Simon Forman probably kindled his interest in conjuring' and 'it was surely Napier's acquaintance with John Dee that induced him to practice it.'[129] Lilly notes that Napier knew Dee 'very well.'[130] Likewise, Dee claimed his interest in angel magic began in 1569 invoking Raphael as well as Michael.[131] The incantations and prayers to summon such angelic assistance are found in many of the books owned by such magicians: as in the angelic operations of Dee, Napier and others 'found the means to conjuring in the works of Lull, Agrippa, the *Key of Solomon*, *Picatrix*, and a library of other medieval texts of baffling authorship and provenance believed by Napier and his colleagues to have been composed in Biblical times.'[132] We know specifically that Napier owned 'Agrippa's book'[133] (most likely the *Fourth Book*, given its technical specifics for such ceremonies), as

125 For more on the life of Dee, and the accusations he faced, see Peter J. French, *John Dee: The World of an Elizabethan Magus*. London, 1987. For more on Dee's magic, see György Endre Szőnyi, *John Dee's Occultism: Magical Exaltation Through Powerful Signs*. New York, 2004.

126 Roos, 'The English Sigil War', 17–43.

127 John Partridge, *Merlinus Liberatus: Being an Almanack for the Year of our Blessed Saviour's Incarnation*. London, 1699, fol. C, last page.

128 *Fourth Book*, 73–107, 95; Sloane MS 3851, f. 61–74 contains most of the *Heptameron*. See *Gauntlet*, 156–179.

129 MacDonald, *Mystical Bedlam*, 18.

130 Lilly, *History*, 227.

131 Skinner & Rankine, *Practical Angel Magic*, 30; Sloane MS 3188.

132 MacDonald, *Mystical Bedlam*, 17–18.

133 MS Ashm. 407, f. 150.

well as "treatises in the hand of his assistant Gerence James"[134] titled *Liber Salamonis* and *Liber Luna*.[135] He also wrote as well as owned several other works of conjuration, including various invocations and rituals to attract angels and enter into spiritual conversation with them,[136] some of which can be found in the Ashmole Manuscripts.[137]

Two apprehensions surface from this historical reflection. Firstly, grimoires were of great interest to astrologer–magicians, who shared, consulted, copied, and annotated them. Secondly, conjuration—to bring forth the attentions of spirits by naming, by gesture, by circle, by timing, by fumigation, and so on—was not so much a separate endeavour from other magical efforts as modern mindsets might consider. Sigils featured the invocated names of spirits. Prayer-charms entreated angelic assistance. When Lilly's treasure hunting around Westminster was disturbed by great uncanny and unsettling winds, the astrologer accounts he "gave directions and command to dismiss the dæmons; which when done, all was quiet again."[138]

However, there were also reports of astrologers calling spirits forth to create rather more vehement effects. Lilly reports his astrological mentor, John Evans, 'was well versed in the nature of spirits, and had many times used the circular way of invocating, as in the time of our familiarity he told me.'[139] He gives two accounts in his autobiography. The first was a classic 'burned fingers' story, in which Evans "had not, at the time of invocation, made any suffumigation, at which the spirits were vexed"—so vexed that, "upon a sudden, after some time of invocation, Evans was taken from out the room, and carried into the field near Battersea Causeway, close to the Thames."[140] He was discovered the following morning by a labourer on his way to work who had to tell the presumably somewhat red–faced conjuror where he had awoken. The second is worthy of repeating in full, for Lilly's typical emphasis on proper conduct, as well as demonstrating a magical operation occurring over several days rather than a specific elected point in time:

---

134 MacDonald, *Mystical Bedlam*, 255 n. 10.
135 Sloane MS 3822.
136 Sloane MSS 3822, 3826, 3679, 3846, 3854; Additional MSS 36674.
137 MS Ashm. 237, f. 190v; Ashm. 244, f. 130–2; Asm. 1790, ff. 112–12v, 113v, 115.
138 Lilly, *History*, 78–80.
139 Ibid., 56.
140 Ibid., 58–9.

There was in Staffordshire a young gentlewoman that had, for her prefer-
ment, married an aged rich person, who was desirous to purchase some lands
for his wife's maintenance; but this young gentlewoman, his wife, was desired
to buy the land in the name of a gentleman, her very dear friend, but for her
use: after the aged man was dead, the widow could by no means procure the
deed of purchase from her friend; whereupon she applies herself to Evans,
who, for a sum of money, promises to have her deed safely delivered into her
own hands; the sum was forty pounds. Evans applies himself to the invoca-
tion of the angel Salmon, of the nature of Mars, *reads his Litany in the*
Common-Prayer-Book every day, *at* select hours, *wears his* surplice,
lives orderly *all that time; at the fortnight's end Salmon appeared, and hav-*
ing received his commands what to do, in a small time returns with the very
deed desired, lays it down gently upon a table where a white cloth was spread,
and then, being dismissed, vanished. The deed was, by the gentleman who
formerly kept it, placed among many other of his evidences in a large wooden
chest, and in a chamber at one end of the house; but upon Salmon's; removing
and bringing away the deed, all that bay of building was quite blown down,
and all his own proper evidences torn all to pieces.[141]

And that, apparently, is what happens when you successfully summon a
Martial angel to resolve a legal dispute. Yet how could spirits *cause* such
things? A cosmological perspective on astrological angelology assists our
comprehension: in order to see this big picture more clearly we must take
a step back and regard a popular work of angelological geomancy.

ANGELOLOGICAL GEOMANCY

Geomancy, chiefly a system of divination by sixteen figures, applies the
'use and rules of astrology'[142]—that is, astrological categories, correspondences and certain techniques—as 'an interpretive system.'[143] Swiss astrologer geomancer Christopher Cattan (whose handbook of the art, translated into English in 1591, swiftly became 'a best-seller which necessitated

---

141 Ibid., 56–8.
142 Agrippa, *Three Books*, 323.
143 Stephen Skinner, *Terrestial Astrology: Divination by Geomancy.* London, 1980, 204.
It is worth bearing in mind that different handbooks of geomancy did not correspond
the geomantic figures and planetary and zodiacal attributions in exactly the same way
across the board.

its reprinting in 1608' and spawned numerous contemporary manuscript copies)[144] cited Thomas Aquinas himself and described geomancy as 'a part of Natural Magicke, and daughter of Astrology'.[145] Agrippa referred to it as 'the most accurate of divinations'[146] and the occult philosopher Robert Fludd (1574–1637) certainly 'defended stoutly the validity of that art.'[147] Stephen Skinner quotes J. B. Craven as asserting seventeenth–century English magicians' networks—specifically name–checking Forman, Napier, Napier's son, Ashmole and Fludd—'formed a sort of succession especially in astrological and geomantic studies'.[148]

Yet it is the rather more ideosyncratic geomancy of John Heydon's *Theomagia: The Temple of Wisdom* which must draw our attention if we wish to apprehend the cosmological import of astrological spirits. Heydon begins his Neoplatonic-cum-'Rosiecrucian' geomancy with this creation story:

> *God the creator of all things, out of the Chaos, which was the bodies of wicked Angels made the Earth, which is divided into twelve equal parts, which over these Ruleth twelve Created Idea's, which bring the vertues and influences of their seven Lords, upon all things created under the Sun: And these vertues or influences we receive, in manner and form following, by sixteen Figures; and they show us also all things past, present, and to come.*[149]

The combination of astrological and geomantic symbolism is cosmogonical, speaking of the profound origin and subsequent ordering of the cosmos. It is directly relatable to the ideas attributed to Trithemius in Lilly's *World's Catastrophe* of the planets as 'Secundarian intelligences' before God the Supreme Creator.[150] Following such theological and spiritual as well as occult significance with which the geomantic figures were thought to

144 Skinner, *Terrestrial Astrology*, 128.

145 Christopher Cattan, *The Geomancie* (London, 1591), 'The Preface to the Authour vnto the Reader', C1.

146 Agrippa, *Three Books*, 324.

147 Robert Fludd, *Historia Macrocosmi*, 'Tractatus Secundus.' Oppenheim, 1618, 718–20; translated in C. H. Josten, 'Robert Fludd's Theory of Geomancy and His Experiences at Avignon in the Winter of 1601 to 1602', *Journal of the Warburg and Courtauld Institutes*, 27 (1964), 332.

148 Skinner, *Terrestrial Astrology*, 131; cf. J. B. Craven, *The Life and Mystical Writings of Dr. Robert Fludd* London, 1902.

149 John Heydon, *Theomagia: The Temple of Wisdom*. London, 1664, p. 1.

150 William Lilly, *The World's Catastrophe*. London, 1647, p. 42.

infuse the very earthy materiality of the universe's nature, operation and contents, the somewhat perfunctory mention of geomantic divination makes such practices almost seem incidental.

Heydon's system of geomancy rests firmly on a committed angelological animism. Heydon does not generally talk, for instance, about the planet Mars or the sign of Aries at all in *Theomagia*—a bold gesture considering the close relation of geomancy and astrology. Instead, he speaks of the Ruler Bartzabel and the Genius or Idea of Malchidael. Considering geomantic efficacy as the result of proper working with spirits is functionally no different from conceiving the system as the manipulation and management of impersonal forces—the actual techniques and symbolic taxonomy and interrelations remain the same. Heydon's angelological explanations locate geomancy within a commonality of Western European magical practice, of a shared view of the spiritual denizens of the cosmos. *Theomagia* has the same planetary spirits listed by Agrippa, with angels in very similar astrological rulerships. So 'Barzabel' is in the *Three Books* as the ruling Spirit of Mars, and Malchidael, like the other zodiacal angels, is listed as being 'set over' one of the twelve signs—in Malchidael's case, Aries.[151]

Heydon also maintains that 'Rosicrucian' operators 'first used holy Deprications, Incantations with other Rites and observations provoking and alluring Idea's of this nature hereunto...'[152] There seems a case to be made for geomancy having a ritual magical dimension to it, along with the rough–and–ready geomantic divination for illnesses and love–life advice. Conversely, Owen Davies has remarked that village cunning-folk and local wizards, traditionally represented as the magic-users least interested in complex Neoplatonic orders and arrangements of angels "would certainly appreciate the detailed practical guide to astromantic and geomantic divination, and the diagrams showing the various signs and characters of the planets and their angels."[153]

Indeed—if readers will forgive me briefly transgressing the limits of England to consider cunning–folk of the seventeenth-century transatlantic world—we find corroborating reports from the British colonies of

151 Agrippa, *Three Books*, 243, 416. There are some exceptions—Heydon sets Amnixiel over Pisces, whereas Agrippa gives Barchiel, which in turn Heydon puts over Scorpio. This may itself be a result of a mistake—the English version of this text originally sets Barchiel over both Pisces and Scorpio.

152 Heydon, *Theomagia*, 2–3

153 Davies, *Popular Magic*, 124.

Chester County, Pennsylvania. Quaker elders, appalled at the magical activities of one Robert Roman,

> *indicted Roman "for practicing geomancy according to hidon [John Heydon]*
> *and divineing by a sticke" and for using occult means to take "the wife of*
> *Henry Hastings away from her husband and children." To support their ac-*
> *cusations, they named three books they found in Roman's possession: "Hi-*
> *don's Temple of Wisdom which teaches geomancy, and Scots Discovery of*
> *witchcraft, and Cornelias Agrippas Teaching negromancy.*[154]

I wish to point out three features of this account. Firstly, this is an excellent short list of the texts contemporary cunning-folk may have used, indeed, most likely did use. Secondly, it demonstrates that the older forms of geomancy with a stick in the dirt—the art being summarised in one contemporary dictionary definition as 'divination by circles in the earth'[155]—seemed to have enjoyed resurgence in the Americas, as opposed to the more genteel pen and paper affairs of English libraries.

Finally, the accusation of not merely divining but working sorcery points to a fundamental elision of divination and enchantment present in all astrological endeavours, whether in popular perception or actual magical practice. To know the hidden workings is to be uniquely privileged to affect outcomes—thus the early modern ban on calculating the nativities of regents, lest those eighth Houses might hold some politically expedient advantage. Furthermore, an image of a thing held power over the thing. The use of astrological charts themselves as talismanic items is not without precedent—when the merchant and astrologer Samuel Jeake (1623–1690) elected a time for the building of a new storehouse, he had this figure 'let into the wall of the building like a kind of talisman.'[156] As I have argued previously,

> *such an engraving should be considered in the context of image magic and*
> *the principle of sympathy. As astrological glyphs were thought to attract the*
> *power of the thing they represented, an election figure adorning the project*
> *for which it was cast becomes as much of a magnet for the forces it depicts as a*
> *mere research exercise. Elections thereby demonstrate the interlinked nature*

---

154 Butler, 333.
155 Henry Cockeram, *The English Dictionarie*. London, 1621.
156 Hunter & Gregory, *Jeake*, 13.

*of astrological knowledge and action applications, and also highlight how as-
trology's rationality cannot be clearly cut away from its magic. Just as knowledge and action are demonstrably fused in knowing when best to act, so too
are astrology and magic a co–dependent admixture of symbol and utility. In
election, the casting of a figure becomes more than measuring, even more than
interpretation—it becomes a ritual in which certain times for action become
sacralised, emphasised as they are underlined with astrological significance.*[157]

Throughout this chapter, I have attempted to show rather than tell the
significance of astrological election. But here I must make pains to mark
it, repeating the judgement of Simon Forman: "I have found by Experience that *all consisteth in the tyme of doinge yt*, for yf the tyme according to
the revolution of the heavens, and aspects of the plannets agre not to his
working, all his works shall be in vaine, for all things ar done in tyme and
bound for tyme."[158] Ashmole seems to show understanding of their affective and operable sorcerous affect when he declared that by "Elections we
may Governe, Order and Produce things as we please: *Faber quisq; Fortunæ
propriæ* [sic]".[159] Once more, Magic joined a guiding hand of Art with the
abundant and earthshaking hand of Nature to swear together.

THE BLACK ROBES OF A DOCTOR

I would like to conclude by bringing up a few features of the *Picatrix* which
should offer us some reflection for modern practice. In the advice of Book
3, Chapter 7, prospective astrological magical operators are instructed to
dress in the manner of someone of the nature of the planet. To perform
Martial ritual, "dress yourself in red garments, and put a red linen or silk
cloth on your head as well as a red skullcap, and hang a sword from your
neck, and arm yourself with all the weapons you can carry; and dress yourself in the manner of a soldier and a fighter", indeed, to conduct oneself
'stand upright on your feet and speak secretly, boldly, and without any

---

157 Cummins, *The Starry Rubric*, 47.
158 MS Ashm. 390 f. 29. Kassell also cites (in *Medicine and Magic*, p. 58 n. 19) Ashm. 363
f. 132v; Ashm. 403 f. 81.
159 Ashmole, *Theatrum Chemicum Britannicum*, 451. The Latin phrase—which might
read 'every man is the architect of his own fortune'—is attributed to the Roman patri-
cian Appius Claudius Caecus.

fear'.[160] In contrast—lest these particularities be taken as standard features of all planetary ritual instruction:

> *when you want to pray to Mercury and ask him for one of the petitions that pertain to him, such as petitions of scribes and regencies of kings, dress yourself in the garments of a notary and scribe, when the Moon is conjunct with Mercury, and proceed in all your actions as though you were a scribe. On your finger put a ring of fixed mercury, because with such a ring Hermes the wise used to work. Sit on a chair of the kind that schoolmasters use, and turn to face Mercury, holding a piece of paper in your hands as though you intended to write on it.*[161]

The operator is instructed to dress and act in the manner of a recognisable personage of the nature of that planet, to wear a ring and carry a thurible of the metal of that planet, and to make fumigations of planetary *materia*. Furthermore, the Martial operator must be 'bold', the Mercurial studious, the Jupiterian pious, the Saturnine 'humble': one's manners, movements, even perhaps what we moderns might call an emotional state, must all reflect the planet's nature.

A sacrifice of a planetary animal is also prescribed, and the operator is specifically instructed to extract and eat the animal's liver. *Picatrix* specifically references the hepatomancy of ancient haruspexy[162] in relation to this idea: the liver is both the looking-glass used to ascertain any impediment to the working at hand and the envirtued *materia* empowering the operator themselves. In Galenic thought, the liver was one of the three governing organs, according with the tripartite faculties of the Aristotelian soul.[163] The fourth-century bishop Nemesius posited the liver to be the seat of all concupiscible passions,[164] and one contemporary commentator claimed Plato argued the liver was 'like a *Looking–glasse*, that it might make a more cleare representation of the *Images of the passions* from thence

---

160 *Picatrix: Atratus*, III.7, 166–7

161 Ibid., 176. Emphasis added.

162 Ibid., III.7, 180.

163 Along with the brain and heart. Galen, *On the Usefulness of the Parts of the Body*, ed. Margaret Tallmadge May (Ithaca, 1968), 4.13, 1, 229.

164 F. David Hoeniger, *Medicine and Shakespeare in the English Renaissance*. London, 1992, 166. The heart was considered the seat of the irascibles. For a seventeenth-century account and refutation of this idea see Nicolas Coeffeteau, *A Table of Humane Passions* (London, 1621), 20–28.

exhibited vnto the soule.'[165] A more complete study of the magic in the passional status of the liver, that is, of early modern occult philosophy of the passions—with their 'expressions' of their 'characters' as both signifier and signified, and their contagious affectivity arising in the imagination to produce wonderful and terrible effects—must await its own dedicated study. For now, I merely wish to note that a ritual conducted in the passional manner of a planet's character culminates in the acquiring, study, and consumption of an organ of divination and passion par excellence.

Evidence seems to demonstrate that, by the seventeenth century, magical dress had significantly simplified. Those attempting to summon angelic spirits generally wore 'a Priests Garments, if it can be'—such as Evans' surplice for his successful operation of Salmon—'but if it cannot be had, let it be of linen, and clean.'[166] Those attempting to summon any other spirits wore black. Funnily enough, Evans is wearing 'black cloaths' when the labourer finds him after being carried off by vexed spirits.[167] The *Excellent Booke*, which deals in an explicit necromancy of consulting with dead magicians by the authority of 'Assasel' as 'the ruler of y[e] deade',[168] were specifically told by a host of spectral mages (amongst with other taboos and instructions) to 'go in a black coat & cloak' in order to do their conjuration.[169]

Black is literally the colour of *melancholy* ('the black bile') and of course mostly associated with the Dark Arts of black magic. Such dark receptive heaviness, the very Platonic qualities of Earth,[170] would sympathetically *pull* spirits to it. This receptivity made dark Earthy people more susceptible to possession by spirits: 'black choler, which is so obstinate, and terrible a thing, that the violence of it is said by physicians, and natural philosophers, besides madness, which it doth induce, also to entice evil spirits to seize upon men's bodies', indeed, 'so great also they say the power of melancholy is of, that by its force, Celestiall spirits also are sometimes drawn into men's

---

165 Helkiah Crooke, *Mikrocosmographia: A Description of the Body of Man Together with the Controversies Thereto Belonging*. London, 1615, 129. Emphasis added.

166 *Fourth Book*, 79. If there were any doubt, this should be 'clean white linen.' *Fourth Book*, 57.

167 Lilly, *History*, 58–9.

168 Add MS 36674, f. 47v. This is clearly a rendering of Azazel, later he is also called 'the Keeper of the Dead Bones'. Add MS 36674, f. 49v.

169 Add MS 3674, f. 59v.

170 'to the Earth [were attributed] darkness, thickness, and quietness.' Agrippa, *Three Books*, 7.

bodies...'[171] The link between Earth and chthonic spirits was further reinforced by wordplay rendering Goetia as 'Geocie', and described as 'being familiar with unclean Spirits.'[172]

Black garments of 'doctors' held Saturnine virtues in *Picatrix*,[173] recalling most immediately that physicians dealt in the inevitability of death. The black garb of an academic doctor might also bring to mind the supposedly sombre cogitations of melancholy *genius* (a term itself denoting both depth of thought and a spirit), a pervasive intellectual, medical and artistic trend in early modern England.[174] Certainly both psychology researcher Robert Burton (1577–1640) and the renowned scholar, priest and astrologer Marsilio Ficino (1433–1499) wrote at length about the melancholies of scholars,[175] and Hamlet after all connects scholarship and spirit conversation.[176] We should however also bear in mind that 'in popular discourse before the twentieth century the title was not restricted to those with a university training', and was also conferred upon 'those who were skilled with herbs and magic'.[177] A doctor—physicist, physician and philosopher—might be a magician almost by default. Certainly to dress in black was to attract shades by the gravity of the grave.

---

171 Agrippa, *Three Books*, 133.

172 Heinrich Cornelius Agrippa, *The Vanity of Arts and Sciences*. London, 1676, 115.

173 *Picatrix: Atratus*, III.7, 159.

174 See Winfried Schleiner, *Melancholy, Genius, and Utopia in the Renaissance* (Wiesbaden, 1991); Douglas Trevor, *The Poetics of Melancholy in Early Modern England* (Cambridge, 2004); Angus Gowland, *The Worlds of Renaissance Melancholy: Robert Burton in Context* (Cambridge, 2006). See also N.L. Brann, *The Debate over the Origin of Genius during the Italian Renaissance: The Theories of Supernatural Frenzy and Natural Melancholy in Accord and in Conflict on the Threshold of the Scientific Revolution* (Leiden, 2002).

175 See, for example, Robert Burton, *Anatomy of Melancholy* (London, 1623). 1.2.3.15 'Love of Learning, or overmuch study. With a Digression on the misery of Scholars, and why the Muses are Melancholy'; Marsilio Ficino, *Three Books on Life*, trans. Carol Kaske & John R. Clark (Tempe, 1998), I.II–X:111–137.

176 William Shakespeare, *The tragicall historie of Hamlet* (London, 1603), I.I. f. 2. Indeed, Horatio is even said to have attended Wittenstein, a university so infamous for demonology its namesake 'letters' linger as a folk euphemism for black magic across Europe.

177 Davies, *Popular Magic*, 74.

BEING THE SPIRIT YOU WISH TO SEE IN
THE WORLD

If this practice of garbing in black has indeed some link to older methods of consorting with specifically Saturnine spirits—often *shades* of the dead themselves—by resembling them, might we perhaps consider other practices whereby the magical operator attempts to frame *themselves* in similitude and sympathy with astrological spirits they conjure? As we have seen, consecration by fume and verse meant vivifying the *materia* with enlivening virtue partly by empowering the operator with that virtue: in a sense, *breathing with*, and thus like, a spirit. Indeed, mouthing prayer-charms such as those attempting to cultivate the 'cosmic infusion of knowledge sought by the liturgy of the *Ars Notoria*'[178] could even mean *knowing* like a spirit.

Furthermore, *Picatrix* and Agrippa both suggest making and charging astrological images in locations of their planetary governance, as 'the places from which come the material of which the image ought to be made, all help arrange things and carry out the work, because all these considerations will influence the result and effect of the planets, and the work will be completed more effectually and marvellously'.[179] So it is 'they that endeavour to procure love , are wont to bury for a certain time the instruments of their art, whether they be rings, images, looking glasses, or any other, to hide them in a stewhouse [brothel], because in that place they will *contract* some venereal [i.e. Venusian] faculty, no otherwise than things that stand in stinking places, become stinking, and *those in an aromatical place, become aromatical, and of a sweet savour.*'[180] By occult doctrines of contagion and exposure apprehending the transmission, storage and manipulation of astral virtue, these locations were themselves places of power which could be used to charge magical objects. The correspondence lists of locations found in every astrological handbook were not merely for decoding information from charts—although this was incredibly useful, and formed part of contemporary cunning–folks' stock trade in finding lost or stolen property[181]—it was also for apprehending and utilising loci and materials to manipulate, store and transmit astral virtues.

178 Fanger, *Invoking Angels*, 2.
179 *Picatrix*, II.7, 157–8.
180 Agrippa, *Three Books*, 96. Emphasis added.
181 Davies, *Popular Magic*, 100.

Moreover, such frequenting of the places of locative astral virtue, in order to work astrological magic, means *haunting*—like these spirits—the locales of these spirits. The astrological ritual magic of *Picatrix* involved appearing and conducting oneself in the manner of a planetary spirit. Consider (which itself etymologically might be rendered 'to constellate with') the planetary Solomonic pentacles chiefly concerned specifically with working with planetary spirits: Saturnine spirits are to be terrified, Martial spirits commanded, the pride of Solar spirits suppressed. A planetary spirit moves as "everything moves, and turns itself to its like, and inclines that to itself with all its might."[182]

This is not simply 'faking it til you make it' or 'method acting.' To swear together with astrological spirits is to align oneself in union, to unlock the circle, to leap out of oneself. There is a treasured place, I contend, in astrological magic for calling something out of ourselves that is bigger than ourselves—for invoking the interior planets that illuminate the very azured vaults of our wholehearted souls.

*   *
*

---

182 Agrippa, *Three Books*, 34.

Thigh of Iron, Thigh of Gold

On Alchemy, Astrology, & Animated Statues

Aaron Cheak, PhD

IN 1990, THE renowned French Egyptologist Philippe Derchain published a study of the texts of *la maison d'or* or 'house of gold' (*ḥt-nb*) from the Temple of Hathor at Dendera, Upper Egypt.[1] Derchain showed how the artisanal traditions of the house of gold and the goldmaker's workshop functioned hand in hand with Egyptian temple cult in the production of living statues. Stemming from traditions stretching back into the deepest antiquity, the specific intermingling of artisanal and theological traditions within the context of Egyptian temple cult penetrates directly to the heart of the origins of alchemy in Ptolemaic Egypt. Here the geographical nexus cannot be ignored, for Dendera is situated along the same bend in the Nile that harbours the grand temple complexes of Luxor and Karnak, the alchemically significant town of Akhmim (birthplace of the alchemist Zosi-

---

1 Philippe Derchain, 'L'Atelier des Orfèvres à Dendara et les origines de l'alchimie', *Chronique d'Égypte* 129 (1990): 219–42. See also: François Daumas, 'L'Alchimie a-t-elle une origine égyptienne?', in *Das römisch-byzantinische Ägypten: Akten des internationalen Symposions 26–30. September 1978 in Trier*. Aegyptiaca Treverensia 2 (Mainz: Philipp von Zabern, 1983), 109–18.

mos), and Nag Hammadi (where the Coptic gnostic and Hermetic codices would be discovered in 1945).[2]

The technical traditions that were developed and employed in Egyptian temple institutions were a vital part of the process by which ritual objects, especially statues, were created, consecrated, and divinised for use in Egyptian temple cult. Needless to say, the ramifications of this simple fact have enormous consequences for understanding alchemy as an art of creation, consecration, and divine animation. In this context, all *materia magica* employed in theurgic and magical praxis must be seen to partake of an identical procedure (a point all the more significant in light of the overwhelming persistence of Egyptian temple cult in the astromagical, alchemical, and theurgic practices preserved in the *Greek Magical Papyri*). In any event, at the heart of this process was the act of creating gods, or rather, material vehicles for divine forces, such as statues and talismans. The art also extended to the reanimation of the dead, an ontological category that, in Egyptian funerary tradition, was closely assimilated to that of the gods/statues themselves.[3]

It is my contention that none of this would have been undertaken in isolation from astrologically significant timings, a point that grows in significance when we realise that the Temple of Hathor at Dendera was the original location of the magnificent zodiacal ceiling—the earliest complete map of the ancient sky—an intricate bas–relief depicting a more or less exact period between 15 June and 15 August of the year 50 BCE. Here more than anywhere, the origins of alchemy, theurgy, and astrology closely cohere.

The present study seeks to explore the dynamics and symbolism of the mouth–opening ritual, and to highlight the alchemical, theurgical, and astrological permutations of this rite within Graeco–Egyptian traditions.

---

2 For a more detailed survey of the history of alchemy, see Cheak, ed., *Alchemical Traditions: From Antiquity to the Avant-Garde* (Melbourne: Numen Books, 2013).

3 Eberhardt Otto, *Das ägyptische Mundöffnungsritual* (Wiesbaden: Harrassowitz, 1960), II, 1. According to Otto, the remaining evidence does not allow us to discern whether a distinction was made by the ancient Egyptians between the statues of kings, the statues of the dead and the statues of gods. It would thus seem that a blending of these realities—royalty, death, divinity—was likely the case. That Egyptian conceptions distinguish little between kings, the dead and gods in fact confirms the picture that emerges from other sources in the study of the dynamics of ancient apotheosis: death, whether initiatory or literal, is fundamentally bound to the process of royal deification.

THE OPENING OF THE MOUTH

The ritual dynamics of divine animation inhered in a specific ceremony known as the *opet-re* (the opening of the mouth and eyes), the quintessential Egyptian rite for consecration, deification, and the infusing of spiritual presence into matter. The opening of the mouth was performed on the dead and upon divine statues so that they were able to receive sustenance through food offerings (hence the opening of the *mouth*) as well as light (hence the opening of the *eyes*). As has been demonstrated by Egyptologists such as Ann Macy Roth, all the symbols of the mouth-opening ritual point to the process of birth and rebirth. By mimicking the birth and maturation of a child, the ritual sought to 'take the newly reborn deceased person through the transitions of birth and childhood, so that he or she could be nourished by the adult food provided in such profusion for Egyptian mortuary cults'.[4] In particular, the ritual emphasises the aspects of the birth and maturation process that affect nourishment: 'the initial connection to the placenta, the severing of the umbilical cord, nursing, weaning, and teething'.[5] This is consistent with the fact that the nourishing force *par excellence* in Egyptian theology was the *ka*, a word which meant not only spirit, but placenta, and whose sense has been translated as 'all that enlivens.'[6] Ultimately, the deep interrelationship between artisanal technology and sacerdotal cult discerned in the mouth–opening ritual becomes comprehensible only when one realises that the verb *meshi*, employed in the sense of 'fashion, create', also means 'to give birth.'[7] The statue animation rite was a birth ritual because consecrated statues were divine nativities.

The very instrument used in the rituals for opening the mouth was assimilated not only to the artisan's chief tool—the adze—but also to the foreleg of the bull. Not only was this the choicest cut of meat used in food offerings, it was, more essentially, the thigh of Seth (*khepesh en setesh*), a potent symbol of vivifying and destructive power deeply instrumental to the death and revivification of Osiris.

4 Roth, 'Fingers, Stars, and the "Opening of the Mouth": The Nature and Function of the Ntrwj-Blades', *JEA* 79 (1993): 60.
5 Roth, 'Ntrwj-Blades', 60.
6 Hornung, *Idea into Image*, 175.
7 *WÄS* II, 137: 'gebären, bilden'.

The Constellation of the Thigh

In order to understand more precisely how the magical process of revivification occurred, we must turn to the scenes from the tomb of Rekhmire, where the adze and the foreleg are assimilated to each other. [8] It is important to emphasise here that the connection between the adze and the foreleg inheres in their close resemblance to the constellation of northern circumpolar stars—*ursa major*—known to the Greeks as ἀρκτος (*arktos*, the 'great bear'), but regarded by the Egyptians as the thigh or foreleg of a bull.[9]

The mouth-opening scenes feature the slaughter of the bull and the removal of its right foreleg; the offering of the foreleg to the statue; and the explicit assimilation of foreleg to the adze. Finally, we see the opening of the mouth proper, which occurs when the adze is brought in direct contact with the mouth of the statue in order to animate it. In these scenes, the foreleg of the bull is specifically assimilated to the adze through the visual resemblance of their forms, thus identifying the nourishing force (the bull, the *ka*) with the creative or shaping force (the iron-bladed statue making tool).

The constellation of the bull's foreleg came to stand, in Egypt as elsewhere, for the 'immortal' or 'undying' stars that never set, revolving around the celestial pole rather than sinking below the horizon. For Homer it was 'the Great Bear that mankind also calls the Wagon' who 'wheels on her axis always fixed, watching the Hunter', and who is 'alone denied a plunge in the Ocean's baths'.[10] The zenith of fixed stars possessed unrivalled symbolic distinction as the deathless summit of the celestial vault, tracing the unmoveable pivot upon which the cosmos was seen to turn.

The 'undying stars' (*meshkhetiu*) were regarded as the origin of meteoric iron (*bia*), which, like 'falling stars', would plunge to earth from their celestial locus as *thunderbolts*. In Egypt as elsewhere, the use of meteoric iron predates the human ability to smelt the metal from earthly ores. We catch a glimpse of this celestial origin in the Greek word *sidēros*, which

---

8 Rekhmire is an Eighteenth Dynasty Egyptian noble whose tomb preserves one of the most complete recensions of the mouth-opening ritual.
9 Roth, 'Ntrwj-Blades', 70; Herman te Velde, *Seth, God of Confusion: A Study of His Role in Egyptian Mythology and Religion* (Leiden: Brill, 1967), 86–9
10 *Iliad*, 18.69–71; cf. also the remarks on Presocratic cosmology in Kirk-Raven-Shofield, 10–17.

means both 'iron' and 'star'. What this means for the mouth-opening ritual is that the iron-bladed adze and the thigh-constellation formed a unity in the Egyptian mind, not only in terms of their form, but in the nature of their cosmic substance. The constellation of the bull's thigh, the adze, meteoric iron, and the thunderbolt all cohere as a single reality: an astral, nourishing, shaping, creative-destructive force. G. A. Wainwright makes it more explicit:

> *The thunderbolt, or lightning stroke, is the most tremendous force in nature for splitting, rending and blasting. A thunderbolt was, therefore, the most terrific instrument the priest could find with which to accomplish his design of forcing open that which death had closed.*[11]

According to the mouth-opening passages from the *Pyramid Texts*, this power comes forth from a very specific god:

> *Horus has opened the mouth of N.*
> *with that with which he opened the mouth of his father,*
> *with which he opened the mouth of Osiris*
> *with the iron* (bia) *that came from Seth,*
> *the blade of iron from the undying stars* (meshkhetiu bia)
> *with which the mouths of the gods are opened.*[12]

Murderer of Osiris, divine criminal, enemy *par excellence*, disturber of the order which Egypt itself sought to exemplify, Seth is nevertheless crucial to a cosmic ecology whereby the transitions between death and life can only be effected after the overmastering power of Seth has made a drastic fissure at the very threshold between existence and non-existence.[13] While Hermann te Velde already saw how the force represented by the foreleg of Seth is pivotal to both the death and rebirth of Osiris, the implications

---

11 Wainwright, 'Iron in Egypt', *JEA* 18 (1932): 7.

12 Faulkner, ed., *The Ancient Egyptian Pyramid Texts* (Oxford: Clarendon Press, 1969), 13–14; Mouth-opening ritual, episode 26, after Otto; cf. scene no. 25 in the tomb-chapel of Rekhmire; scenes 46 and 36; Roth, 65.

13 Seth's role in the cosmic ecology: Hornung, Chaotische Bereiche in der geordneten Welt', *ZÄS* 81 (1956): 28–32, Velde,Seth', in *Lexikon der Ägyptologie*, ed. Helck and Eberhard (Wiesbaden: O. Harrassowitz, 1972), col. 909: 'But as limited disorder was accepted as essential to a living order, S. was accepted and venerated as a god with whom one had to come to terms'.

of this observation are seldom drawn.[14] The central ontological changes that inform the Osirian drama are achieved precisely through the power of Osiris' most feared *enemy*. 'Viewed in this way', remarks te Velde, 'Seth is not only a murderer and demon of death, but also assists the resurrection of Osiris. This would mean that he is the demonic initiator, who leads his brother to life through death by violence.'[15]

Ontogeny Recapitulates Cosmogony

The mouth-opening ceremony pivots around the dangerous transition from death to life, from chaos to cosmos, from non-existence to existence. Given this, it is no surprise to find distinctly Sethian symbolism encoded into the instruments that effect the transition between these states. Indeed, it is entirely fitting for a god who presides over liminal regions, dangerous transitions, and violent initiation. More specifically, Roth lays bare how this vital transition was deeply bound to the ritual symbols of human birth. In doing this, she draws out the fundamental connections between the process of birth and the solar journey, an insight first made by the neglected Dutch *Religionshistoriker*, Bruno Hugo Stricker. For the Egyptians, *ontogeny recapitulates cosmogony*. The genesis of the being reflects genesis of the cosmos.[16] Human genesis is thus homologous to the journey of the solar divinity through the heights and depths of the heavenly expanse—moving through the celestial and subterranean worlds like the sun through the zodiac.[17]

The New Kingdom underworld books such as the *Amduat* (literally, 'what is in the underworld') and the *Book of Gates* begin with the sun's setting in the western horizon and conclude with its rising on the eastern horizon.[18] During the interim, the solar barque moves through the depths

14 Velde, *Seth*, 84–91.
15 Ibid., 98.
16 Renggli, 369: "Kosmogonie und Embryologie, Makro– und Mikro–kosmos werden beliebig miteinander verglichen. Anders ausgedrückt: die individuelle Entwicklungsgeschichte ist eine Rekapitulation der Schöpfung der Welt."
17 Renggli, „Der Sonnenaufgang als Geburt eines Babys: Der pränatale Schlüssel zur ägyptischen Mythologie. Eine Hommage an den holländischen Religionshistoriker Bruno Hugo Stricker", *International Journal of Prenatal and Perinatal Psychology and Medicine* 12, no. 2 (2000): 377; Roth, 'Pss-Kf', 138 with n. 126.
18 See Hornung, *Texte zum Amduat* (Genève: Editions de belles-lettres, 1987–1994). Other notable underworld books from this period include the *Book of Caverns* and the

of the earth, traversing the twelve hours of the night, which form the structure of the text. The underworld (*duat*) is essentially a place of regenera-
tion. It is also a place of ultimate destruction. Despite or perhaps because
of such dangers, however, the nightly descent of the sun into the depths of
the netherworld allows the solar divinity to be revitalised. This takes place
in the primordial waters of Nun. It occurs precisely at the sixth hour: the
nadir of the journey, corresponding to midnight.

One of the most specific points of convergence between the solar cosmogony and the human birth rite is the identification of Apep, the pri-
meval chaos serpent, with the umbilical cord. The god Apep, whom the
Greeks called Apōphis (Ἀπωφις), embodies a deep, eternally regenerating
menace to the existence of the gods (and by extension, the cosmos which
they create and animate). Every night, Apep threatens to extinguish the
very cosmic order that the gods embody, to envelope them utterly in the
waters of limitless darkness into which the gods must descend nightly with
the sinking of the sun. In so doing, this snake-formed god of increate darkness ultimately represents the negative or destructive valence of the same
primordial waters that actually give rise to the creator god and hence to the
Ennead and cosmos in the first place. The positive or generative valence
of the primordial waters is embodied as the god Nun, who together with
Apep, constitutes the very matrix in which reality and existence gestates.
While Apep functions to *negate* existence, at the same time he forms the
conditions which existence must emerge from.

Because Egyptian religious texts are predominantly underworld books,
their precise concern is with the dangers of this descent into the *duat* (*katabasis*). The most crucial moment in this transition culminates immediately before dawn, which is to say, before birth or emergence (*anabasis*).
Hellenistic astrologers such as Vettius Valens and Paulus Alexandrinus
referred to this threshold (the exit from the *duat*) as the 'gate of Hades'
(*Haidou pulē*), and assigned it to the second 'house' (*topos*). In this hour,
Seth, the inveterate enemy of the gods, advances to the prow of the solar
barque as the only deity with the strength to divide the Apep serpent in
two, inaugurating the cosmogonic scission, and liberating the solar divinity
and his entourage from the threat of extinction. 'The creation of the child',

---

Book of the Earth, while in the Armana period, the *Book of Nut*, and the *Book of the Night*
recapitulate the same essential themes. For a useful survey, see Hornung, *The Ancient
Egyptian Books of the Afterlife*, 26–135.

comments Roth, 'thus mimics the creation of the world, which is accomplished daily by cutting the snake's body of Apophis in two.'[19]

It is important to note, with te Velde, that Seth performs this pivotal cosmogonic role not because of any latent benevolence; rather, this occurs as a precise manifestation of the overmastering violence of his nature, above all, his *strength*. Seth, as his epithets suggest, is the separator, divider, and butcher. He corresponds closely to Arēs-Mars, the planetary divinity presiding over conflict, strife, and separation. The reality embodied by Seth ultimately instigates the very rupture between the chaos of non–existence represented by Apep, and the existent cosmos represented by the solar theophany.[20] As such, Seth is a necessary enemy to both domains, the *limen* or threshold at the edge of reality, a threat to non-existence as to existence.

In accordance with Stricker's connection between ontogeny and cosmogony, the primordial waters are recapitulated as the amniotic fluid that encompasses the developing foetus. The process of birth proceeds through the breaking of this amniotic membrane, enabling the baby to emerge from the womb. Birth is brought to definitive completion with the severing of the umbilical cord, through cutting the newborn off from the placenta. The Sethian *limen* or threshold between non–existence and existence is thereby recapitulated and crossed at the precise moment of human birth.

In the mouth-opening ritual, a birthing knife known as the *pesesh-kef*—also fashioned from meteoric iron and hence specifically assimilated to Seth—was the instrument which physically enacted this separation between child and mother.[21] To the Egyptian conception, cutting the child off from its matrix of gestation was equivalent to cutting the child off from its *ka*, which in addition to 'double, image, and manifestation', also meant *placenta*. To be born, then, was to be separated from a vital source of *nourishment*. Thus, upon birth, the sustaining *ka*-substance from the primordial amniotic waters needed to be replaced by nourishment taken through the mouth (i.e. *milk*, later food); consequently, the mouth needed to be

19 Roth, 'Pss-Kf', 139.
20 Seth as separator.
21 For evidence pertaining to the *pesesh-kef* knife: Walsem, 'The Pss-Kf: An Investigation of an Ancient Egyptian Funerary Instrument', *Oudheidkundige mededelingen uit het Rilksmuseum van Oudheden te ...* 59 (1978). For convincing interpretation of this evidence: Roth, 'Pss-Kf', passim.

'opened' so that the child could be nourished, weaned, and ultimately forced to cultivate independence.[22]

Thus, just as Seth is the god that kills Osiris, so do his instruments and symbols—the thunderbolt, meteoric iron, birthing knife, bull's thigh, circumpolar stars—revivify him. The severing of the umbilical cord with the birthing knife represents the pivotal demarcation: the child is separated from the placenta (*ka*) with an instrument of meteoric iron, and must take its own nourishment through the mouth. The new being is now able to be vivified with divine power, and the *khepesh* or foreleg is presented as a food offering to nourish the newly born entity. No longer able to draw sustenance from the placenta, it must, after suitable maturity is attained, nourish itself on the power embodied in the thigh. As we have seen, this is much more than a premium cut of meat. It is in reality the undying power by which the gods vivify the dead, consecrate cult-images, and transmit theocratic strength to warrior-kings. Like the lightning strike, it is the most unadulterated current of celestial force in the cosmos. Given the bivalence of this force, it is no surprise that its potent destructive power is commensurately balanced by its ability to revivify, immortalise, and deify.[23]

Opet and the Thigh

At the very centre of the Dendera Zodiac, the thigh of the bull (*ursa major*) is depicted alongside the goddess Opet, a divinity who provides an important key to the rites of death and rebirth with which the mouth-opening ritual was concerned. Opet is a hippopotamus-formed goddess presiding over birth and suckling. In her Theban context, she serves as protectress over the birth of the god Amun (Zeus). In the Opet festival, whose epicenter was the temple of Amun at Luxor, her role was to ensure that the cosmic dangers that beset the annual rebirth of Amun through the apotheosis of the pharaoh were allayed.

---

22 To ensure that the child is able to breathe and feed, the newborn's mouth must first be cleared of the mucus which gathers there prior to birth; the ideal and natural object for this was the little finger. As Roth maintains, the *ntrjw* blades, because of their symmetrical form and duality, are consistent with the ritual forms and uses of the little finger inserted into the mouth.

23 Cf. Plutarch's account of Alexander's mother's womb being sealed by a thunderbolt—here bespeaking its generative power—after being inseminated by Zeus in the form of a serpent.

Opet is a threshold being, and typical of the liminal divinities that in-habit regions far from established order, she takes on a monstrous appear-ance: to her hippopotamus form are wedded the tail of a crocodile and the paws of a lion. In many respects Opet partakes of the same animal forms as Seth; it is therefore appropriate that, in exploring the function of Opet, the presence of Seth is naturally evoked. Indeed, Seth himself was often depicted as a (male) hippopotamus, an animal vilified and hunted because of its devastating power to decimate precious crops. As such, Seth forms a destructive complement to the generative (female) hippopotamus god-dess, Opet (much as Apep forms the destructive compliment to Nun in Egyptian cosmology).

Opet is also the Egyptian term for 'opening', as we have seen through the *opet-re*, the 'opening of the mouth'. The connection to the mouth-open-ing rite is by no means accidental, for the hippopotamus goddess herself is known to play a significant role in restraining the destructive valence of the *meshkhetiu*, the Sethian constellation of the bull's thigh that kills and revivifies. In doing this, she functions to hold back the murderous force of Seth in order to facilitate the creative valence of rebirth.[24] Opet thus possesses a close relationship to the bull's thigh, which goes a long way to explaining their depiction together at the centre of the Dendera Zodiac.

We have seen how Seth clearly participated in the rites of cosmic and royal rebirth by slaying Apep and cutting the umbilical cord. However, he also played another, perhaps more fundamental, role in the process of birth. Seth is often invoked in the magical papyri and depicted on magi-cal gems in contexts which link him specifically with the opening of the womb, an act which could have both negative and positive connotations. As Ritner has shown, Egyptian gynaecological conceptions saw opening and closing as two necessary activities which regulated the normal func-tioning of the uterus:

> *Opening is required for expulsion of the menses, conception, and birth. Nega-tively, it may signal hemorrhaging and abortion. Closing may halt such*

24 Cf. Meeks, 'Ipet (Jpt)', in *Lexikon der Ägyptologie*, III, col. 173: 'Occasionnellement *Jpt* incarne la constellation de l'hippopotame ayant un crocodile sur son dos et dont la fonction est de retenir la Grand Ourse (*Mskhtjw*), constellation sethienne, afin qu'elle ne puisse retourner dans l'autre monde troubler Osiris'. ('Occasionally *Jpt* embodies the constellation of the hippopotamus having a crocodile on its back, whose function is to detain the Great She-Bear (*Mskhtjw*), the Sethian constellation, so that it is not able to return into the other world to disturb Osiris').

menorrhage and stabilize the egg, but it may also prevent delivery. Neither activity is inherently positive or negative. Both must be regulated to ensure the health of any woman.[25]

What these various mythic contexts suggest is that Opet's restraining of the bull's thigh at the celestial pole acts to facilitate birth in a very specific way: by preventing the Sethian disruptions of hemorrhaging and abortion and thereby regulating the opening of the womb in order that it may dilate at the opportune time.

The Man with the Golden Thigh

Another revealing example of the thigh as symbol of divine rebirth occurs in the Pythagorean doxographies. In classical antiquity, Pythagoras of Samos was regarded, at least by his disciples, as 'no ordinary man but a god'; a being of 'higher than mortal nature and origin'.[26] More specifically, he was revered as the Hyperborean form of Apollo.[27] Significantly, the visible sign of Pythagoras' divine nature was a golden thigh.

The sixth-century Neoplatonic Theurgist, Iamblichus, left an account of Pythagoras' life in which Pythagoras reveals his divine nature to Abaris, the high priest of Apollo. In this account, Abaris, an intriguing figure in his own right, arrives from Hyperborea ('beyond the northern winds') and presents a golden arrow—the symbol of his god—to Pythagoras:

Pythagoras, however, accepted the arrow, without expressing any amazement at the novelty of the thing, nor asking why the arrow was presented to him, as if he really was a God. Then he took Abaris aside and showed him his golden thigh, as an indication that he was not wholly mistaken.[28]

---

25 Ritner, 'A Uterine Amulet in the Oriental Institute Collection', 221.

26 Iamblichus, *Vit. Pyth.* 28.140: 'The Pythagoreans derive their confidence in their views from the fact that the first to express them was no ordinary man but a god'. Cf. *Aristotelis Fragmenta Selecta*, ed. W. D. Ross (=*AFS*), 130–3; Ael. *V. H.* 4. 7: 'Pythagoras used to teach that he was of higher than mortal nature and origin' (=*AFS*, 131).

27 D. L. 8. 1.11: 'He is said to have been an awful person, and it was the opinion of his disciples that he was Apollo, come from the Hyperboreans' (=*AFS*, 131); Ael. *V. H.* 2.26: 'Aristotle says that Pythagoras was hailed by the people of Croton as Apollon Hyperboreios'.

28 Iamblichus, *Vit. Pyth.* § 19; Fildeler and Guthrie, eds., 80. NB: *quote continues.*

Like the bronze sandals worn by Empedocles and other initiates within the purview of Pythagorean tradition, the golden thigh has been seen as a symbol of descent into the underworld, of initiatory death and rebirth, and of emergence as a god.[29] As Cook points out, the detail of divine incarnation presupposes the philosophical death of Pythagoras as well as his consequent rebirth as an avatar of Apollo. The golden thigh thus highlights Pythagoras' divine nature in a very specific sense.[30]

As to the *arrow* received by Pythagoras, it confirms the association with Apollo that is garnered from the thigh. The bow and arrow, along with the lyre, are the sacred instruments of Apollo. *The Homeric Hymn to Apollo* informs us that it was with an arrow that Apollo slew the serpent Python. As René Guénon points out, this arrow is equivalent to the thunderbolt (*vajra*) with which the Vedic god Indra kills the demonic serpent, Vrtra: 'the thunder-wielder, he kills the dragon'.[31] Once again, the overarching symbolic references point to the primordial motif of *drakontomachia* (serpent slaying) and here one cannot overlook the deep coherence that the slaying of Python has with its Egyptian counterpart: the slaying of Apep and the rebirth of the sun.

Sagittarius and the Thigh

The mysterious connection between the golden thigh of Pythagoras and the arrow of Abaris alerts us to an intriguing detail from traditional medical astrology. Demarcating a fundamental homology between microcosm and macrocosm, the foundational texts of Hellenistic astrology provide us with a consistent set of correspondences between the signs of the zodiac and human physiology. From the head to the heels, the body recapitulates the zodiac from Aries to Pisces. According to this schematic, the thighs are said to be ruled by Sagittarius—the archer.

The origins of iatromathematics (medical astrology) are first attested to by the Roman poet, Marcus Manilius (first century CE), who, in Book II of his *Astronomicon*, connects 'Sagittarius' (*centauro*) with 'the thighs'

---

29 Kingsley, *Ancient Philosophy*, 289–91.
30 Cook, *Zeus: A Study in Ancient Religion* (Cambridge: Cambridge University Press, 1914), II, 223–5; Burkert, *Lore and Science*, 159–61; Dodds, *The Greeks and the Irrational* (Berkeley: University of California Press, 1951), 163 n. 43; Eliade, *Shamanism*, 45 ff, 53.
31 See the discussion of 'Symbolic Weapons' in *Fundamental Symbols*, 125; *Rg Veda*, 1.32.

(*femina*).[32] Similarly for Vettius Valens (120–175 CE), 'the archer' (*toxotēs*) rules 'the thighs and groin' (*mēroi boubōnes*).[33] But just as the symbolic connection between thigh and arrow evokes the motif of (re)birth, so too does the astrological signification. For Valens, the wider significations of Jupiter, the planetary ruler of Sagittarius, include 'childbearing' (*teknōsin*) and 'engendering' (*gonēn*); in addition to ruling the thighs and feet of the external body, he also rules the sperm (*sporas*), uterus (*mētras*), and liver (*hēpatos*) of the internal body.[34] These details cohere deeply with the humoural physiologies of eastern as well as western medical tradition, in which the marrow of the femur is seen as continuous with cerebrospinal fluid and semen. According to this conception, the thighbones contain the very root of the generative principle and govern everything to do with longevity. A similar idea continues in the work of modern Hermetic philosophers such as René Schwaller de Lubicz, for whom the femur holds the immortal mineral remains that survive combustion and putrefaction, forming the very pivot of palingenesis. In alchemy, the ashes of the femur—the largest and most dense bone in the body—are especially significant for they preserve the fixed alchemical salt from which the entity may rise again like a phœnix. It is thus the key to bodily resurrection.

We need not look far in the mythology of Zeus/Jupiter before we find some unusually specific connections to the themes we have been exploring. In Euripides' *Bacchae*, Zeus fathers the god Dionysus with a mortal lover, Semele. Before the god is born, however, Hera, ever-jealous, tricks her husband into appearing before his mortal consort in the fullness of his divine form. Zeus consequently reveals himself as the thunderbolt (*keraunos*), the divine fire that 'burns away mortal parts', and Semele is incinerated. Dionysus, however, survives due to his immortal nature, and Zeus rescues the unborn god from his mother's mortal ashes and places him in a womb or cavity in his thigh:

> *And Zeus the son of Cronos*
> *Ensconced Dionysus instantly in a secret womb*
> *Chambered within his thigh* (mērō),
> *And with golden pins closed him from Hera's sight.*[35]

32 Manilius II.463: '*Centauro femina accedunt*'.
33 Vettii Valentis, *Anthologiarum Libri*, Guilelmus Kroll, 2.36.110–11, 37–1.
34 Kroll, Liber I, Kap. 1, p. 2, lines 24–34.
35 Euripides, *Bacchae*, lines 94–98 (tr. Philip Vellacott); Dodds, *Euripides Bacchae*, 6–7.

Dionysus, who is consequently referred to as the 'thigh-bred' (*mero-traphēs*), gestates in and is born from the thigh of his divine father as in a womb.[36] While this entire episode may seem strange, it agrees with what we learn from Valens: in addition to the thigh, Zeus rules semen and the womb, taking on both paternal and maternal functions.

The Theophany of Mithras

To bring matters back to the topic at hand, one final example of a golden thigh must be mentioned. It comes from the so-called 'Mithras Liturgy' in the *Greek Magical Papyri*. Herein we find an explicit description of theurgic ascent (*anagōgia*) in which the initiate ascends to the company of gods by breathing in their fiery emanations. Before him the seven Fates appear as virgins with the faces of asps, followed by the seven 'Pole Lords of heaven' (youths with the faces of black bulls). The initiate greets the latter as 'guardians of the pivot', who 'turn at one command the revolving axis of the vault of heaven', sending out 'thunder and lightning', 'earthquakes and thunderbolts'. All of this occurs during the 'good hours of this day', suggesting an auspicious astrological timing.[37] After the initiate greets the seven Lords, the manifestation of Mithras-Helios occurs:

> *Now when they* [the Pole Lords] *take their place, here and there, in order, look in the air and you will see lightning bolts going down, and lights flashing, and the earth shaking, and a god descending, a god immensely great, having a bright appearance, youthful, golden-haired, with a white tunic and a golden crown and trousers, and holding in his right hand a golden shoulder* [foreleg] *of a young bull: this is the Bear* (Arktos) *which moves and turns heaven around, moving upward and downward in accordance with the hour. Then you will see lightning bolts leaping from his eyes and stars from his body.*[38]

---

36 LSJ, 1129: *AP* 11.329 (Nicharch.); Strabo, 15.1.7; Eust. ad D.P. 1153; also *-trephēs*, *Orph. H.* 52.3. Cf. Herodotus. 2.146.2; Arrian, *F. G. H.* 3.592 (localising the birth in Bithynia); Theocritus 26.33 (in Drakanon; cf. *H. Hymn.* 1.1). Cf. remarks in E. R. Dodds, ed., *Euripides Bacchae* (Oxford: Clarendon, 1960), 79.
37 *PGM* IV. 680–86.
38 Ibid., 694–704.

Here, in a Greek text dated, on linguistic and paleographic grounds, to the early fourth century,[39] a bull's foreleg is identified with the Bear (*Arktos*, or *ursa major*).[40] Moreover, the wielder of this foreleg is seen to descend from the celestial pole while giving forth lightning bolts. The links to the mouth–opening instrument are clear—a bull's thigh from the celestial pole whose substance is that of the thunderbolt. In this connection, it is hardly coincidental that at the very epicentre of the Mithraic mysteries proper—and at the literal centre of its iconography—is the *tauroctony*: the life-giving bull-sacrifice which engenders renewal and rebirth, precisely the function of the slaughter of the bull and the offering of its thigh to the statue in the Egyptian mouth-opening ritual. Depictions of the *tauroctony*, which famously portray Mithras slaying the bull, are frequently surrounded by the signs of the zodiac, and often feature Sol, Luna, the five planetary divinities, along with symbols of the constellations, further supporting the circumpolar nature of the central motif.

THE TELESTIC ART

Hieratic Neoplatonists such as Proclus referred to statue animation as the telestic art (*telistikē*, literally [the art of] 'perfection' or 'completion'). They used it as a general synonym for theurgy, which means 'divine work', or the 'work of the gods'. More precisely, however, they indicated the central process of *anagōgia*, in which the divine fire of Helios would purify the initiate from the accretions of human generation and corruption, raising them to participation in divinity (*theōsis*). According to the rituals of the telestic art, statues, symbols, and sages alike become infused with purifying divine presence through the principles of cosmic *sympatheia*.

The principle of divine *sympatheia* is particularly replete throughout the *Greek Magical Papyri*, which preserves, among other things, a spell for animating cult images of Helios inscribed on a magic ring. In this instance, the temple statue is replaced by a ring inset with a heliotrope (a gemstone

39 Though, as Betz notes (*Mithras Liturgy*, 9), the text's composition probably came together over the preceding two centuries, from both older and younger sources. Moreover: "the text is thoroughly Hellenistic-Egyptian—without any traces of Christian, Christian-gnostic, or Neoplatonic influences—, although traditions of Middle Stoicism are apparent, as is a certain closeness to Hermeticism."

40 See Fauth, "Arktos in den griechischen Zauberpapyi", *ZPE* 57 (1984). Cf., however, Betz, *Mithras Liturgy*, 184–5 with refs.

sympathetic to the sun) upon which images of the god Helios, and a radiant scarab encircled by an ouroboros, are inscribed.[41] According to H. J. Thissen, the name *Ouphōr*—one of the *voces magicae* used in the rite—specifically derives from the Egyptian phrase *opet-re*, 'to open the mouth'.[42] What is more, Ian Moyer and Jacco Dieleman have suggested that the ring consecration rite exemplifies the miniaturisation process described by Jonathan Z. Smith, whereby practices originally employed within temple contexts by 'priests' are scaled down for use by 'magicians'.[43] Not only does the inscription on the gemstone function as the cult-image, in this connection the inscribed gemstone is in fact referred to as a *statue*. This is significant because it demonstrates one way in which ritual practitioners from Egyptian temples consciously adapted and transmitted their native traditions beyond their original cultural contexts; in the case of the ring consecration—a quintessentially talismanic rite—it demonstrates the adaptation and preservation of the mouth-opening ritual in particular.

To the extent that talisman creation is equivalent to the consecration of images, it coheres with the Egyptian understanding of magic, which was predicated upon the imagistic basis of Egyptian theology. As we have seen, the fashioning of a statue was the means by which the cult image of a god was formed (born). This image, when animated with divine presence, was equivalent to the living manifestation of that god into physical existence on earth. Accordingly, giving birth and the fashioning of 'living images' were regarded as magical acts of creation, a point which we understand more precisely when we realise that the Egyptian term for magic, *heka*, derives from the verb *hwi-* ('to strike, consecrate') and the noun *ka* ('double, image, manifestation').[44] Thus, the process of consecrating the

41 *PGM* XII. 270–350.

42 See H. J. Thissen, 'Ägyptologische Beiträge zu den griechischen magischen Papyri', in *Religion und Philosophie im alten Ägypten: Festgabe für Philippe Derchain zu seinem 65. Geburtstag am 24. Juli 1991*, ed. Verhoeven and Graefe, *Orientalia Lovaniensia Analecta; 39* (Leuven: Department Orientalistiek/Peeters, 1991). See also Hopfner, I, § 808.

43 See I. Moyer and J. Dieleman, 'Miniaturization and the Opening of the Mouth in a Greek Magical Text (*PGM* XII. 270–350)', *Journal of Ancient Near Eastern Religions* 3, 1 (2003): 66 ff; Smith, 'Trading Places', in *Ancient Magic and Ritual Power*, ed. Meyer and Mirecki, *Religions in the Greco-Roman World* (Leiden: E. J. Brill, 1995).

44 Heka as the consecration of images: Ritner, Velde, "The God Heka in Egyptian Theology," *Jaarbericht ex Oriente Lux* 21 (1970). *Ka* as double, image and manifestation: Kaplony, "Ka," in *Lexikon der Ägyptologie*, ed. Helck and Eberhard (Wiesbaden: O. Harrassowitz, 1972).

ka or image of a god—which could mean a king or priest as much as a statue or talisman—by striking its mouth with the iron blade of an adze, is fundamentally assimilated to a process of magical consecration and animation: the infusing of an image with divine, vivifying power in order that it may act as an extension of the god to whom it is consecrated. Alongside invocations and offerings, astrological timing necessarily played a critical role in determining the *energeia* of the god awakened within the material substance.

The word talisman comes into European languages from Arabic *tilsam* (plural *tilsaman*), which is in turn derived from Byzantine Greek *telesma* 'talisman, religious rite, payment'. The roots of the word *telesma*, however, run deeper, deriving from the ancient Greek verb *teleiō*, which means 'to perfect, complete, accomplish'. This expression is related not only to the telestic 'art of perfection', it is also synonymous with the mysteries (*mystēria*). In ancient Greek, the word *myein*, 'to initiate [into the mysteries]' is interchangeable with *telein* 'to perfect, complete, accomplish'.[45]

With respect to the Egyptian provenance of the telestic art, it is significant that both of these terms—perfection and mystery—neatly encapsulate the literal and implied meaning of the name of the god Amun (Zeus/Jupiter). As Egyptologist Erik Hornung has pointed out, the name Amun (*imn*) means 'the hidden one', but the idea of hiddenness itself was closely bound to the idea of primordial perfection: Amun is the 'hidden one' precisely by virtue of being 'the perfected one'.[46] This is because the concept of perfection was bound not to the visible world (Amun-Re as *deus revelatus*),[47] but to the mysterious world of 'hiddenness', the invisible world underpinning phenomena (Amun-Re as *deus absconditus*). Here the primordial nature of Amun forms the benefic, creative potential of the primordial darkness, balancing the malefic, destructive darkness represented

---

45 Liddel-Scott-Jones, τελει-οω (*telei-oō*), 'make perfect, complete, accomplish; bring to perfection or consummation'; *teloi*, 'mysteries' (*mysterion*); cf. Erman/Grapow, *Wörterbuch* I, 83ff, *imn*, 'verborgen sein' (to be concealed); *imn.t*, 'das Verborgene, das Geheim' (the concealed, the secret).

46 See Erik Hornung, *Idea into Image: Essays on Ancient Egyptian Thought*. New York: Timken, 1992.

47 In this regard, cf. Atum, whose name means the 'finisher'. Both Amun and Atum must be understood as representing different phases of the cosmogonic process; Atum as 'finisher' is more related to manifest perfection, the culmination of cosmogenesis, whereas Amun is the primordial, unmanifest ground of being, the roots underpinning the manifestation of cosmogenesis.

by Apep.

The idea or perfection as primordial hiddenness has a number of ramifications for the conception of initiation expressed by the word *telein*. Although the word seems to point to the meaning of 'completion, end-point,
perfection' (*telos*), and the mysteries may be understood accordingly as
means of 'perfecting' human initiates, in Latin the word is rendered as
initium (whence initiate), which means precisely the opposite: the beginning point.[48] We may surmise that the deeper ground upon which these
opposites rest is the hidden place where 'beginning' and 'end' meet, the
alpha and the *ōmega*, neither of which reside within linear time (the historical realm of visible manifestation grows *out of* the primordial darkness in
Egyptian cosmology). Because this reality is 'beyond' time, conventional
language can only describe it in terms of time's extremes: its beginning
and end-points. Given these considerations, the purpose of 'initiation' may
be defined as the ability to move from the visible level of creation to the
invisible *roots* of creation, while the purpose of magic may be defined as the
ability to shape the former in the image of the latter. Astrology may be understood as the cosmological paradigm that *mediates* between these realms.
In any event, the ability to reveal the hidden divinity present within visible
matter, and to help unfold its workings, touches on the deeper purpose of
talismanic magical practice.

The Path Up and the Path Down

In so far as talismanic processes embody a precise juncture of metaphysical and material realities, they may be recognised as Platonic. For Plato,
form (*eidolon*) is immaterial, while substance (*hypodochē*) is formless. Together they create *formed substance*, or *material form*, which is what we perceive with our senses. In the same way, the creation of talismans involves
an equivalent juncture of immaterial form (a planetary divinity) with unformed matter (a substance sympathetic to that divinity within the chain of
being). The talismanic body is thus a material receptacle that has taken on
the qualities of the divine form 'impressed' upon it—a process frequently
likened to a seal pressed into wax. Through this process the essence of the
god descends into, or is awakened within, matter.

Just as planetary influences are crystallised into bodily beings, so too

---

48 Initiation, from *in* + *iter*, literally, '[he/she] goes in'; compare *ex-iter*, '[he/she] goes
out.'

is the human soul seen to descend into material embodiment via a similar process. Among the Hermetic and gnostic texts of late antiquity, however, the seven planetary spheres are regarded as binding forces that enslave us within the cycles of generation and corruption. Within this schematic, we find a number of references to the vices that the human soul acquires in its descent into material existence, each of which is associated with a particular planetary sphere. 'When souls descend', remarks Marcus Servius in his commentary on Virgil's *Aenid*, 'they draw with them the sloth of Saturn, the wrath of Mars, the lust of Venus, Mercury's passion for money, and Jupiter's desire to rule'.[49] Cosmologically, the kingdom of the 'seven' (*hebdoas*) shuts the soul off from the eighth sphere (*ogdoas*), the divine totality or fullness (*plerōma*) from which the soul originates. However, although the planetary forces trap us in the sublunary world, they also form the steps of the ontological ladder by which we may extricate ourselves from samsaric existence. By climbing the seven planetary spheres and relinquishing the bonds of astral determinism instilled in us through the process of embodiment (*ensōmatosis*), the planetary vices may be transformed into antidotes.

All of this is to suggest that, while the creation of statues and talismans replicates the process of birth, it is not the birth of a mortal body that is at stake, for this is simply another body bound by sublunary forces. Rather, it is the creation of an immortal body—a vehicle for spirit (*ōchema pneuma*) or body of resurrection (*anastasia sōma*)—free from the leaden accretions of planetary descent. Paradoxically, this is a body that has a presence in the material world, and yet transcends it. This point becomes more understandable when we realise that, unlike Platonic dualists (for whom philosophy was an escape from a demonic, spiritually devoid cosmos), hieratic Neoplatonists such as Iamblichus held that matter and nature were derived from, i.e. created by, a divine principle, and that the modalities of nature were *extensions* of divinity. The phenomenal cosmos for Iamblichus is a theurgic act in itself, the visible portion of the entire spectrum of divine activity. Moreover, the soul's dual nature as mean term between mortality

---

49 Servius, *In Aen.* 6.714; cf. *Corpus Hermeticum* 1.25 (Poimandres), where the Moon gives physical growth and decay; Mercury, malicious artifice; Venus, lust; the Sun, ambition to dominate; Mars, reckless audacity; Jupiter, greed and aggrandizement; and Saturn, falsehood. See also Kurt Rulolph, *Gnosis: The Nature and History of Gnosticism*, (HarperSanFrancisco, 1987), 67 ff; Ioan P. Culianu, *Psychanodia: A Survey of the Evidence Concerning the Ascension of the Soul and its Relevance* (Leiden; Brill, 1983), 48–9; Nicola F. Denzey, *Cosmology and Fate in Gnosticism and Graeco-Roman Antiquity: Under Pitiless Skies* (Leiden: Brill, 2013), 113 ff.

and immortality gives it the privileged position of being able to participate directly in both worlds.[50]

CONCLUSION

The planetary theurgy of divine images, especially as expressed in the *Corpus Hermeticum*, had already drawn the rebuke of Augustine (354–430 CE), who branded it heretical, and the telestic art became a central point of contention in the polemics of early Catholicism against paganism. Nevertheless, the far-ranging influence of these traditions would see the telestic rites revived in the precepts and practices of Islamicate, Renaissance, and Persian Illuminationist Hermeticism. It is thus important to recognise that the connections and continuities that we have established here between statue animation, the *symbolique* of the thigh, and the telestic art, are all foundational to the hieratic practices that fed and informed these later cultural traditions.

After Justinian closed the Platonic academy in 529 CE, the animation of divine images via Hermetic principles emerged most distinctly in the Islamicate world. Most intriguing are the accounts of the 'star worshipping' Sabians of Harran, who held the *Corpus Hermeticum* as a sacred work, and formed one of seven cities, each of which was dedicated to a planetary divinity. In the ninth century, the Sabian mathematician and translator Thābit Ibn Qurra (826–901 CE) wrote a work called *De Imagibus* (On Images), which together with the eleventh century *Picatrix* (*Ghāyat al-Ḥakīm*, or 'Goal of the Wise') form the most important primary sources of practical planetary magic. In fifteenth century Europe, the telestic arts would be further revived—along with the Platonic academy itself—in the Renaissance Hermeticism of Marsilio Ficino (1433–1499), who famously translated the Hermetic and Platonic texts into Latin and integrated the theurgic doctrine of sympathies into a consistent system of magical correspondences. The deeper alchemical principle of the immortal *corpus resurrectionis* also continued down into modern times. In the nineteenth century Shaikhī school of Illuminationist Sufi theosophy, Shaik Ahmad Ahsaī (d. 1826) speaks to the heart of the alchemical opus when he speaks of a 'spiritual body [...] which is not formed of the sublunar Elements, but from the four Elements of the world of Hūrqalyā [the world beyond the plan-

50 Gregory Shaw, *Theurgy and the Soul*, 16.

etary spheres], which are seventy times nobler and more precious than the Elements of the terrestrial world.'[51] Our examples may be multiplied, but enough has been said to highlight the threads of a very rich tapestry whose warp and weft arises from the still deeper rhythms of the ancient world.

* *
*

---

51 Epistle addressed to Fath-'Ali Shāh Qājar, Shah of Persia (1797–1834)', Jawāmī' 'al-kalim, vol. 1.1, 5th risāla, 122–4; trans. Henry Corbin, *Spiritual Body and Celestial Earth* (Princeton, New Jersey: Princeton University Press, 1977), 198.

𝔇ark 𝔐atter

Mallorie Vaudoise

IT IS OUR bias as astrologers to look up at the infinite sky and see only stars. Knowingly or not, we often neglect the dark vault into which they are set. This is one symptom of a bias that runs deep within our culture. We are trained to ignore the dark, the feminine, the queer, the Other. And none more so than the dead, whose invisible presence acts as our own Primum Mobile. The dead are the backdrop for our own rise and set, and for the conjunctions and oppositions we make with one another along the way.

Physicists hypothesize that dark matter and dark energy constitute 95% of the materialist Universe. This is a majority that deserves our attention, so we may at the very least understand the nature of our environs. What, then, are the fundamental *metaphysical* properties of the space between and beyond the stars, this so-called dark matter? How do we come to know this seemingly unknowable nonsubstance?

The Western astrological and magical traditions refer to darkness in several guises. There is the ecliptic, the path traced by the sun through the cosmos. The ecliptic itself is dark and thus, in a sense, unknowable. Like physical dark matter, we understand it by the proxy of visible objects. There are also the houses, an alternate and complementary way of dividing space relative to the earth. As we shall see, astrological elections frequently rely on the relationship between the dark houses and their visible domicile rulers. Descriptions of how to understand and apply these technologies of darkness are found dating back to Babylon and persist through Hellenistic and later European texts on astrology.

Running in parallel to the development of this astrological technology are themes of blindness and invisibility emerging from a tradition of magical praxis with distinctly chthonic connotations. Though they are most certainly older, we find these themes in the Greek Magical Papyri. Dating from the 2nd century BCE to the 5th century CE, the Greek Magical Papyri are roughly contemporaneous with the Hellenistic tradition of astrology. Looking at the themes of darkness, space, blindness, and invisibility in these seemingly unrelated bodies of literature may yield new insights regarding foundational elements of both, as well as their descendants, which include later treatises on astrology and magic such as the *Picatrix* and the European grimoire tradition.

Let us begin our inquiry by exploring the treatment of empty space in Western astrology. Within an astrological chart, space is measured by the ecliptic. It is along this band that we locate the celestial bodies, so considering how the ecliptic is defined in traditional sources might provide us with some perspective on the nature of that space. There are various ways to measure ecliptic coordinates, many of which are intended to complement rather than replace one another in practice. These include the familiar zodiacal signs, the decans (subdivisions of the zodiacal signs into three ten-degree spans), the bounds (subdivisions of the zodiacal signs into five uneven spans), and the lunar mansions (which divide the ecliptic into twenty-eight or twenty-nine spans, entirely independent of the zodiac). Trying to find a consistency across these systems or some universal underlying pattern yields no fruit.

These sets of divisions are further diversified by the distinction between the tropical and sidereal zodiacs. During the period in which Hellenistic astrology was being developed, these calculations more or less aligned, so tropical Aries was located in the same region as sidereal Aries. But over the centuries these signs have shifted due to a phenomenon known as the precession of the equinoxes. At the time of this writing, the two are separated by a growing offset of about twentyfive degrees. However, Hellenistic astrologers understood the difference between the tropical and sidereal zodiacs, as well as the phenomenon of precession, and concluded that both systems were equally valid. In his *Anthologies*, Vettius Valens gives evocative descriptions of the zodiacal signs which combine sidereal and tropical reasoning. For example, he describes Taurus as:

> *...feminine, solid, lying in the sun's spring tropic, full of bones, with some limbs missing, rising backwards, setting straight down. This sign lies for the most part in the invisible sky. It is calm. From its first degree to 6° (the section of the Pleiades) it is worthless, even destructive, diseaseproducing, thundering, causing earthquakes and lightning flashes. The next two degrees are fiery and smokey. The right part (toward Auriga) is temperate and cool. The left parts are worthless and changeable, sometimes chilling, at other times heating. The head (to 23°) is in a temperate atmosphere, but it causes disease and death for living things. The rest is destructive, worthless, diseaseridden...*[1]

Here we see a reference to 'the sun's spring tropic', as well as sidereal logic which involves the reputations of the stars within the constellation of Taurus and the constellation's orientation as it rises and sets. It is through the proxy of celestial bodies that astrologers usually come to understand the ecliptic. In the example above, Valens derives the signification of an empty space, the thirty degrees of the ecliptic we call Taurus, by observing the visible bodies within it in much the same way that physicists infer the properties of dark matter by looking at its effect on the visible matter. But can we really say we understand something, if we only ever consider it in relation to something else?

We recognize that there are multiple systems for describing the ecliptic, and that many of these systems are meant to be applied in tandem. This inconsistency does not harm our understanding, but rather, it reveals the nature of darkness as the presence of legions. This is perhaps even closer to the truth than any description of dark matter derived from the observation of visible bodies. Legion is the nature of darkness in relation to itself. The decans in particular have a reputation for being haunted by ghostly legions which stretches back into antiquity.[2]

Most importantly, it should be noted that all of these diverse systems—the two zodiacs, the decans, the mansions, et cetera—render empty space comprehensible, not by filling it, but by *dividing it*. These divisions of dark

1 Vettius Valens, *Anthologies* trans. Mark T. Riley, Book I, p. 3. Last accessed 8/30/2015 at http://www.csus.edu/indiv/r/rileymt/Vettius%20Valens%20entire.pdf.
2 Coppock, Austin. *36 Faces: The History, Astrology, and Magic of the Decans.* Three Hands Press, 2014, p. 24.

or invisible space can be channeled through ritual action into the visible universe, where they can then be subjected to the same manipulation as any visible matter.

Picatrix, an Arabic text that entered the European astrological tradition when it was translated into Latin in 1256, provides a wealth of astrological talismans which do just that. Talismans are perhaps the most prominent form of explicitly astrological magic within the Western tradition. They require careful timing and a deep understanding of astrological theory in order to execute. By examining practical instructions for how to elect the opportune moment to harvest and preserve the fruit of celestial influences, we can infer something about the nature of these forces. We can also see principles of astrological reasoning at play which go otherwise unmentioned in theoretical texts, including the more theoretical chapters of *Picatrix* itself.

One of the most salient features common to many of the elections given in Book I, Chapter 5 of *Picatrix* is the house lords. The lord of a house is the domicile ruler of the sign in which the house cusp lies. The relationship between the domicile and its ruler is sometimes compared to that of a house and its master. Consequently, the relative dignity or debility of a planet will impact the fortunes of those signs it rules:

> *For if the ruler of the sign is well located, that planet about which we are inquiring also shares in a part of the good fortune of the host's joy. But if the ruler of the sign is dejected in any way, that planet about which we are inquiring, even though placed in a fortunate house, will be hindered by the dejection of that other planet which is the ruler of the sign. This you can easily observe from human behavior. If you enter anyone's home by invitation and the master of the house has just been blessed with an increase in good fortune, you too become a participant in his good fortune, for you share in the happiness of the good fortune of your host.*[3]

I would argue that, in magical practice, the relationship between the houses and their domicile rulers reaches even farther than the housemaster analogy implies. *Picatrix* , for example, lists a number of elections in which the house rulers appear to function in much the same way that personal concerns or volts do in various schools of folk magic. The part stands in

---

3 Julius Firmicus Maternus, *Mathesis*, Book II, Ch. 22: 89, ed. and trans. James Herschel Holden. Tempe, AZ, 2011, pp. 6970.

for the whole, and thus whatever virtues that part is brought into contact with—whether beneficent or baneful—also affect the whole. A simple example from *Picatrix*:

> *An image to generate peace and love between two people. Make two images under the ascendant of the question, and make fortunate the ascendant and tenth house, and remove malefics from the ascendant, and make the lord of the tenth house fortunate and applying to the lord of the ascendant by a trine or sextile aspect.*[4]

We can infer some of the logic behind these instructions. The client is being represented by the domicile ruler of the Ascendent, whereas the one with whom they wish to foster peace and love is represented by the tenth house. These planets are then united by a trine or sextile, which are regarded as aspects of harmonious communion. This is a curious magical formula through which the dark matter of a house is channeled into the visible universe, thereby making it subject to manipulation through visible action. By using a signifier in the form of a domicile ruler, new relationships between spaces become possible. The Ascendant and the tenth house will, by definition, always be roughly square to one another. However, when the Ascendant and the tenth house are embodied by planets, they are liberated to form any aspect. What the magician is doing through these talismanic elections is nothing short of remapping the landscape of heaven.

In another example from *Picatrix*, we see how the relationship between house lords plays out when two talismans are being cast in relation to one another:

> *Now I will explain how you should make a twofold image. If you do this for two friends, make the eleventh house of the first image the ascendant of the second image; and if you wish to generate friendship between man and wife, make the ascendant of the second image the seventh house of the first image. And make it so the lord of the ascendant of the one who will return the friendship makes a good aspect with reception to the lord of the ascendant of the*

---

4 *Picatrix*, Book I, Chapter 5, trans. John Michael Greer and Christopher Warnock. Lexington, KY, 2014, p. 40.

other image. Then join the images and bury them in the place of the one who is to have friendship and they will be friends as before.[5]

The detail of placing the seventh house of the first image as the Ascendant of the second is well worth noting. The obvious implication is that a link is being forged between the target's seventh house of marriage and the desirous party. But there is something truly beautiful about how this works in practice: in doing so, the whole chart is rotated 180°. Is there any more accurate way to capture the feeling of falling in love, than turning someone's world upside down? Does love not turn Hell into Heaven, and Heaven into Hell?

This particular example seems tailormade to illustrate the principles of sympathetic magic as explicated by Frazer. The act of tying the two images together to produce a bond of affection employs the Law of Similarity: the cord resembles love itself, which keeps two people together, whether in friendship or romance. The detail of burying the bound images in the home of the target employs the Law of Contagion. Presumably, the spell grows stronger when the target walks near or over the images.

Spells employing the act of tying, adhering, or otherwise joining images in order to produce bonds of love are rife within Western magic. A survey of GrecoRoman love magic from the sixth century BCE through late antiquity reveals the recitation of incantations over bound images to be a popular motif in spells intended to produce erotic frenzy. A gentler parallel exists in contemporary spells designed to produce affection, wherein cords are often knotted without binding images.[6]

We also find these mechanisms at play in much later grimoires, including that of 17th century London cunning man Arthur Gauntlet. Gauntlet's workbook describes a spell 'to gain the love of Man or Woman':

Take a piece of virgin Parchment as broad as your hand and make in it two images The one of thy self the other Of the woman or man Then with the blood of the little finger of thy left hand write on thine own Image thine own name. And on the other his or her name... You must make it so that when you close the Parchment the Images may be right over one another. Make thine own Image on Friday the first hour that [Venus] governs And make the other

---

5 Ibid., p. 40.
6 Christopher A. Faraone, *Ancient Greek Love Magic*. Cambridge, MA, 1999, p. 28.

the Friday following In the same hour This done put the Images under your foot three times a day removing it to the other foot.[7]

The similarities with the example from *Picatrix* are stunning. These images are created using a rough astrological election: the planetary day and hour of Venus, who rules love and pleasure. Interestingly, even though the election for these images is the same, as in *Picatrix* Gauntlet's instructions state that the images should be made on different days. The two images are bound, and affect the situation through contagion, albeit with the operator rather than the target.

Unlike the author of *Picatrix*, Hellenistic astrologers did not employ a set of houses separate from the zodiacal signs. Instead, they numbered the signs one through twelve, starting with the sign rising on the ascendant, which is referred to as the *horoskopos*. The numbering proceeds in the counterclockwise direction, ending with the sign that has just risen in the twelfth position. In this context, the signs were referred to as *topoi* (singular *topos*), which means simply 'places'. In order to avoid confusion with the houses more familiar to contemporary readers, I will continue to refer to them using this term.

The significations of the twelve *topoi* underwent some evolution over the centuries spanned by the Hellenistic tradition. However, one of the most consistent themes within the extant literature, from Valens in the second century to *The Book of Hermes Trismegistus* in the sixth, is the malevolent reputation of four of the *topoi*. These are the second, sixth, eighth, and twelfth *topoi*, in which we are warned repeatedly that the malefics will do their worst and the benefics can do no good. Valens summarizes the evil done thusly:

The 2nd: manner of living, Gates of Hades, shaded place, giving, receiving, community. ...The 6th: the place of slaves, injuries, enemies, ailments, weaknesses. ...The 8th: death, benefits from fatality, idle place, lawsuits, weaknesses. ...The 12th: place of foreign countries, enmities, slaves, injuries, dangers, courts of judgment, ailments, death, weakness. Each place, then properly produces what it signifies...[8]

7 *The Grimoire of Arthur Gauntlet*, ed. David Rankine. London, UK, 2011, p. 151.
8 Valens, *Anthologies*, Book IV, p. 80.

What do these *topoi* have in common that has earned them all such a consistently evil interpretation? They are not considered to be in aspect with the *horoskopos*. Hellenistic aspect doctrine expanded on Greek optical theory. This is evidenced by the etymology of the terms used in both Greek and Latin in relation to the angles formed between planets and their significations. The lack of aspect between the second, sixth, eighth, and twelfth *topoi* meant that the *horoskopos*, the signifier for the native in astrological charts, could not see the powers located within these four houses. Robert Hand recapitulates this nicely:

> ..the Latin word *aspecto* and its Greek originals, *epimartureō*, *martureō*, *theōreō*, and *epitheōreō*, are all words meaning 'to look at' or 'to see'. Two bodies standing in the same place cannot actually "see" each other. Therefore, the conjunction cannot properly be thought of as a "looking at."...This logic also extends to things that stand directly next to each other. If I stand right next to you, and we look in the same direction, it is difficult for you to see me. For this reason, signs on either side of a given sign were held not to "look at" each other. The signs that were six and eight signs away were also not regarded as "looking at" the 1st sign. The logic of this is not so clear, but, in general in ancient astrology, signs and their opposing signs were regarded as having similar characteristics. So if the 2nd and 12th signs did not "look at" the 1st sign, the 8th and 6th were not regarded as "looking at" the 1st sign either.[9]

Thus, certain *topoi* are considered malefic because they either cannot be seen or share in the essential nature of something else that cannot be seen. It may be worth asking ourselves, why is the unseen evil, or at least, dangerous in the Hellenistic worldview? We find a similar fear regarding the dangers of the unseen in the doctrine of planets in aspect, which are classified as either overcoming or hurling rays. In an aspect between two planets, the one located in a sign earlier in the zodiac is said to be 'overcoming' the later planet, in the sense that it has some kind of tactical advantage over the other. This other planet is said to be 'hurling rays' at its aggressor. We understand this relationship by likening it to that of a predator, who initiates an attack, and its prey, who fights back. This predatorprey relationship is particularly important for the astrologer to consider when malefic planets or harsh aspects are involved. The recurring theme under-

9 Robert Hand, 'Whole Sign Houses: The Oldest House System.' Reston, VA, 2000, p. 4.

stood for both bad *topoi* and the doctrine of overcoming within aspects is that invisible forces within a chart are considered aggressive, malefic, and unpredictable.

Invisibility is a shamanic skill in cultures throughout the world. The predatorprey relationship enacted in the astrological doctrine of overcoming and hurling rays adds a new dimension to our understanding of this ability, glossing it in terms of the hunt which our preagricultural ancestors regarded as sacred. Within a shamanic worldview, we first learned to become invisible from the same tutelary spirits who also taught us how to hunt. The shaman or magician retains this knowledge and with it the responsibility for maintaining relations with the spirit world. The skill of becoming invisible is later attested to in the Greek Magical Papyri. It is also a common theme in the spirit lists and spells found in later grimoires, including the *Grimorium Verum*, the *Lemegeton*, and the *Grand Grimoire*. This is one strand of continuity from pre-agricultural shaman, to ancient magician, to grimoire operator.

Although invisibility appears as a consequence of some other rites within this corpus, the Greek Magical Papyri contain only two spells whose sole purpose is to render the operator invisible: PGM I. 222231 and PGM I. 247–262. The first of these petitions Helios, the sun god: 'Make me invisible, lord Helios, AEO OAE EIE EAO, / in the presence of any man until sunset, IO IO O PHRIXRIZO EOA.'[10] The appeal to the sun should make sense to magician and astrologer alike, as the sun renders all things on earth visible or invisible according to its rise and set. Even the planets become invisible when they approach it, a condition known to astrologers as 'combustion'. In Greek, the word for invisibility, *amaurosis*, literally means 'darkening.'[11]

Interestingly, both of the invisibility spells of the Greek Magical Papyri make use of *pharmakon* (i.e. drugs or herbal preparations, in this case ointments) to produce invisibility. *Pharmakon*[12] is also the vehicle of choice for spells which produce 'evil sleep', blindness, and death. It is perhaps not surprising to find a connection between invisibility and death in magical texts dating from or strongly influenced by late Antiquity. Apollonius of Rhodes, Virgil, and Ovid all recount the tragedy of Orpheus, who journeys to the Underworld to rescue his fair Eurydice, only to lose her once more

10 *The Greek Magical Papyri in Translation*, ed. Hans Dieter Betz, p. 9.
11 Stephen Skinner, *Techniques of GraecoEgyptian Magic*. Singapore, 2014, p. 214.
12 Skinner, p. 244.

when he violates the sole stipulation for their return to life: he turns around and looks at her. Deeper knowledge of the link between invisibility and the chthonic powers may help us understand how the significations of the four evil houses developed during the same period in which the Greek Magical Papyri were being written, even if those texts do not directly employ the *topoi* in spellwork. The fact that each of these four 'invisible', unaspected *topoi* has associations with injury and death is an elaboration on this connection with the Underworld, which concerned ancient Mediterraneans inasmuch as it was rife with beings that needed to be propitiated to avoid such tragedies. Often, these propitiatory sacrifices were the domain of the same type of itinerant magicians who authored the Greek Magical Papyri.

Plutarch describes this type of sacrifice, albeit to disparage the practice, in an essay in Book II of his *Moralia* titled, 'On Superstition.' He recounts how superstitious people, upon waking from troubled dreams (perhaps related to the 'evil sleep' invoked in the Greek Magical Papyri), are diagnosed by 'conjurers and imposters' as being under the influence of 'the troop of dire Hecate'. They then call in a magical specialist who performs purificatory rites and has the afflicted individuals wash themselves in the ocean and spend a full day sitting on the ground.[13] Both ocean and earth have chthonic properties.

As the aforementioned leader of the restless dead, the goddess Hecate was propitiated through sacrifices or invoked during ritual purifications. She received a monthly supper which coincided with the night of the new moon,[14] that is, when the moon itself becomes invisible through conjunction with the sun. PGM LXX. 4–25 describes a propitiatory rite performed through the agency of Hecate syncretized with the Babylonian goddess Ereshkigal. The spell instructs the magician to perform certain incantations and gestures at the crossroads, then to "turn around and flee, because it is at those places that she appears."[15] The implication of this warning is clear: even when invoking a chthonic deity and performing a magical operation through their agency, there is still a risk associated with seeing that deity. Extending this logic back to astrology, while the denizens of the second, sixth, eighth, and twelfth *topoi* are dangerous because they are unseen, it might be even more dangerous for them to come into view.

13 Plutarch, *Moralia*, trans. Frank Cole Babbitt. Cambridge, MA, 1928, p. 461.
14 Jacob Rabinowitz, *The Rotting Goddess: The Origin of the Witch in Classical Antiquity*. Brooklyn, NY, 1998, p. 109.
15 Betz, p. 297.

The name given to the second *topos* by Hellenistic authors is 'the Gates of Hades', a reference to both the Underworld and its ruling deity. The word itself means 'sightless'. The connection to darkness and invisibility was explicit for speakers of ancient Greek. It is an appropriate name for the second *topos*, as this is the last *topos* in the chthonic hemisphere of an astrological chart. It is the next to rise over the Ascendant and be reborn into the middle world. Likewise, the eighth *topos* may be so strongly associated with death because it is the next *topos* to go down through the Descendant. This is a reminder that the Gates of Hades open in more than one direction. We have passed through them before in returning to this world, and will pass through them again when our time here comes to an end.

This metaphor can be extended to the sixth and twelfth *topoi*, which as we have already seen were believed to share in the essential nature of the second and eighth due to their opposing locations. When we consider the Ascendant and Descendant as points of anabasis and katabasis respectively, the sixth *topos* becomes the place of the recently dead and the twelfth *topos* becomes the place of revenants. This hypothesis seems to be supported by the name of the twelfth *topos*, *kakodaimon*, meaning 'evil spirit'. We might consider the twelfth *topos* to be the place of frightful Underworld spirits such as the furies or Erinyes, who would travel in this world to punish certain crimes, notably murder and oathbreaking.[16]

Like Erinyes and other beings that properly belonged to the Underworld, the recently dead were also accorded a malevolent reputation. Elaborate rituals of mourning were required to ease the transition into the Underworld, a tradition from Magna Graecia which was preserved in Italian *pianto rituale* until fairly recently. The consequence of improper burial or insufficient lamentation was considered devastating to both the recently deceased and the living. Rites performed on behalf of the recently dead and the grave consequences of avoiding them have been explored extensively by the work of Sarah Iles Johnston.[17] This could explain some of the significations of the sixth house, which include illness and injury, two signs of attack by the restless dead.

The challenge posed by dark matter is to train ourselves to honor the unseen. We must recognize that space, rather than being defined by emp-

---

16 Sarah Iles Johnston, *Restless Dead: Encounters between the Living and the Dead in Ancient Greece*, Berkeley, CA, 1999, p. 2324.
17 Johnston, p. 3681.

tiness, or lack, or the desire to be filled, has as much agency and potency as the stars themselves. This realization opens new horizons of novel and practical celestial magics. We have considered how dark matter manifests in astrology as empty space, blindness, and invisibility. A close reading of traditional sources reveals how empty space is almost exclusively described in relation to visible objects, rather than being understood on its own terms. Little can be said about the true nature of this space, but we have hopefully glimpsed it out of the corner of our eyes, or remembered it like a dream, and we know it as legion. We have learned that it gives form and meaning as it is divided and channeled into visible matter through talismanic elections. In the practice of talisman-making, astrological theory and pragmatic folk magic combine; wisdom and action inform one another.

As we have seen, for Mediterranean magicians in the early Common Era, invisibility was inseparable from the Underworld, the dead, and the chthonic gods. These chthonic beliefs and practices shed a new light on contemporary astrological doctrine, even though they are attested to by largely separate literary traditions, and likely practiced by different social classes. Those wishing to explore this connection further would do well to make note of the importance ascribed to purificatory rituals by the magical tradition. Purification is a necessary precaution for the sorceror looking to practice safely. But, if we accept that there is some underlying connection between the four evil *topoi* and the chthonic energies employed by the magician, this opens new avenues of astrological remediation. A querent whose natal chart reveals heavy afflictions in the second, sixth, eighth, or twelfth *topoi* can be instructed to alleviate these conditions through propitiatory sacrifices or purifications. The true proof or rejection of this hypothesis can only come through praxis.

*　*
*

The Planetary Viscera of Witchcraft

Daniel A. Schulke

THE DOCTRINES OF astrological correspondence hold that the celestial bodies—their light, motion and occlusion—extend their *numen* through all of creation. In addition to the stars, the more planets imbue their corresponding terrestrial progeny with the foison of their rays, lending them signs, characteristics, and allied magical powers. Although all planetary emanations interpenetrate terrestrial phenomena, some are more distinct and concentrated in their worldly concrescences, and thus the planets' 'dominion' and 'subjects' are established. By understanding this planetary governance, the adept of Natural Magic may make use of a rich and highly specialized occult taxonomy, and directly observe how these planets cause their 'children' to rise and fall with their tides. These powers may also be deliberately harnessed in concord with the laws of the heavens, using specified and highly attuned magical operations. The station of human–planetary congress thus moves from observational and interpretive to active enchantment, and the diviner of the firmament becomes the astral magician. Yet not all planetary power is beneficent to mankind, and the same may be said of magic.

For centuries, the figure of the witch haunted the margins of magic, religion and the human imagination, the personification of illicit magical practice. Dwelling within the cloistered enclave of midnight, she is depicted as being engrossed in the sorcery of the abominable, dismembering corpses for her maledictive poisons, blaspheming the sacraments of religion and consorting with every manner of malevolent spirits. Standing naked before the moon with unbound hair and the accoutrements of erotic magic, she embodies a nocturnal sexuality, transgressive not only for its embrace of the hidden order of night, but also for its unfettered state. As the hunched and cowled hag, she presents a wholly inhospitable face, her time–contorted flesh being the ruination of her nubility: the power of age-born wisdom, disease, affliction, fate, and the curse. She turns, and reveals yet another of her aspects: the Queen of the Sabbat, consort of the Devil, being noble and tutelary, the dispenser of occult learning and the giver of ecstatic vision. Whether through the art of attraction or repulsion, the witch's powers to seduce, disorient, poison and destroy have provided countless inspirations for literature, religious homily, and esoteric symbol. Apropos her misdeeds amid the twilight, her enduring *visage* is framed by the Moon, planets and stars.

Like the practices of witchcraft, astrological magic also possesses an ancient pedigree, and has long indwelt the esoteric scaffolding of occult practice. The planetary quintessences, their movements, interrelations, and constant intercession in human events, naturally magnetized the attentions of sorcerers and mystics, and as astrological science gained magical authority, it was inevitable that its principles would penetrate other forms of magic. Doctrines of planetary correspondence mapping celestial virtues to terrestrial bodies, and for reckoning magical times and seasons, were natural branches of the astrological tree, bearing the fruits of celestial philosophy that further enriched the occult traditions they encountered. In almost all eras, astrological magic and witchcraft were contemporaneous; the former considered a noble art, the latter an aberration often punishable by death. In some historical instances, the noble arts of astrology and the damned of the witch were even conflated. Although divided by the distinction of magical legitimacy, it is likely that both witchcraft and astrology initially emerged from a common nexus of primordial humanity's mystical interaction with the night.

After passing through periods of repudiation and contempt by scholars, in recent years, both witchcraft and astrology have been deemed worthy subjects of academic discourse once more. This shift in the scholarly winds was perhaps best summarized by Michael MacDonald:

> *Until the 1970s the main historical problem posed by early modern astrologers was why in the world anyone fell for them. But since the publication of* Keith Thomas's Religion and the Decline of Magic *(1971), it has become impossible to see astrologers as simply objects of ridicule. For he showed that astrology was actually a central—if controversial—feature of the intellectual and social history of the early modern period, especially the history of medicine, which has become a branch of both.*[1]

Similarly, witchcraft scholarship has undergone a kind of renaissance, moving beyond rational materialist embarrassment at religious mass–hysteria, to understanding the varied roles of iconography, class, gender relations, local folk custom, folk magic, and syncretic religion, among others. What was formerly regarded as fairy-tales and irrational fears has been shown to be a more complex phenomenon, involving pervasive belief complexes and actual magical practices. Yet, other perspectives on both witchcraft and astrology are lacking, particularly from the vantage point of the magical practitioner, and it is in the spirit of new these reformed investigative approaches to these subjects that I offer my own astrological considerations of the witch and her art.

In particular, I shall focus on three planetary emanations which most succinctly inform and empower the essence of the historical witch, and more importantly the magical practices of witchcraft itself. Specifically, the emanative qualities of the Moon, Saturn, and Venus. Likewise, because astrology served not only as the basis of divination and high magic, but also of philosophy and art, I will also consider how these planetary powers permeated and helped to define witchcraft. Additionally, I will briefly discuss some tentative links between witchcraft and astrology worthy of consideration.

The ancient reality of witchcraft, manifesting in diverse ways across time and locus, presents formidable challenges in cohering a consistent magical

---

1 'The Career of Astrological Medicine in England', in *Religio Medici: Medicine and Religion in Seventeenth Century England*, Ole Peter Grell and Andrew Cunningham, eds., Scolar Press, Aldershot, 1996 p. 62.

phenotype. This inconsistency, as I shall argue later, forms its own type of identifying marker and is thus linked with the shifting countenance of the Moon. The same is true for its practitioner: the figure of the witch. Like her magical power of shape-changing, the witch presents a different face to the analytic foci of each who scrutinize her, providing ample evidence for theories and speculations, and more importantly, a mass of voidful lacunae upon which to project them. The looking-glass of the epidemiologist will reveal one image, the scholar of medieval Jewish magic another, and the social historian yet one more. A modern astrological inquiry into witchcraft is no different, and could follow many investigative rubrics, but like other specialized windows into the phenomenon, the inchoate nature of the witch should be borne in mind. Thus, in any consideration which sincerely accords her such power, we must be cautious.

Although witchcraft has been primarily attributed to women (males practicing unlawful magic were often, but not always, referred to as sorcerers), men were charged with the crime of witchcraft as well as women, though usually comprising a smaller fraction of the accused.[2] Where magical practices are concerned I will focus on sorcery utilized by either gender, but the figure of the witch as practitioner will be treated principally as the sorceress, or female practitioner, of unlawful magic.

Likewise, although the practices of the witch can be traced back several millennia, I will focus upon the late medieval to early modern period, a time when her characteristics were richly cohered, and during which her power over mankind was greatest (not surprisingly, this era also tracks closely to a period of great influence for the astrological art). Finally, although it has exerted great power over the human mind, I will treat witchcraft less as a psychological phenomenon, focusing more upon its magical qualities and actual practices.

---

2 In certain regions and eras, the number of men accused or convicted of witchcraft was equal to or greater than women, such as Finland. See for example Anterro Heikkenen and Timo Kervinen, "Finland: The Male Domination." in Bengt Ankarloo and Gustav Henningsen, eds. *Early Modern Witchcraft: Centres and Peripheries.* Oxford University Press, 1990, pp. 319–338.

WITCHCRAFT: AN EXILED MAGIC

At its point of origin, we may consider witchcraft first a maledictive and illicit magic, a spell or sorcerous operation for causing harm, a type of sorcery known from remote antiquity. It was often the case that the witch existed as both a legal and theological construct, and it was in early examples of these literary genres that the witch was often defined. In many depictions of witchcraft there is also is a sense that, due to its perverse or 'backward' characteristics, the rational order of Nature, everyday life, religion and lawful magic are being turned on their heads.

An early example preserved in the written record is the Sumerian *Kaššapu* and *Kaššaptu*, often translated in modern English as 'warlock and witch.' *Uš*, the Sumerian word for witchcraft, also means 'spittle' and 'phelgm' as well as poison. The logogram denoting *Uš* also represents *tu* and *mu*, the two basic words for 'spell' and 'incantation.'[3] Anti-witchcraft trials were conducted in Sumeria, and death was a frequent penalty for the guilty; Sumerian anti-witchcraft rituals such as *maqlû* bear testimony to the seriousness with which *maleficia* was addressed. Witchcraft of this kind included coercive spells, love magic, hate magic, effigy magic, *and zikurudû* ('cutting of the throat magic').[4] This taxonomy, augmented with the powers of necromancy, passed through ancient Greek figures such as Erichtho and Medea, to the complex assemblage of the late medieval witch as a night-traveling sorceress.

The early twentieth century saw the rise of Margaret Murray's witch-cult theory articulating earlier hypotheses of accused European witches representing the remains of a pre-christian fertility cult, a theory which gained some initial academic support, but was later vociferously rejected. Some writers have seen in the figure of the witch a community scapegoat, while others have attempted to explain the origins of the witch-phenomenon as mass-hysteria, or in terms of class or gender warfare. Still others have favored the theory that the witch and her power are rooted in dissociative visionary frenzies brought on by hallucinogenic drugs, whether ingested accidentally, such as the infection of grain with ergot (*Claviceps*

---

3 Tzvi Abusch and Daniel Schwemer, *Corpus of Mesopotamian Anti-Witchcraft Rituals*, Vol 1. Brill, 2011, p. 4.

4 To this constellation of sorcerous activity we may also add *Kadabbedû* ('seizing of the mouth magic'), *Dibalû* ('distortion of justice magic') and *Ziru* ('hate magic'), among others.

purpurea) or the deliberate use of psychoactive ointments or brews. In-deed, as early as the 1580s—amid the very thick of European witch trials—Johann Weyer, a student of Heinrich Cornelius Agrippa, was advancing the argument that some cases of witchcraft arose from the narco-psychosis induced when depraved old women ingested mixtures of plants such as Darnel,[5] Opium, Henbane, Mandrake, and kindred plants.[6] Notably scarce in monotypic theories of European witchcraft were examinations of the intersection of popular magic and folklore endemic to specific areas.

Scholarship emergent in the late 20th century, however, began to un-cover certain trial records which did not accord with the usual clerical or demonological descriptions of the Sabbat. The testimonies of the accused were anomalous and unexpected, and began to suggest to a prehistoric origin for some aspects of the medieval witches' Sabbat, possibly a pre-pagan spirit cult with shamanic features.[7] This general stratum would seem to have been widespread in Europe, with examples found in the Ital-ian Alps, Sicily, Hungary, and Corsica, among others. Classic elements of the Sabbat that were previously understood primarily as the products of inquisitional fabulism—such as sexual intercourse between witches and the devil, or the round dance of midnight—have been located in historical contexts that defy typical patterns of accusation, and indeed present them in positive (rather than abominable) contexts.[8] Similarly, a defining fea-ture of the witches' Sabbat, the nocturnal 'flight' to the place of Assembly has been found in the context of European folk traditions of the present day, such as the night-traveling *mazzerei* of Corsica.[9]

Additionally, despite all attempts at eradication, whether by religion or science, folk magic—which includes such actions as spell-craft and charming—has continued in many places in the world up to the present day. In such contexts, there is ubiquitously found a taxonomic division of 'beneficial' and 'harmful' magical activities, the latter frequently regarded

5 Darnel (*Lolium temulentum*), a plant in the grass family whose ingestion is linked with narcosis and extreme torpor. Its complex of alkaloids is thought to arise through the action of an endophytic fungus.

6 *De praestegiis daemonum*, 1583. Published as *Witches, Devils and Doctors in the Renais-sance*, MRTS, 1998, pp. 225–228.

7 Carlo Ginzburg, *Ecstasies: Deciphering the Witches Sabbath*. 1991 (1989).

8 Gustav Henningsen, "The Ladies from Outside: An Archaic Pattern of the Witches Sabbath." In Bengt Ankarloo and Gustav Henningsen. *Early Modern Witchcraft—Centres and Peripheries*. Oxford University Press, 1990, pp. 191–215.

9 Dorothy Carrington. *The Dream Hunters of Corsica*. Weidenfeld & Nicolson, 1995.

as witchcraft. Physical remains of such malefic operations, such as curse bottles, poppets and amulets, bear archaeological testimony to this reality. Thus, in places where folk magic was practiced, and witchcraft accusations arose, there was, at the very least, both a conception of abominable magic and those who practiced it, as well as a rich trove of magical methods for combatting it.

In modern magic, the link between astrology and witchcraft is present, but tenuous. Calculating a horoscope, as well as forecasting auspicious planetary transits, was part of the folk magic skills of the cunning man and wise woman, with medical remedies, protective magic, angelic conjuration, and spells of unbewitching. Likewise, among Scottish cunningfolk the expression 'planet-struck' is recorded as a term in reference to ill omen, disease or misfortune afflicting cattle.[10] Cecil Williamson, who was a twentieth-century British practitioner of cunning-folk type magic, demonstrated traditional knowledge of cursing and maledictive practices clearly categorized as witchcraft. Despite this, he was also well-versed in astrological magic, and created many planetary talismans for his clients, several beautiful examples of which are currently preserved in the Museum of Witchcraft and Magic in Boscastle, Cornwall.

As an additional consideration, witchcraft has also been characterized as an inversion or degradation of the legitimate rites of religion, an attitude which animates demonological literature during the period of the European witch trials. A variant of this bias prevails today within many occult circles, often couched in quasi-moralistic terms. Kenneth Grant, who considered medieval witchcraft a degenerate and 'puerile' form of an ancient and sophisticated astral magic, is but one example.[11] In Grant's analysis, witchcraft is a relict technology of Lunar or 'Moon' Magick, in which the female principle was exalted over the male.

10 Robert Kirk, *The Secret Commonwealth of Elves, Fauns and Fairies.*
11 Kenneth Grant, *Aleister Crowley and the Hidden God.* 'The Witches' Sabbath and the Reincarnation of Primal Obsessions.' *Starfire*, 2013 (1973) pp. 125–138. One cannot distance Grant too far from witchcraft however, given the amount of space he devotes to the subject in his writings, and his rôle in promulgating the Sabbatic doctrines of Austin Osman Spare.

WITCHCRAFT AND ASTROLOGY

In considering witchcraft and the planetary tides which suffuse its sorcerous power, it is perhaps useful to recall some of its curious historical associations with astrological magic. The 300 BCE *Book of Enoch*, in which is narrated the fall of the heavenly angels known as the Watchers, contains the germ of both arts. The rebel angels took human wives, and proceeded to teach them various forbidden arts, sciences, and magic. Among these were various astrological disciplines, including stellar and planetary divination, as well as reading signs from eclipses and meteors.[12] Later Christian scholars would ascribe to these angels the introduction of evil into the world, and the emergence of sorcery and witchcraft itself.[13] Also found within *The Book of Enoch* is a section called 'The Astronomical Book' or 'Book of Heavenly Luminaries' which narrates the prophet Enoch's passage through the heavens, as guided by the angel Uriel. This narrative compiles astronomical data and descriptions of the wonders of the firmament.

Despite the *Book of Enoch's* characterization of astrological magic and divination as forbidden arts, its angelic origin is as important as its supposed corrupting influence on humanity. Among the Ancient Hebrews, although the belief in astrology was condemned in the scripture,[14] textual and archaeological evidence suggests that it was a valued practice, and its belief accepted.[15] In medieval Jewish magic, the angelic star, or celestial angel, is embodied in the entic personage of the *memuneh*, the 'heavenly deputy' or 'appointed one.' The idea reflects individual celestial agents as governors or intercessors in specific worldly phenomena, including people, animals, plants, minerals, and events. The jurisdiction of the *memunim* was accounted as so pervasive that each second of time, as well as each grain of sand, has its own presiding angel, charged not only with governance but direct advocacy in the celestial courts. In this context, the concepts of 'angel', 'prince', and 'star' were often used interchangeably.[16] Magical spirit-operations of the *memunim* pervade the *Sefer Raziel*, where alignment between the angelic and astrological is significant.

---

12 I Enoch 8.

13 See, for example, John of Damascus' eighth-century *Sacra Parallela*, published in 1577, in which demons are also listed as the source of deceptive dreams.

14 For example, Deuteronomy 4:19

15 Ann Jeffers, *Magic & Divination in Ancient Palestine & Syria*. Brill, 1996, pp. 150–1.

16 Joshua Trachtenberg, *Jewish Magic and Superstition*, University of Pennsylvania Press, 2004 (1939) p. 69.

In common with those accused of witchcraft, astrologers did come under legal suspicion and accounts survive of their trials and executions. The influence of the planets and signs of the zodiac upon various parts of the human body was promulgated by the Christian ascetic Priscillian (d. 385), who was tried, then later executed, for sorcery and immorality. Under torture he did not confess, but also did not deny that he had

> *studied obscene doctrines, held nocturnal gatherings even of disgraceful women, and prayed naked.*[17]

Priscillian's doctrines continued to flourish some two centuries after his death, such to the point that the 'Priscillianian doctrines' of astrological fate and melothesic anatomy were made anathema by the Roman Church.[18] Among early medieval theologians, astrology was often included in a larger group of illicit divination arts, all ultimately proceeding from evil spirits.[19] Remarking on the beliefs of popular magic at the time, Marsilio Ficino wrote:

> *...they say that images fashioned and directed for the ruin of some other person have the power of a bronze and concave mirror aimed directly at him, so that by collecting rays and reflecting them back, at close range they completely incinerate him, and even at long range they make him blind. From this has arisen the story or belief which supposed that by the machinations of astrologers and the witchcraft of magicians, people, animals, plants can be planet–stricken and waste away.*[20]

Astrology, as both an intellectual and occult foundation, endured into the early modern era as a licit branch of Natural Magic. In this environment it was thus possible for Porta to compose and publish his *Magia Naturalis*, describing the finer details of such things as the composition of witches' flying ointments, while at the same time the witchcraft persecutions churned out a sodden waste-ground of human destruction. Despite the ac-

---

17 Haig Bosmajian, *The Freedom Not to Speak*. NYU Press, 1999, p. 20. Though long predating the *Canon Episcopi* and witchcraft trials of early modern Europe, the description here is evocative of the witches' Sabbat.

18 First Council of Braga, 561.

19 Richard Kiekhefer, *Magic in the Middle Ages*. Cambridge University Press, 1989, p. 11.

20 *Liber de Vita* III: 20.

ceptance of the Celestial Art, most prominent astrologers at this time were accused of witchcraft.[21] The renowned and successful London astrologer John Lambe, who was bludgeoned to death by an angry mob in 1628, had, earlier in his life been found guilty of witchcraft.[22]

THE MOON

Of the planetary forces aligned with witches and their art, perhaps none is so compelling in the imagination as the Moon, allied to feminine power, and an element present in depictions of the witches' Sabbat. Vettius Valens attributes to it both conception and the powers of marital bonding,[23] components essential for the magical formulation (and casting) of spells. Despite this power of drawing together, the Moon also governs the shifting tides of temporality. The principle is embodied in the Aristotelian concept of the sublunary sphere, which defined the realms below the Moon as impermanent, shifting, and polymorphic.

This contrary, mutable nature is evident during solar and lunar eclipses, events often allied with a usurpation of the temporal human order, both of which are united and defined by the location of the lunar nodes. In his master work *On the Composition of Signs, Images and Ideas*, the renaissance magus Giordano Bruno remarks that among the throng who stand *opposite* to Luna's court are "...Immobility and the contraries of way and Mercury's Chariot, Fate, Parca, Nature and God."[24] This characterization of the Lunar emanation resembles that of the witch, being unnatural, unlawful, and against divine principle. In the modern era, Andrew Weil has remarked on the altered state of mass–consciousness accompanying total solar eclipses, as well as attendant institutional hysteria.[25] This contemplation would

21 Michael MacDonald, 'The Career of Astrological Medicine in England', in *Religio Medici: Medicine and Religion in Seventeenth Century England*, Ole Peter Grell and Andrew Cunningham, eds, Scolar Press, Aldershot, 1996 p. 77.
22 *A Brief Description of the Notorious Life of John Lambe*, London, 1628.
23 *Anthologies*, I.
24 Giordano Bruno, *On the Composition of Signs, Images, and Ideas*, Book 2, ch. 12.
25 Andrew Weil, *The Marriage of the Sun and Moon*, Houghton–Mifflin, 1980. Lunar eclipses were taken as especially ominous events for the Jewish people, see Joshua Trachtenberg, *Jewish Magic and Superstition*, University of Pennsylvania Press, 2004 (1939) p. 69.

seem in agreement with an authority no less than John Dee himself, who hinted at the moon's suspect nature in 1568:

> *If anybody should wish to learn what the sun's light can accomplish through the moon, or what the moon can do by itself when not steeped in the sun's sensible rays, he can find out by catoptrical skill from the full moon and from the period of darkness following a total eclipse of the moon. It is unnecessary to point out that he may adapt the same kind of experiment to other problems.*[26]

Epitomizing lunar sorcery is the ancient practice of the Thessalian witches known as 'drawing down the moon', exacted by reflecting the full moon in a vessel of water, and using the resulting liquid in various enchantments and magical preparations. This concentrated substance, known as *lunare virus* or 'lunar slime', was densely imbued with the lunar emanation, and considered a quintessential 'witch substance.'[27] Lucan remarks on it in *Pharsalia*:

> *Lowered by incantation [the Moon] suffers greatly until, almost on the earth, she drops foam on the herbs below.*[28]

The sorceress Erictho's necromancy re-animates the corpse with a hell-broth of ingredients that include a panoply of venomous herbs, animal parts, and the 'moon-liquid' of concentrated lunar virtue. Diverse specializations of this ritual, identified with witches, have been recorded in modern Morocco, with the resulting lunar spume being used to bewitch victims.[29]

As the celestial governess of liquids, water, and the cyclic ebb and flow of tides, the Moon (together with the Sun, her consort) also governs the

---

26 John Dee, *Propaedumatica Aphoristica*, LIII.

27 Bengt Ankarloo and Stuart Clark, eds. *Witchcraft and Magic in Europe: Ancient Greece and Rome.* University of Pennsylvania Press, Philadelphia, eds. 1999, p. 223. Other forms of this rite more allied to parlor tricks are attested; these include accurate prediction of total lunar eclipses at which time the witch convinced others she had drawn down the moon from the sky and hidden it.

28 Lucan, *De Bello Civili*, 6.505f, trans J. D. Duff, quoted in Ankarloo and Clark, Op. cit. The witch Sinathea, appearing in Theocritus' third century *Pharmakeutriai* ('The Witches') addresses her spells and incantations to the full moon in the sky, as well as to Hecate in the infernal realms.

29 Edward Westermarck, *Ritual and Belief in Morocco*, MacMillan, 1926.

thickened sap of the sexual fluids, and the efflux of blood in man and woman critical for sexual arousal. Here, it is worthy of mention that the powers of Lunar engorgement would also be essential in formulating another class of ancient curse, that designed to cause impotence in men. Agrippa aligns the moon with "menstruous blood, of which are made wonderful strange things by magicians..."[30]

Of direct concern to the intersection of lunar astrological magic and witchcraft is a seventeenth century lead curse-tablet found near Dymock, Gloucestershire, inscribed with markedly Lunar arcana. In addition to a spoken curse, it includes the Seal of the Moon, the sigillae of the Supreme Intelligence of the Moon, the number 369 which is the Lunar Magical Constant, and the name of Hasmodai, its allied Demon.[31]

The magical fascia cohering this example of lunar *maleficia* also extends into twentieth century occult theory. In his modern reformation of the Tarot, Aleister Crowley associated the Moon Atu with terror, abomination, uncleanness, and sorcery:

> In this Trump, her lowest avatar, she joins the earthly sphere of Malkuth, the culmination in matter of all superior forms. This is the waning moon, the moon of witchcraft and abominable deeds. She is the poisoned darkness, which is the condition of the rebirth of light.[32]

Though best known in esoteric circles for his exposition of magical theory and practice, as well as the occult philosophy of Thelema, Crowley was also an astrologer, well versed in astrological principles and horary process.[33] This afforded him an additional esoteric foundation and vista on magic, astrological arcana underpin much of his magical writings, such as *The Book of Thoth*, and its associated Tarot.[34]

The Moon also governs a complex of concepts including Drugs, Illusion, Transformation and Dreams, intimately associated with the witch and her magical arts. This is dramatically illustrated in the series of correspon-

---

30 Henry Cornelius Agrippa, *Three Books of Philosophy* 3:26 ed. Tyson, Donald, Llewellyn 1993 notes 2 and 5.

31 Merrifield, pp. 147–148.

32 *The Book of Thoth*. Samuel Weiser, 1974 (1944), p. 112.

33 Hymenaeus Beta, in his introduction to Crowley's *The General Principles of Astrology*. Weiser, 2002 (1927, 1930), xvii.

34 Extensive planetary and astrological principia also permeate *The Vision and The Voice*, as well as his book of magical correspondence *Liber 777*.

dences arrayed as the Moon, Morpheus, Poppy, Morphine, and Dreaming. This illusory aspect is also depicted in the famous *Children of Luna* images, in which deception, stage magic, and carnival tricks are all assimilated to the Lunar potencies. An especial power of the witch is shapeshifting, particularly the power to assume the form of a nocturnal animal and go forth in the night undetected. Crowley delineates a biune form of the Moon, with Artemis as the Virgin Moon, and Hekate as the Evil Moon.[35] Kenneth Grant, a student of Crowley, was more explicit in terms of the Moon's links with witchcraft:

> *...the formulae of the whore is connected with the Moon of witchcraft, Black Magic, and the dark sorceries of sterile and malevolent entities such as Echidna, Lilith, Melusina, Lamia, certain aspects of Kali, Kundry, "and the Fairy nature generally." This comes closer to the popular conception of the whore as a vehicle for sterile lusts, nosogenous and vampiric. Unlike the true whore or beloved, she cannot form a gateway through which the magician is able to contact sources of real power; her way is limited to the world of glamour, of illusion, and the treacherous realms of the astral planes which skirt the Qliphoth—the world of shades or shells.[36]*

Grant accounts 81 as the number of witchcraft, and being allied to the power of the Moon. Being the sum of 99, it also forms the Magic Constant of the square of the order of 9 for Saturn, used in texts of Arabic planetary magic such as as–Ashraf Umar's *Kitāb al-Tabsira fī 'ilm al-nujûm* ('Enlightenment on the Science of the Stars').[37] Regardless of the Moon's inconstancy and proclivity for change, it was relied upon for the timing of important magical operations; much of the 'experiments' or spells populating the fifteenth century grimoire of necromancy *The Munich Handbook* prescribe not only specified planetary hours for the rite, but also moon phases.[38]

35 *777 and Other Qabalistic Writings.* Weiser Books 1973 (1912, 1955) p. 85.

36 Kenneth Grant, *The Magical Revival.* Starfire, 2010 (1971) p. 136.

37 Petra G. Schmidl, 'Magic and Medicine in a Thirteenth-Century Treatise on the Science of the Stars.' *Herbal Medicine in Yemen*, Ingrid Hehmeyer and Hanne Schönig eds., Brill, 2012.

38 Kiekhefer, *Forbidden Rites: A Necromancer's Manual of the Fifteenth Century.* Pennsylvania State University Press, 1997.

SATURN

Classical attributions of the planetary dominion of Saturn include Death, Disturbance of Mind, Disease, Decrepitude and Melancholic Temperament. Also attending the Saturnian emanations are derangement, obscenity and distortion—particularly of mind and body—and this aspect permeates witchcraft at every level, from the appearance of the witch herself to the sorceries of the Sabbat. This state of opposition, inversion and derangement has been used to characterize the essence of the witch and her art as 'other' or 'otherness' in occult writings of recent decades focusing on witchcraft.[39] The powers evident in this characterization also lie at the roots of heresy, an important part of the witchcraft complex.

Albertus Magnus described the seventh planet as 'an enemy to mankind,' and noted that it also governed 'mutation,' both essential characteristics of the witch–figure in multiple strands of historical conception.[40] In the astrological taxonomies of the late medieval period, the retinue of characters falling under the planetary dominion of Saturn increasingly included the dead, magicians, and witches.[41]

Saturn was also accorded governorship over dark, forlorn and hidden places, whose ponderous atmospheres carried the signatures of bane, infection or a status of exiled place at the margins of acceptable dominion. Characterizing the Saturnian influences upon certain *genius loci*, the celebrated astrologer William Lilly wrote of the planet:

> He delights in Deserts, Woods, obscure Vallies, Caves, Dens, Holes, Mountaines, or where men have been buried, Churchyards, &c. Ruinous Buildings, Cole-mines, Sinks, Dirty or Stinking Muddy Places...[42]

The places thus characterized are also in alignment with the gathering-places of witches. Seven hundred years earlier, the medieval collectanea of planetary sorcery *Picatrix* or *Ghāyat al-Ḥakīm* mentions Saturn's especial governance of "black mountains, dark valleys, basements, wells, graveyards

---

39 See Austin Osman Spare, *The Witches Sabbath*, Fulgur, 1992; Andrew D. Chumbley, *Azoëtia: A Grimoire of the Sabbatic Craft*, Xoanon, 1992; Daniel A. Schulke, *Lux Haeresis*, Xoanon, 2011, and Peter Hamilton-Giles, *The Witching-Other*, Atramentous Press, 2016.
40 Albertus Magnus, *Book of Secrets*. Michael R. Best and Frank R. Brightman, eds. Weiser, 1999.
41 Zika, *Appearance*, p. 214
42 William Lilly, *Christian Astrology*, 1647.

and the wilderness," as well as abominable flavors such as the wild pear. This juxtaposition of burial grounds and ruins—mythical haunts of the witches and their diablerie—with atrocious victuals brings to mind the so-called Witches' Supper, in which the remains of the dead were consumed in a nocturnal ritual of necro-cannibalism. The Saturnian elements present in this juxtaposition of magical elements call to mind the arresting image of Francisco Goya, *Saturn Devouring His Son*.

Cursing, an action of malefic magic sometimes characterized as martial, in witchcraft has less in common with warfare and more with predation and parasitism.[43] The act of the bewitching curse is in fact an invocation or projection of baneful forces, such as death, bereavement, decay, and disease, all of which are Saturn's domain.

The Renaissance magus Giordano Bruno, whose knowledge of the minutiae of the planetary powers and attributes was exhaustive, addressed many of the magical qualities of the planets in his 1595 book *On the Composition of Signs, Images and Ideas*. The book may be considered to contain the marrow of Bruno's advanced systems of memory, occult semiotics, and planetary philosophy, presenting highly detailed and obscure minutiae of planetary correspondence. Within the Field of Saturn, we find the Witch, in addition to the related magical visages of Poisoner, Necromancer, Enchanter and Jew.[44] One of Saturn's attendants is described as:

> *An old woman with bent back, severe countenance, hollow eyes, not very steadfast in spirit, disgusted with time, knocking her weak spirit on Dis' silent gates, her breasts fallen, limbs broken, stomach shriveled, breathing weak, pulse trembling through all her joints.*[45]

The ancient strands interweaving the planet Saturn, the Sabbath, and sorcery have been explored by Moshe Idel, who examined their relation to the rite of the Witches' Sabbat, and the possible contributions of medieval Jewish astro-magical conceptions to witchcraft.[46] This trajectory of

---

43 Exceptions occur with the *benandanti* of the Italian Friuli who went forth by night in armed troops to battle sorcerers in spirit for the fertility of the land, people, and crops.

44 Giordano Bruno, *On the Composition of Signs, Images, and Ideas*, Book 1, 2:13.

45 Bruno, 5, Book 2, 4 (141)

46 Moshe Idel, *Saturn's Jews: On the Witches' Sabbat and Sabbateanism*. Continuum, 2011. Indeed Saturn, in Hebrew *Sabbatai*, is 'seventh', seven being a number recurrent in ancient Jewish magic, and accorded great power.

research adds yet another layer of complexity to our understanding of the witches' primordial rite, and suggests its capacity as a carrier of occult traditions and practices from Judaism and Islam, as well as Christianity and the prehistoric strata of ecstatic spirit-cults proposed by Ginzburg.

A common witchcraft accusation was the magical destruction of crops, often by the use of magically-prepared powders, spoken incantations, or the summoning of storms. This zone of witchcraft activity presents a dual strand of Saturnian planetary governance: the agrestic art of agriculture, wresting crops from the earth, and its associated concern of infertility, barrenness and crop failure. The witch's historical power of being able to castrate, or to otherwise cause impotence, is also part also of the Saturnian complex, in alignment with his ancient association with Cronus the Titan.[47]

Like a witch's destruction of crops or a field's fertility, laying waste to a city is an assault on civilization, and the influence of Saturn in the *Picatrix* features several such operations:

A TALISMAN FOR THE DESTRUCTION OF A CITY OR LOCATION.

It is made in the hour of Saturn and through that you may bring misfortune to the city ascendant, to the ascendant's master, and to the house of the ascendant. Additionally you may drop Al-Su-ud and the poles from the triangle of the ascendant. Bury it in the middle of the city.[48]

The state of infertility levied by curse-blasted crops is, in essence, a derangement of sexuality, an unnatural mutation of the procreative drive, the latter governed by Venus. Sexual distortion and monstrosity, a defining feature of the witches' Sabbat, was also identified in the astrological nativity from early times. The renaissance Jewish astrologer Yohanan Alemanno, quoting an earlier unnamed source, remarked on this phenomenon:

The astrologers said that Sabbatai/Saturn, when in alignment with Nogah/ Venus, points to ugly and repulsive intercourse, especially with relatives, like a mother, sister or a daughter.[49]

---

47 The complex of arcana is also allied to the Moon.
48 *Picatrix* I:5. Ouroboros Press, 2002, p. 32.
49 MS. Oxford–Bodeliana 2234, fol. 118a, Quoted in Moshe Idel, *Saturn's Jews*, Continuum, 2011, p. 71.

In further consideration of the Saturnian agricultural mystery, the linkage between the seventh planet and witchcraft-power is particularly striking when considering its associated pharmacopeia. These are the so-called 'hexing herbs' of Europe, historically linked with witches' poisons, and the 'flying ointment' prepared from them for ritual use. These baleful Plants of Saturn, the best known of which are Henbane, Poison Hemlock, Aconite, Monkshood, Hellebore, Scopolia and Mandrake, epitomize the planet's magical emanation on multiple levels. A shared characteristic of all such plants is extreme toxicity, as well as derangement of the mind and corporeal senses. The benumbing states arising from these plants, a fraction of which is anaesthesis when taken at therapeutic dose, are also marked by their ability to distort time perception, a feature which has led me to refer to them as *chronophagoi* or 'time-eaters.'[50]

Aleister Crowley remarked on the foul and obstreperous nature of the Saturnian plants when discussing their use in formulae of magical suffumigations:

> *There is little difficulty in recognizing Saturnian perfumes; the difficulty on practice is to find one which is at all tolerable to the sense of smell. In magical work of the kind which borders upon the material plane, large quantities of incense are necessary and incantation becomes difficult when the magician is being rapidly asphyxiated.*[51]

As anyone who has compounded suffumigants using the more poisonous of the Saturnian herbs can attest, even if the greatest care is taken in their preparation and use, the resulting atmosphere is oppressive, terrifying, caustic and anathema in every way to the human physium: perfectly aligned with certain aspects of the planet's power.

Still other accretions of Saturnian botanical lore and folk use, such as Poison Hemlock's ancient reputation as an anaphrodisiac, for suppression of sexual development, and causing sterility, align with the ponderous Saturnian arena, both in agricultural contexts and human health. Using Lilly's correspondences and passing into the column of Saturnian zootypes, we find the Owl, Cat, Toad, Serpent, Bat, Hare and Mouse, all nocturnal creatures associated with the witch and her art.

---

50 Schulke, *Viridarium Umbris. Xoanon*, 2005, p.
51 *777*, pp. 117–118.

VENUS

The Lady Venus, who commands the vigor of growth and procreation, also extends her authority into the realm of witchcraft, albeit of a different nature to her counterparts. Presiding over the especial affairs of women, sexual pleasure, and allure, as well as appearance, aesthetic and marriage, it is the love potion and other erotic sorcery that best emblematize Venus's interface with the witch. These planetary principia are, in general, aligned in the astrological sources, ancient and modern. Noting the especial resonance of Venusian power with magic, the *Picatrix* referred to her as the granter of wishes, while Albertus Magnus associated Venus with the concepts of 'lover' and 'stranger,' both applicable to magnetic incongruity of the witch-figure. Observing the problematic aspects of Venus in the nativity, Aleister Crowley remarked:

> *A badly afflicted Venus will often cause the native to be profligate, indolent, without shame, and wholly abandoned, and open to every species of lust and depravity.*[52]

Erotic astral magic, an extensively developed genre of sorcery in the middle ages, was governed by the planetary emanation of Venus, and gained with her favor. The associated folk magic of love charms, potions and secreted aphrodisiacs were, and still are, the purview of witchcraft. Ironically, as Richard Kiekhefer has noted, practitioners tried for erotic magic were typically women accused of using their sorcery against men, while most surviving manuscripts of erotic magic specify the operation is to be performed by a male, in order to gain the affections of women.[53]

In European witchcraft, the characterization of the female witch was frequently aligned with the Venusian principle.[54] Vergil's *Ecologues* spoke of the witch Amaryllis, whose knot-spell incantation included the exultation "I weave the chains of Venus."[55] In Nider's *Formicarius*, a demonological manual influential during the period of the European witch trials, the

---

52 *The General Principles of Astrology*. Weiser, 2002 (1927, 1930), p. 219.
53 Kiekhefer, *Forbidden Rites: A Necromancer's Manual of the Fifteenth Century*. Pennsylvania State University Press, 1997, p. 79.
54 see Charles Zika, *The Appearance of Witchcraft*. Routledge, 2007. The wild ride of the witches in Diana's troop culminated at the mythical Venusberg, or 'The Mount of Venus.'
55 Vergil, *Ecologues*, 8.77–78.

erotic ritual trance of the witches is said to arise from the Lady Venus.[56] The witches of the Basque region, who frequented cemeteries and strewed graves with fragrant herbs, were observed to bathe in the foam of the Mediterranean sea, from which Venus was born, retiring to the seaside caves in which they held their Sabbats.

> *This mixture of grown girls and young fishermen can be seen at the coast of Anglet, covered by a cape and totally naked underneath, jumping into the waves. This allows Love to get her hooks into them, takes them into her net, inviting them to fish in this churned up water, and inspires in them as much desire as they have freedom and comfort. Wet all over, they can go and dry off in the neighboring chamber of love, which Venus seems to have intentionally provided for this singular occasion on the seashore.*[57]

The latter portrayals emphasize the powers of youth, love, and attraction which constitute compoenents of erotic magic, and the aspect of the witch in maidenhood in particular.

Witches, both as the inhabitants of popular imagination, and those folk magic practitioners inspired or conflated with the archetype, practiced a number of kinds of herbal magic, including a magical knowledge of plants, their stewardship and preparations. As the governess of gardens, bowers, and the pleasant green spaces of the horticultural world, Venus rules the natural effulgence of the plant world and that living sap which animates it. The garden, with its pleasant appeal to the senses and aesthetic delights, is to be distinguished from the 'taming' of the primordial wild inherent in the Saturnian fields, where the forces of death are present even as the rows of grain are seeded. Beyond its organizational rationales, the horticultural magic of gardening bears much in common with the witch's art of allure and seduction.

In Marsilio Ficino's *Liber de Vita*, it is surely a kind of Venusian witchcraft the planetary persona of Mercury references when speaking in astrological allegory to the elderly:

> *Venus endowed you with only one pleasure, and that harmful, with which she harms you but profits those to come, little by little draining you as it were*

---

56 Cited in Zika, *The Appearance of Witchcraft*.
57 Pierre DeLancre, *Tableau de l'inconstance des mauvais anges et demons*, 1612. Trans. Harriet Stone and Gerhild Scholz Williams. MRTS, 2006.

through a secret pipe, filling and procreating another thing with your fluid and leaving you finally as if you were an old skin of a cicada drained upon the ground, while she looks after the fresh cicada. Don't you see that Venus generates a fresh being living and endowed with sense, from your own matter? She steals from you, therefore, the youth, life, and sense, from your whole body, I say, through pleasure of the whole body, that she may from thence make a whole body.[58]

Crowley would seem to be in accord with Ficino when he articulates the complications of the so-called Venus Aversa.[59] The attribution of Venus as having governance over the life-giving juices is in accord with her dominion of erotic arousal and the love-potions of the witch, but the flow, as Dr. Ficino's Mercury warns, can certainly go both ways. This echoes a kind of witchcraft spell of the early modern era I have heard referred to as 'willie-withering spells,' magical curses cast upon men intended to prevent erections.[60] Power over erection and flaccidity is the stock and trade of erotic sorcery, and has much in common with such revered folk magic as the blood-stopping charms of European folklore and the Pennsylvania Dutch, which can arrest severe bleeding in the absence of a surgeon.[61]

PLANETARY POWERS AGAINST WITCHCRAFT

The constructions of unlawful, malefic or deviant magic ascribed to witchcraft during the early modern period come into sharper focus when we consider the great number of magical remedies and rituals used against them. Put another way, although surviving textual documentation of actual 'witchcraft' practices are rarer than texts of 'licit' magic, we may posit their existence given the large number of attested anti-witchcraft magics and cures for bewitchment. The archaeological record is particularly rich with such artifacts as witch-bottles, curse-tables, thorn-pierced effigies and, in some cases, talismanic textual fragments.[62] The diversity of these

58 *Liber De Vita* 2:XV. Mercury continues later, saying of Venus: "She destroys what has been made in order to construct from them what is still to be made."
59 *777*, pp. 63–64
60 The author is indebted to sister H. for this reference.
61 James K. Kirkland, et al, eds. *Herbal and Magical Medicine: Traditional Healing Today*. Duke University Press, 1992.
62 Ralph Merrifield, *The Archaeology of Ritual and Magic*. New Amsterdam, 1987, *passim*.

artifacts as well as persistence of folklore well into the present century, attest to the pervasive belief in witchcraft and a nuanced understanding of magical methods to counter it. We may glimpse these sovereign and protective remedies according to their exposed station in the light: we may not know exactly what lies in their shadow, but we know it is there.

Planetary correspondences reveal an additional layer of arcana when investigating anti-witchcraft magic. Herbs with ancient anti-*maleficia* properties, such as Rue and St. John's Wort, are often governed by the Sun; and in other cases Mars, such as Chile (for its punishing fire), Garlic (for its aggressive stench) and Hawthorn (for its spines, often used to pierce effigies of counter-witching). The Solar herbs may be seen as utilizing the magical principle of fortification, a defensive strategy of strengthening the corpus, while the Martial herbs take an offense approach, allied to the drastic medical actions of surgery or military bombardment. A great champion of Solar plants (together with those of Jupiter) was early renaissance philosopher and astrologer Marsilio Ficino.[63] Indeed, many of his herbal preparations in *Liber de Vita* (1490) are Solar-Jupiterian in nature and are kindred to the famous Mithridatum or Theriac medicines, the ancient preservatives against all types of poison.

SUMMATION

Saturn governs the essential witchcraft magic of Poisons, Sterility, and destructive curses, as well as being the planetary agency often cited in authoritative magical texts as empowering sorcery, or illicit magic. Additionally, there is a prominent Saturnian exudation governing the Dead which permeates witchcraft, both in terms of their presence as spirits at the Sabbat and the necromantic magic used to summon them. Venus, in turn, lends her virtues to the vast array of erotic magic, particularly love charms, and the supra-sensorial pleasures of the 'White Sabbat.' The Moon, with its station as the feminine nocturnal lamp, provides its protean force to magics of shapeshifting and, in more ancient traditions, cursing.

All three planets contain elements of the witch's sexual arcana: Venus for allure and the eroto-procreative effusion, the Moon for mesmeric flux. In contrast to these elements are Saturn's chthonian sexual power to raise

---

63 'When you fear Mars, set Venus opposite. When you fear Saturn, use Jupiter.' *Liber de Vita* 3:VI.

the field, but also lay it waste, embodied in the concepts of sterility and castration. This 'hexing trine' of powers provides an excellent understanding of the planetary forces which permeate aberrant magic in general, and especially witchcraft, and should serve as a basis not only for further understanding of the strange magic of the nocturnal Sabbat, but its emanative application within the Circle Bound.

*   *
*

CONTRIBUTORS

AARON CHEAK, PHD, is a scholar of comparative religion, philosophy, and esotericism. He received his doctorate from the University of Queensland in 2011 for his work on French Hermetic philosopher, René Schwaller de Lubicz, and served as president of the international Jean Gebser Society from 2013–2015. He has appeared in both academic and esoteric publications, including *Light Broken through the Prism of Life* (2011), *Alchemical Traditions* (2013), *Clavis* (2014), *Diaphany* (2015), and *The Leaf of Immortality* (2017). He currently directs Rubedo Press from the rugged west coast of New Zealand, where he maintains an active interest in tea, wine, poetry, typography, and alchemy.

FREEDOM COLE is a practitioner of Jyotiṣa, Āyurveda and Yoga therapy. He is initiated into a traditional Jyotiṣa lineage which traces back to the royal astrologers of Odisha, India. Freedom is the author of *Science of Light*, volumes I and II, as well as numerous articles. With his training in Sanskrit, Vedic philosophy, modern psychology and two decades of practice, he is able to translate ancient principles into practical application. Freedom is presently working on a PhD focused on applying the framework of Yoga and Āyurveda to modern clinical psychology. His work can be found at shrifreedom.org.

AUSTIN COPPOCK is an astrologer and author based in Ashland, Oregon. Austin's writing on astrology and magic has appeared in journals such as *The Mountain Astrologer* and *Clavis: Occult Arts, Letters and Experience*. He has spoken at conferences and events throughout the United States, including the Esoteric Book Conference and the United Astrology Conference. Austin is a regular guest on podcasts which deal with astrology and the occult, such as Rune Soup and The Astrology Podcast. Additionally, he served as President of The Association for Young Astrologers, from 2012–2016. Austin's ground-breaking work, *36 Faces*, was published by Three Hands Press in 2014 and has since met with both popular and critical acclaim. He continues to regularly publish articles on astrology, as well as offer online classes and consultation services through his website austincoppock.com.

ALEXANDER CUMMINS, PHD, is a professional diviner, consultant sorcerer, and trained historian. He received his doctorate in the history of early modern European magic from the University of Bristol. His research specialties include geomancy, grimoires, cunning-craft, and folk necromancy. Dr. Cummins can be found and booked for consultation at www.alexandercummins.com

DR. BENJAMIN DYKES is a leading traditional astrologer and translator of Latin and Arabic who earned his PhD in philosophy from the University of Illinois, teaching at universities in Illinois and Minnesota. In 2007 he published Bonatti's complete *Book of Astronomy*, and since then has translated and published numerous traditional works in all areas of astrology, including the introductory *Traditional Astrology for Today* (2011). He also has 25 years' experience in the Western esoteric tradition (focusing on the Golden Dawn), and recently co-wrote *Astrological Magic: Basic Rituals & Meditations* (2012). He currently offers the *Logos & Light* philosophy lectures on MP3 and speaks to astrological audiences worldwide. In 2018 he will release a major course in traditional natal astrology. See: www.bendykes.com.

DEMETRA GEORGE holds a MA in Classics from the University of Oregon. She looks to classical antiquity for inspiration in her pioneering work in mythic archetypal astrology, ancient astrological techniques and history, and translations from Greek of primary source texts. She lectures internationally and leads pilgrimages to the sacred sites in the Greece, Italy, Egypt, and India. Her forthcoming book *Ancient Astrology in Theory and Practice* will be released in 2018.

JOHN MICHAEL GREER is the author and translator of more than thirty works on occultism and operative magic, and served for twelve years as Grand Archdruid of the Ancient Order of Druids in America (AODA). He blogs at www.ecosophia.net.

J. LEE LEHMAN has a PhD in Botany from Rutgers University. She is author of eleven astrology books, including *The Magic of Electional Astrology* (2014). She is a Tutor for the School of Traditional Astrology, both in horary, and in a medical course which she has designed. Lee was the recipient of the 1995 Marc Edmund Jones Award, and the recipient of the 2008 Regulus Award for Education.

JASON MILLER (INOMINANDUM) has devoted 25 years to studying practical magic in its many forms. He is the author of the now classic Protection and Reversal Magick as well as *The Elements of Spellcrafting*, *The Sorcerer's Secrets*, *Sex Sorcery and Spirit*, and *Financial Sorcery*. He also runs the Strategic Sorcery Training Course, Take Back Your Mind Program, and The Sorcery of Hekate Training. He lives with his wife and children in the New Jersey Pine Barrens. Find out more at www.StrategicSorcery.net.

ERIC PURDUE is a writer, astrologer, and olorisha. He has published articles in the first volume of *The Ascendant* (AYA 2014), and a translation of a section of Khunrath's *Amphitheatrum Sapientiæ Æternæ* (2016, Viatorium/Ouroboros). Eric's new translation of Agrippa's *Three Books of Occult Philosophy* will be published in 2018.

DANIEL A. SCHULKE is an herbalist writing on the subjects of Natural Magic, Alchemy, and Occult Herbalism. His articles have appeared in the occult journals *The Cauldron*, *Abraxas*, and *Starfire*. He is the author of *Veneficium* and *The Green Mysteries*.

MALLORIE VAUDOISE is a spiritualist, diviner, and herbalist based in Brooklyn. She studied Computer Science at Brown University and Hellenistic Astrology with Chris Brennan. Her writings on Southern Italian magic and religion can be found at ItalianFolkMagic.com.

*   *

*

INDEX

INDEX

✷
✷   ✷

The Celestial Art was published in May, 2018 by Three Hands Press. This first printing is comprised of two thousand seven hundred and eighty copies in total. Of this are two thousand trade paper editions printed offset and sewn with colour covers, seven hundred thirty standard hardcover copies bound in ultramarine cloth with colour dust jacket; and fifty deluxe hand-numbered copies quarter-bound in black goat and hand-marbled endpapers, with slipcase.

SCRIBÆ QUO MYSTERIUM FAMULATUR

✷   ✷
✷

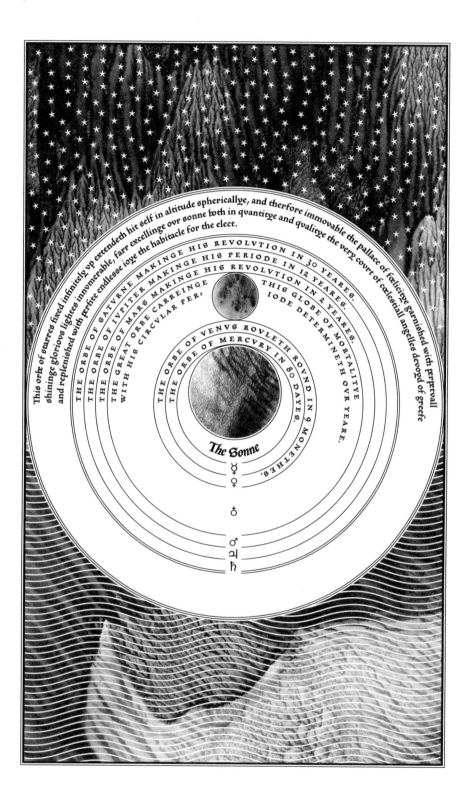

This orbe of starres fixed infinitely vp extendeth hit self in altitude sphericallye, and therfore immouable the pallace of fœlicitye garnished with perpetuall shining glorious lightes innumerable, farr excellinge ovr sonne both in qvantitye and qvalitye the very covrt of cœlestiall angelles devoyd of greefe and replenished with prfite endlesse ioye the habitacle for the elect.

THE ORBE OF SATVRNE MAKINGE HIS REVOLVTION IN 30 YEARES.

THE ORBE OF IVPITER MAKINGE HIS PERIODE IN 12 YEARES.

THE ORBE OF MARS MAKINGE HIS REVOLVTION IN 2 YEARES.

THE GREAT ORBE CARREINGE THIS GLOBE OF MORTALITYE
WITH HIS CIRCVLAR PERɪ IODE DETERMINETH OVR YEARE.

THE ORBE OF VENVS ROVLETH ROVND IN 9 MONETHES.

THE ORBE OF MERCVRY IN 80 DAYES.

The Sonne

☿
♀

☾

♂
♃
♄